Decrypting Sovereignty as Archism

Decrypting Power and Coloniality: Philosophical Perspectives from and through the Global South

Series Editors: Ricardo Sanín-Restrepo, Marinella Machado-Araujo, Angus McDonald, and James R. Martel

The theory of encryption of power (TEP) proposes a fresh understanding of how the use of language monopolizes and hides power, preventing access to it through the denial and neutralization of differences based on class, race, and gender. It argues that coloniality exists because it encrypts power; hence the theory develops insights alongside and in parallel to decolonial theory and critical and subaltern studies. The central claim exposes how, in the name of the people, the people are made vulnerable to dispossession and exclusion, and how in the name of democracy, democracy is undermined and potentially destroyed. Theorizing encryption challenges the linkages between liberalism and colonialism, capitalism and sovereignty, constitution and economy, and their claims of necessity. The insights produced can be brought to bear on such phenomena as information circuits of disinformation on social media platforms, artificial intelligence, weapons, technologies of surveillance, and data mining.

Titles in the Series

Decrypting Sovereignty as Archism: Moving Toward a New Democracy, edited by James R. Martel and Ricardo Sanín-Restrepo

Decrypting Political Theology: Genealogy, Tendencies, Antagonisms, by Andityas Matos

A Hopeful Political Imagination: Courage and Fantastic Critique in the Age of Meltdown, by Oscar Guardiola-Rivera

Decrypting Justice: From Epistemic Violence to Immanent Democracy, edited by Ricardo Sanín-Restrepo, Marinella Machado-Araujo, and Sabelo J. Ndlovu-Gatsheni

Decrypting Sovereignty as Archism

Moving Toward a New Democracy

Edited by
James R. Martel and Ricardo Sanín-Restrepo

BLOOMSBURY ACADEMIC
NEW YORK • LONDON • OXFORD • NEW DELHI • SYDNEY

BLOOMSBURY ACADEMIC
Bloomsbury Publishing Inc, 1359 Broadway, New York, NY 10018, USA
Bloomsbury Publishing Plc, 50 Bedford Square, London, WC1B 3DP, UK
Bloomsbury Publishing Ireland, 29 Earlsfort Terrace, Dublin 2, D02 AY28, Ireland

First published in the United States of America 2026

A catalog record for this book is available from the Library of Congress.

ISBN: HB: 978-1-6669-7871-1
ePDF: 979-8-216-25359-4
eBook: 978-1-9787-6882-6

Series: Decrypting Power and Coloniality: Philosophical Perspectives from and through the Global South

Typeset by Newgen KnowledgeWorks Pvt. Ltd., Chennai, India

Contents

Introductory Dialogue on Archism and Encryption

James R. Martel and Ricardo Sanín-Restrepo

Introduction[1]

We conceived this book as a platform for diverse voices to explore archism and the theory of encryption of power (TEP)—to explore their connections and capacity to deal with the intricacies of power, especially in today's world that seems to be looking into a dark endless abyss of pain.[2] Knowing that what could prevent a leap into mass annihilation lies in what the people can collectively imagine and do. What the people can collectively imagine and do is far from being a desire or wishful thinking of the authors of this book; on the contrary, as we will prove, it is the ontological condition of the world.

In the face of the insane and sadistic violence that the few are inflicting on the many, can we still offer hope from words? We think it is the only way—that is, not words alone (words are never alone). Words, in this case, perform a spiritual task: the task of bringing forth, of bringing to presence what is absent, what power as domination needs to hide and obliterate in order to be, or rather in order to destroy. So, we are referring to words that are organized from action and that organize action at every turn. Action that must be taken against the powerful elite colluding for the mass destruction of ecologies and systemic genocides to flatten the world into fitting into their depraved dystopian view of the world.

Hence, the question put on the head of a pin is, is it still timely or even valid to discuss sovereignty? A term that seems to carry the scent of mothballs with it. We believe that not only does sovereignty still hold a magnificent weight, but within its secret chambers rests the blueprint of emancipation and the key toward changing this state of things. How so? Let's start by looking at how the book's editors clarify archism and the theory of power encryption, which will help us understand the topic better.

When starting this dialogue, we realized that our concerns with the origin, exercise, simulation, occlusion, and commonality of power not only shared the same atmosphere but were charged by the same equalitarian spirit. While we noted terminological divergences, we questioned whether these were mere semantic preferences or reflections of deeper conceptual differences. We were not sure if, parodying a famous song, it was a case of “you say leisure /ˈliː.ʒɚ/ I say leisure ˈle.ʒə/ I say privacy /ˈpraɪ.və.si/ ˈyou say privacy prɪv.ə.si/.”

One thing was evident: the dynamic and ever-changing nature of our subjects—“power,” “oppression,” “potentiality,” and “liberation”—demanded a multiplicity of tools, networks, and perspectives. Equally significant were the effects these varied modalities had on the collective populations, specifically what the TEP has termed “the hidden people.” This shared axiom serves as the foundation of our work.

Terms such as archism, transcendent models, potentia, nonarchism, and the hidden people all converge around shared concerns, perspectives, and themes: forms of power that manifest as oppression under the guise of freedom. This includes the progressive and effective separation of being from power, with the latter entrenched into formidable institutions like the State or the economy, which present themselves as necessary and immovable. As we observed, this dynamic underscores the need for immanent difference to empower itself in ways that can confront and surpass restrictive forms of sovereignty. Consequently, it leads to a precise ontological understanding: being is either contingent or it cannot exist, and necessity must be overcome through a dense web of self-organizing, unqualified subjects.

Both projects identify the eruption, at some point in modernity, of an overarching and overdetermining form of power that encroaches on every human action and absorbs all living energy, returning a frozen image of itself as the only truth. This leads us to discover a plethora of historical and living practices of self-organization of the people that require another sensitivity, another set of registering tools on our behalf to unleash their power and let them show us the way toward equality and radical democracy.

In so many forms of nonarchist organizing—in Indigenous forms of collective self-organization such as the *ayllu* in the Andean Highlands and the Zapatistas in Chiapas; in communities that stem from what Cedric Robinson calls the Black Radical Tradition such as the revolution and its aftermath in Haiti and the Black Panthers in Oakland; in the organizations that crop up in the West such as ZAD in France, NoTAV, as well as the larger practice of autonomism in Italy—we see endlessly diverse and radically unrelated forms of organizing and taking power that are nonetheless linked by their common form of resistance to both archism and encryption.

Eschewing the gladiatorial tradition of Western zero-sum philosophical debates where one must die and only one can prevail, we embraced the principle of abundance, knowing that the multiplication of voices and actions would foster theoretical rigor and precision for all involved. Theoretical rigor and precision are not the stuff of a solitary genius speaking in one voice (another archist trick!) but of a thick social brain of multiple inputs-outputs and of interconnectedness of diversity, something that only comes from the collective itself in all of its complex, internally contradictory, agonistic, and wildly powerful forms.

One of the main tenets of the TEP is that there is no world unless it is fashioned by all the differences that can produce and communicate differences. This implies an infinite and dynamic process of production, ideas, relations, viewpoints, and actions, precluding any definitive closure, inhibiting anyone standing up and declaring “this is it, this is the world." Consequently, we both reject any notion of a final, authoritative interpretation of the world. Our shared motivation is to demonstrate that the world not only *can* be otherwise, but that it *must* be otherwise (and in some fundamental ways, it already is otherwise). This nonarchist stance (in Martel's parlance) signifies our commitment to a world comprised of infinite, interwoven realities, rejecting any singular, ultimate vision. Therefore, we view our diverse terminologies, stemming from varied theoretical traditions, personal backgrounds, and methodological approaches, not as limitations but as sources of depth and intensity. Indeed, difference is to be expected and welcomed in theorizing that opposes domination and the imposition of false unities onto the rest of the world. These differences facilitate rich intersections, generate diverse potentialities for action and designs, but most importantly, it ultimately zeroes in on power as oppression (or *potestas* in Sanín-Restrepo's parlance) as a unique and precise manifestation; consequently, it allows us to focus with precision on it and sets us in a better position to deal with it, making it more malleable and comprehensible.

It is this methodological and theoretical diversity precisely that arrests power as oppression and does not let it reconfigure as one more simulacrum.[3]

Thus, we are not voices describing the ebb and flow of the people or the multitudes from above but are entrenched within it as a movement and potentiality. In fact, the pose of speaking above or beyond the people is itself redolent of archism and encryption, the stuff of secrecy and lies.

Allow us then to begin our dialogue on archism and the TEP.

Necessity and Contingency

RSR: You begin your latest book (Martel forthcoming) stating, "This is not a book about failure." I love this beginning. One of the main ideological or aesthetic claims against critical theory is that it is pessimistic, that it unearths the unpleasantness of life and offers little hope in exchange. The main feature of TEP (and I believe this is the cornerstone of our agreement and common struggle) is to demonstrate that things can be otherwise, that we are not predestined to obey and mimic models of oppression, that we can melt the structures of power that dominate us and create a better world. This is not simply wishful thinking or a particular political agenda. TEP offers this as an absolute ontological truth (please see section "The Ontological Foundation of Being and Politics" later for the hard proof).

Power is fundamentally understood through the tension between contingency and necessity. Contingency describes changes that may occur without predetermination, while necessity refers to inevitable changes dictated by an unknown model. This liminal space between the possible and the predetermined is where the drama of power unfolds. As previously established:

> While contingency is the unleashing of immanence, generation, transitions, and creativity; necessity is the sovereign grip of every definition of time and space

> from a predefined point zero. While in necessity, the contingency of the future is captured in what is presently actual; contingency is the edge where possible and impossible are to be decided. Contingency is always the unbound multiplicity of becoming. Hence, there is no expression of difference that is not contingent as there is no negation of difference that does not always fall back into necessity. Contingency and necessity are then the gridlocks of power, that is, of what is possible and impossible. (Sanín-Restrepo 2018, xi)

The world is only a world where it is comprised of every being that produces difference; hence the world is contingent, because anything can happen without a preexisting transcendent model that predefines existence and action.

The consequence is quite simple: Where there is necessity there is no freedom; more than that, there is no possibility of change (becoming). Our capacity for self-expression, collective belonging, and shared creativity is entirely dependent upon contingency.

Power when exercised as oppression—whether termed archism or potestas—relies entirely on a grounding in necessity. This reliance is crucial for its ability to dictate and define being, becoming, and belonging, thereby establishing a paradigmatic moment wherein the political is neutralized and power is appropriated.

Hence, the world is either contingent, and then we can all create the future through imagination and collective action, or it is necessary, and we are trapped in someone else's fate, a destiny defined by invisible and untouchable forces that shape us at every moment. A nightmare lived in wake.

As you affirm:

> I am one of those who believe that participation in political and economic life constitutes two forms of activities that all humans have the ability to be expert in. Unlike brain surgery, which takes a lot of training, or engaging in sports or artwork that some people have more facility than others, politics and economic activity, because they come out of our ontological condition, are something that we are all equally "good at." (Martel forthcoming)

Exactly, imposing something like talent or virtue to exercise politics is tantamount to qualifying life, conditioning beingness and thus imposing a telos to a community.

As we have stated:

> The ontological condition of the political (of what counts, of how things communicate) lies in the absence of conditions or qualifications beyond difference to belong to the body politic. If the latter is true, politics can only exist in democracy (Rancière 2001)—a non-place where meaning is potentiality, being is unqualified, and everything is yet to be decided. (Sanín-Restrepo and Machado-Araujo 2025, 17)

At this point the discussion is centered on the most fundamental philosophical questions of all: what is possible and what is impossible, the very limit of what can be and what cannot be. Western politics' monumental weight is on two things: (1) Anything that comes forth or emerges in the lack of a transcendent model of existence that presupposes it is an aberration, a nonbeing. And (2) that nothing new is possible, not really, not outside its own stringent models. We are doomed, destined to be ruled, to obey, to leave everything in the hands of the sovereign speaking through a few mouthpieces of selected experts that outline the extension of our reality.

To break this imposition from the root, TEP sees itself as a complement to two major contemporary works. First, Quentin Meillassoux's *After Finitude* proves, in absolute terms, that the only necessity is contingency, which means that everything, even the sacred principles imbedded in (formal) science such as cause and effect, is in fact contingent. This leads to the central conclusion: reality is radically contingent. Anything is possible. The laws of physics could change, and the universe could be completely different. There is no underlying necessity that governs existence. Second, David Graeber and David Wengrow's *The Dawn of Everything*. The "two Davids," as you happily call them, demonstrate in historical and anthropological terms that necessity is an imposition of archism, that things can not only be different than they are (blind obedience, oppression, fate), but that they have been different for the majority of human history. Human history is a permanent flow of beautiful social and political experiments of freedom and equality; Western modernity built a wall of necessity around it to keep it at bay while declaring that their own particular, fractured, and nimble truths (the State, the police, the rule of law) are absolutely necessary.

As the TEP incorporates these insights and adds a reading of Aristotle's composition of potentiality and actuality in a completely different light from the traditional, and even against the grain of radical tradition (Negri and Agamben, see Sanín-Restrepo 2016), it finally proves that contingency (whose name in politics is democracy), as the infinite extension of intense difference, is necessary in all possible worlds. As the theory proves, "Democracy, as the only materiality of politics, casts forth the most beautiful paradox of philosophy: politics is the question of all questions, because it is the question of who can formulate questions, of who counts" (Sanín-Restrepo 2016, 2). Politics can only be considered when all worlds are possible stemming from the mere unqualified existence of beings, all beings.

As a conclusion, while Meillassoux demonstrates that reality is fundamentally unpredictable and without reason, and thus everything is logically contingent, and the two Davids demonstrate that there is no historical necessity, TEP proves that if there is a hint of necessity in politics (e.g., the necessity that the strong command the weak, the necessity of a State), then politics is but a simulacrum. Or, put another way, being is ontologically contingent, which leads to it being free to create, and, thus, any solidification of power that stands as necessary (the State, the constitution, money, etc.) is but simulacra.[4]

JRM: I am in full agreement about the relationship between tyrannical power and the sense of necessity. In a way, the idea of necessity is itself the birth pang of encryption because it offers a constant excuse for why, although it is "clear" that the people are sovereign, some necessity or other (which is only ever known by those in positions of authority) requires a strong intervention from above. Necessity, and with it a series of endless crises, is how the people are tamed and rendered docile. The people's power is always just around the corner, about to be instantiated, but it never quite is. This accords with Schmitt (although I hate to agree with anything that he says) about the idea of the *katechon*, the State as a guard against impending catastrophe. It is also the source of the idea of the state of exception.

What is crucial, I think (and I know you think this too), is that this necessity is always false. The crisis is always manufactured (not that it is not a real crisis at certain times, but its source always comes from the unjust authority of archism), and there is always a series of ruses by which such power is enabled. Contingency, on the other hand, just like human ontology, is in fact the real situation of the world. Everything is contingent. This can be seen in the beautiful diversity of so many instances of nonarchist polities. Nothing is ever only what it must be, everything is subject to change (as Lauren Olamina, the prophet in Octavia Butler's majestic *Parable of the Sower*, says, "God is Change" (1993, 3)). To me, this is very good news because it means that archism, and hence encryption, cannot last forever. Sooner or later, it must dissolve itself into the absolute contingency that it is always trying to fight against.

In *The Arcades Project*, at several points, Benjamin tells us that, although what I have been calling archism always purports to be breathlessly rushing toward the future, in fact it is a static hell.[5] It uses things like fashion to provide a sense of motion, but the entire point of both archism and encryption is to capture the world in its static embrace and to prevent change—and contingency—from occurring.

To the beautiful books that you mention, I would add one that I recently came across, Kristin Ross's *The Commune Form* (2024). In that book, Ross argues that the key modality of resistance is not in this or that ideology or any specific content or local practices but rather the commune form itself. I find this a really intriguing idea and note that this form, which remains prevalent in so many Indigenous communities today, is also the form that leftists in the Global North adopt as soon as they encounter a revolutionary situation. I think this form, which I like to call "continuous assembly," best expresses human ontology and is the political form that best captures the nature of contingency. Those who are organized in this way have their working life double as a political forum where they can learn to trust one another—not in an individual and subjective way but in a collective and objective way—in order to find their own political counter-power. I also think that a big part of encryption—maybe the biggest secret of all that it hides—is that in order to end this unjust power dynamic, no new political form has to be invented, just as no new political subject has to be produced. Instead, people must readopt the commune form that encryption does everything that it can to eliminate.

One key way that this elimination happens—and this fits in really well with the way you describe things—is to turn what could be in fact communal forms into something else. Thus, so many ways that people are organized today under conditions of encryption, the workplace very much included, are not recognized as being political spaces. Perhaps more accurately, the forces of encryption work very hard to ensure that these spaces remain depoliticized and disparate. Accordingly, the opportunity for resistance is not realized. When people gather together it is not to make collective decisions but rather to hear from their bosses what they must do next, or to have a "social" where people may gripe about conditions but not plan ways to take back their collective power. The hidden people are right there, even in some ways, already occupying the right form; but without a realization of this space as being what it is, encryption turns the very means of its overcoming into a source of its own ongoing power.

Archism and Transcendent Models

RSR: I want to contrast our choices of the use of conceptual tools. Where you use "archism," I use "transcendent models," and "potestas" as its byproduct (though sometimes I use "arché"). Where you use "nonarchism," I use "radical democracy" or "Energeia." Here, I will try to highlight and intensify our communalities while drawing attention to an important difference in our views of archism-potestas through the construction of the hidden people and their indelible link with sovereignty.

I believe the philosophical backbone of the theory of encryption is its transformative use of the concept of *Energeia* that alters what we know of power. Consequently, I synthesize my arguments from *Decolonizing Democracy* in this regard further below to try to tie it all together.

There is an interesting discussion regarding names here. The obvious path would be to ask why you chose nonarchism and not straight anarchy or a more nuanced term such as an-archy (as Schürmann did interpreting Heidegger[6]).

You define archism as "As the word implies—the ancient Greek verb ἄρχειν or *arkhein* from which it is derived means both to rule and to begin—archism is about hierarchy, about top-down political domination and a sense of serving as an origin (for power, for action, etc.)" (Martel forthcoming).

Here are the first coincidences between your archism and transcendent models according to the TEP: they are institutions designed to posit hierarchy, preserving inequality, establishing harsh preprogrammed but movable lines of inclusion and exclusion, and the existence of experts that keep its core alive. In archism, as you put it, "deeply hierarchical model of politics that includes many variants such as liberal democracies as well as fascist and authoritarian models but all of which share an abiding interest in preserving forms of political and economic inequality and, in particular, the practice of capitalism" (Martel forthcoming). Here we can see further how both transcendent models and archisms cross the same axes. (1) They institute the unfoundable, that is, they impose a false origin as the sacred matrix of all that exists within. (2) An unexamined and impossible teleology[7] imposes qualifications of what a people must be. (3) They elevate a particular form of being and doing into an inscrutable eminence that overdetermines every action in a particular society. (4) They are built to preserve and, I would go further and say, fatten the privileges of the few, and those few are the ones that built the power form in the first place.

I know that you tried to push away from the name "anarchy" due to its Western progeny. You explained this very beautifully in your conversation with David Wengrow

(Martel forthcoming). Nevertheless, I believe there is something more powerful here. What I sense in your choice of nonarchism is that it thrusts beyond ontological or political diagnoses and immediately implies action, praxis; it denotes that the action of a permanent assembly is in itself nonarchist. How collective power is the one that does away with hierarchies and false models of power. Beyond the immediate choice to reject archism, the suffix "-ism" itself offers a critical perspective. This suffix denotes doctrines, States, or practices, highlighting the inherent process of "ism"—of formation of followers and doctrines. Applying this to "archism" it suggests not just a state of being ruled but also the active pursuit and justification of such a condition. The creation of an "-ism" inherently involves the formation of a distinct identity, a rallying point that both unites and divides, that directs toward want or identity. When applied to "archism," it means a form of societal autophagy, where the system consumes itself in the tendency, but also a manifestation of pure solipsism where existence is owed to obedience, and the focus becomes an isolated, self-referential view of a total immersion in said obedience that carries both poles you are displaying: hierarchy and an utter lack of confidence in the power of the people.

On the other hand, the suffix "ist" of "nonarchist" denotes an adherent to a practice; hence the practice of the nonarchist implies a continuity and permanence as you say it; it has "a very mundane, workaday aspect" (Martel forthcoming).

Now, you state that archism

> arose along with the development of Western capitalism and which has dominated our planet for the past 500 years. Even though it has not usually had (or sought) a name, archism is the scourge that has been battling and or suppressing non archism throughout its history via forms of capitalism, colonialism (both internally and externally to the West), slavery, genocide, white supremacy, heteropatriarchy and many related phenomena. (Martel forthcoming)

I completely understand why demarcating the past 500 years makes sense as the historical frame for archism; it is where Western history shuts down alternatives, imposes its own worldview, and establishes its destiny as world destiny. And I agree this has to be the shuttering—or in our lingo encrypting—event.

Nevertheless, through TEP, we believe that within these 500 years another phenomenon—that is absolutely its progeny—arises and changes dramatically the forms of power and beingness in a way that reshapes power as potestas, making it almost impenetrable, pushing us to rethink liberation and radical democracy.

Hidden People and Sovereignty

RSR: We are referring to a powerful and defining sleight of hand: the simulated fusion within modern constitutions of the concept of the people and sovereignty that creates a quantum leap of power as potestas (or archism) into an unsuspected dimension of deep entrenchment and impermeability.

As I previously stated:

> The galvanization between coloniality and liberalism creates the most sophisticated and impermeable machine of power in history. We can formulate it simply: "the people must be both the exception and the (simulated) sovereign!" Coloniality achieves the most extraordinary exploit: it establishes the people as sovereign as it immediately seizes their sovereignty as absolute power (constituent power). All of this is done while maintaining the simulacrum of popular sovereignty as the political and legal axiom of the people. Therefore, it paradoxically merges the hidden people as sovereign and exception. (Sanín-Restrepo 2016, 202)

Only in late coloniality, and through modern US paradigm-ready-made-constitutions, do the people become both the (simulated) sovereign and the index of the state of exception, that is, the excluded (the hidden people).

When modern constitutions make the people the sovereign, they are creating a useful paradox where the people can be killed, displaced, or starved … in the name of the people themselves. This, I believe, is the most sophisticated form of power as potestas we have ever witnessed.

How is it achieved? There is a fundamental split at the core of politics. While "the people" (not God, not the monarch, not the nation State) are considered the core of modern politics and law, their structure is fundamentally fractured.

> In modernity the key to encryption is the conversion of the concept of the people into a synecdoche. Accordingly, a false totality (the people of human rights and constitutions, the included) become to symbolize and falsely represent an impossible infinity (the excluded, the hidden people). (Sanín-Restrepo and Machado-Araujo 2020, 24)

The people as a totality is a *pars pro toto* synecdoche. An arbitrarily constituted part (white people within a nation State) stands for and defines an impossible infinity (the marginalized people, the forced migrant). The concept of "the people" works by symbolically combining what a body politic discards and what it lacks. This unrepresentable "excess" remains logically outside the grasp of any form of representation.

This system has materialized within the framework of modern constitutions. It operates on a core paradoxical structure: the construction of "the people" as simultaneously the exception—those systematically excluded and marginalized—and the (simulated) sovereign (those that are not only included but who are the core legitimacy of every exercise of power).

> "We the people," is the most splendid and horrifying fusion of power and sheer violence under an impermeable armor of legitimacy. The people become the transcendent and mystic model of their own exclusion, of the war to subdue and expropriate them. Injustice is naturalized as justice. The outside becomes the

> inside, as the exception becomes the (simulated) sovereign. (Sanín-Restrepo and Machado-Araujo 2025, 16)

The "people as a synecdoche," where a privileged group is made to represent the totality of the people, effectively obscures and denies the existence and agency of the "hidden people," who, in their paradoxical position, embody the inherent contradictions of power and sovereignty.

> However, the hidden people have to be falsely included to give consistency to the fantasy of the totality. The crucial point is that the people as a whole can only exist and exercise power, if and only if, it keeps that other zone of the people "hidden." (Sanín-Restrepo 2016, 44)

Modern constitutional sovereignty is therefore characterized by the strategic merging of the "hidden people" as both the exception and the (simulated) sovereign, achieved through the creation of a "simulacrum" of popular sovereignty.

The most notable consequence of this fusion is the impenetrability of sovereignty as it turns it into the perfect autopoietic machine. As you see, a deeply unethical and powerful structure is created. It uses the global recognition of a vulnerable population (the idea or abstraction of the hidden people) as both its source of power and the reason for their potential destruction. Any attempt to fight it simply makes it more powerful and immune. The power of the people is neutralized and disenfranchised in their own name.

> The ambush of the power of the people follows a simple logic: make the people the sovereign, devolve sovereignty to a norm, deactivate the people within the norm, capture its energy in legality, deny their access to language, and expel their bodies to the triturating machine of the market. (Sanín-Restrepo 2016, 40)

In another chapter, Marinella Machado-Araujo and I will closely analyze the deep consequences this brings for power, liberation, and sovereignty. For example, what it means for resistance and critique. What it means for the fetishization of power (responding to what you beautifully constructed as leaderism/followerism) that becomes a form of narcissism. As power is supposedly in the people, we get something like people adoring the model of themselves, which is a simulacrum. We delve into how this narcissism, when exposed, draws politics necessarily to a radical breaking point of violence.

The first question it raises is: what does the building of the hidden people as the key act of sovereignty, or rather its fusion with sovereignty, mean for archism? Second, we are before a very precise form of hierarchy that reproduces specific kinds of models. Sovereignty/hidden people is an odd form of transcendent model, it is paradoxical. And, like any transcendent model, it shapes reality; it casts regimes of truth; it creates trauma, fear; it gives weight to choices, it imposes epistemological regimes as tribunals. But the paradox is intensified when the model of mimesis is the elevation of the people to a model.

Your profound study of Kant's passage of the "Critique of Judgement"—where he makes an analogy of the stars and the universal moral law—unpacks how a transcendent model is erected through *transcendental imagination* as the purest form of eminence of a simulacrum, of something build in reality that actually comes from a void, an imposition of something uniquely subjective. The "higher self" awarding itself the moral law from the universal. As you stripped it down to its bare bones, the thing is quite simple: the stars are real while the universal moral law is not. The consequence you draw is powerful, you call this "a parasitic transference of reality from the actual object to the immaterial one." Now, for the sake of argument, imagine what would happen with that parasitic transference when the sovereign (simulated, of course) ceases to be a divine abstraction like God, the monarch, or the nation and it turns into the people. What transcendent image is awaiting adoration and mimicry? (again, not God or a monarch). The first answer that comes to mind is that it produces a kind of narcissism, an exaggerated and aberrant love of one's image that once saturated or leading nowhere turns its monstrous head into what you call *leaderism* and creates these monsters that are now walking the earth as "presidents" and "CEOs."

As you put it, "Kant's internalization of Numa's ruse becomes much more difficult to dispel. After all, we can rebel against a king (and often do) but how do we rebel against our own self (or at least what we take to be our own self)?" (Martel forthcoming). This is the point of the fusion of the hidden people and sovereignty. The fact is that you cannot rebel against yourself and the rules you have legitimately created. And thus, there is an outsourcing of guilt that ends in impotence.

Regarding our conversation. As a first consequence, we hold that sovereignty is still the point zero of potestas (or archism), and, as such, it cannot be simply wished away, it must be confronted from a paradoxical place of inclusion/exclusion and normality/exception. This, I believe, exhibits a significant difference with your vision of both the function of sovereignty and of archism itself, at least regarding the moment of its emergence and its role in history.

JRM: I agree that there is a great deal of overlap and convergence between the idea of archism and TEP. The way I think about it, archism is the name, or at least a name, for the phenomenon as a whole with the idea of encryption explaining both the method and the means by which archism is perpetuated and sustained.

In terms of the term "nonarchism," the idea is to describe every system of political, economic, social, and cultural self-organization that is not marked either by archism or by encryption. In one sense you could call it a form of political decryption although in some cases the communities that I am interested in, like the *ayllu* in the Andean Highlands and the community of collective farmers that emerged in Haiti after the Haitian Revolution, have been fighting encryption for the past 500 years in the first case and the past 200 years in the second. One of the key ideas of nonarchism, and I think this fits in really well with what you have to say about decryption, is that it is based on human ontology, that is to say, on the fact of human plurality. This basic fact means that any politics that is worthy of its name must reflect the actual people in their actual life, not just as a set of individuals but also in terms of all of the cross-cutting identities and forms of community that are present in a real and material way.

Arendt makes a great deal of this when she writes, "the hope for man in his singularity lay in the fact that not man but men inhabit the earth and form a world between them. It is human worldliness that will save men from the pitfalls of human nature" (1986, 175). In practice, however, Arendt does not follow through with the logic of her own convictions in that she allows for the Ancient Athenians—who are one of her ideal communities—to exclude women, slaves, and nonnative people from Athenian politics. In this way, I think she does fall into the logic of encryption, albeit in a partial way, but the thing about encryption is that it is all consuming. Just as you can't be "a little bit dead or a little bit pregnant," you also cannot be a little bit encrypted. She allows for some part of "the people" to stand in for all of the people, and even though she accords to *these* people a great deal of power, rights, and equality, the fact that other people are excluded from their own "peoplehood" means that they have become, in effect, a hidden people.

It is true that ancient Athens occurred in a time before archism arose as a phenomenon, but the potential for both archism and encryption has always been present. Yet, although many of the most basic tenets of archism were founded in ancient Greek thought, the real malignant form of archist power did not emerge until much more recently, taking its form through the European conquest of much of the rest of the earth, the spread of colonialism, slavery, genocide, and ultimately global capitalism.

I really like your point that when the parasitical transfer of reality that we see in Kant's theory, wherein the subject is able to transcend their own body and the world around them by annihilating it, at least as a thought exercise, and transferring its fleshy reality to the metaphysical, noumenal self, is applied to the people as a whole—as a sovereign entity—that is an ultimate expression of archist power. One of the reasons that the frontispiece of Hobbes's *Leviathan* is so important is that it seeks to give us an image of just this, a giant figure looming over the landscape whose body is composed of the people (lots of little heads all turned inwards—with a few exceptions—toward their sovereign master). The ambiguity of that image—is it the people that compose the sovereign, or is it the giant head that looms over all which constitutes the reality of power relation?—seems to me to capture precisely how encryption works. Ambiguity, which is also the specialty of liberal politics and theory, allows for a sense of engagement and involvement that works to actively disempower the people as such.

As you put it so well, "The power of the people is neutralized and disenfranchised in their own name." Hobbes is the one who says that you cannot rebel against the sovereign because you are yourself the author of that power and the sovereign is only ever acting in your name. While this may seem to be a ruse, one thing that I have always appreciated about Hobbes is the way he is far more honest than those who follow him (especially Locke). It's interesting that at the dawn of the era of encryption there was at least one person who effectively said, "you are all going to be encrypted!" The power of encryption is such, however, that even such a blunt warning was not enough to dispel the power of encryption itself. It is not just a matter of "exposing" encryption as such. It requires that the people form their own forms of collective power that act to usurp the power that archism has stolen from them and continues to steal.

Transcendent Models

RSR: The essence of encryption rests in how capitalism manipulates communal spaces and the concept of social space itself, flipping it on its head. Over time, spaces have morphed into zones of fear—whether it's the office, the university, or the transformation of the sociality of urban areas into a shopping mall. Today, this dynamic extends even further through the screen, disenfranchising individuals politically in profound yet understated ways.

Encryption operates subtly yet powerfully, transforming spaces originally designed for social interaction into zones dominated by consumption, fear, and compliance. This transformation suppresses the ability to communally articulate ideas that challenge the status quo, demanding obedience instead. We are thus before a process that becomes a crucial mechanism for the consolidation of power.

Every space now appears to be constructed and governed by a transcendent model. The office demands efficiency and obedience; the university molds individuals into compliant entities; and the broader world operates as a neatly packaged arena of consumption. This is ever so evident in the first world and bleeds over as a desire for development in the third world.

Now we are able to get a better grip of what we mean by transcendent models and how their role is to dictate the conditions of "beingness" and thus of power.

Transcendent models refer to the abstract, ideological, and violently imposed frameworks that legitimize and perpetuate power. They are the site of encryption, they create a sense of inevitability or naturalness around existing power relations, while they are accepted as just, necessary, normal, or even desired.

As I have stated:

> Since Plato, politics is predefined through extenuating conditions of belonging to the body politic. Insofar, "to be" corresponds to an already existing qualification of life, an inner split within forms of identity where some are welcomed into politics and some are excluded according to qualifications that are detached from beingness but to which beingness must conform in order to be. We have thus the definition of potestas: potestas is the negation of power through the stratification of the conditions to exercise power. The element that above all defines potestas is the arrangement of systems of identity through the permanent construction of transcendent models (presupposition) to define life. (Sanín-Restrepo 2018, xxii)

Genuine politics, therefore, can only exist within a democratic space, a nonplace where meaning is fluid and potential, where being is unqualified and unconstrained, and all possibilities remain open and subject to ongoing negotiation. In stark contrast, transcendent models—operating from a seemingly invisible and inscrutable vantage point—dictate the conditions of being, demanding unquestioning obedience and creating a rigid inclusion-exclusion hierarchy. These models, manifested in abstract yet powerful ideas such as "homeland," "nation," "man," "race," and "rights," generate simulacra that stifle the expression of authentic political agency and limit the potential for transformative change.

Hence, we understand that being is not disconnected from power,[8] but that power comes from beingness, and every being exercises power by the mere fact of existing. Consequently, this "presupposition" is the key to understanding agency: "to be is to exercise power," but this power is always channeled through a predefined, necessary presupposition.

It is important to note the *protean* nature of transcendent models. Sometimes they are found in discourses (human rights), political slogans (MAGA), institutions (the State, the constitution), beliefs (liberalism), procedures, and principles (especially in law, rule of law, legality). The point for TEP is that the creative power of difference is hidden, better yet simulated, by institutional structures that impose fixed and static models of identity and difference, such as the State, the law, or the constitution. The primordial role of transcendent models is to create simulacra (of difference, of people, of life), acting as forms of encryption that prevent or condition the expression of political agency.

As Rancière beautifully puts it:

> Thus the logic of arche presupposes a determinate superiority exercised upon an equally determinate inferiority. In order for there to be a political subject(ivity), and thus for there to be politics, there must be a rupture in this logic. (2001, 3)

JRM: Yes, I love how TEP helps us to distinguish between false forms of social organizing and real ones. This is critical, I think, because, as you show, the false shows are used to convince us that we have access, freedom, equality, and so on, when we do not. The notion of encryption encourages us to first of all not trust what we think we are seeing before our eyes but to rely instead on a kind of second sight that may have atrophied from disuse but is still part of our makeup as human beings. That second sight is attuned to the hidden people because, even if hidden, they are still the people. In the very same way, for Benjamin, although archism—his word for it is mythic violence—produces mere life, at the very same time we are all part of the group that he calls the "living," a source of dynamism and power that archism and encryption parasitize. You can see the congruence between these theories in that the hidden people are also "the living," the radical embodiment of resistance that is always available to thwart the domination of archism.

This is also once again why I am interested in the intervention of Kristin Ross. In her view, I think the commune form is *as itself* relatively immune to the lies and phantasms of encryption. The form itself, if recognized and engaged with as such, is a material, real-life praxis that serves to undermine the top-down and false nature of communication under conditions of archist encryption. That is something I'd like for us to think more about together, whether the form can save the content, as it were, or provide protection from archist predation.

RSR: Our projects are both anti-teleological and anti-hierarchical. They reject necessity as an illegitimate imposition, asserting instead that the true order of politics lies in utter contingency.

Furthermore, our differences are confluent and merely require further dialogue. For instance, while you locate the emergence of archism at the beginning of modernity, I argue that modern constitutions, with their fusion of sovereignty and the people, introduce a novel form of oppression—what we term the proper encryption of power. Consequently, this novelty demands new forms and conceptual frameworks to adequately address it.

My question, then, is whether this shifts your perspective on two points:

1. The emergence of archism.
2. Your position that there are good forms of sovereignty.

JRM: You raise some very important and interesting questions. As for the emergence of archism, in thinking about this further with you, I do think that archism, for all of its attempts to avoid change at all costs, is, of necessity, changing all of the time. One of the key insights of the Italian autonomists in the 1970s was that it was not the capitalists who were driving the nature of capitalism but rather worker resistance. Because of the endless forms of resistance to encryption, it makes sense to me that archism too is always changing (and not of its own accord). Also, in terms of dating the origins of archism, it's a bit complicated because I think archism has always been a possibility, not just in the Global North but all over the world. One of the things I love about *The Dawn of Everything* is that it shows that archism, or at least something like it, sought to emerge at many times in human history. The two Davids claim, for example, that Cahokia, a powerful city in modern-day Missouri, was a very top-down and violent and oppressive society. They argue, however, that Cahokia was brought down by a popular uprising to resist it. So, I'm very ecumenical about the timing of the dawn and rise of archism. I think that we both agree that the past 500 years have been an unmitigated disaster for the planet and for the animals, plants, and people that live on it.

As for the nature of sovereignty, I think that depends on how you define it. The sovereign forms of the Global North are terrible, and I don't think there is a "good" form there at all. But Indigenous forms as well as forms that emerge from what Cedric Robinson calls the Black Radical Tradition have practiced different versions of sovereignty, which I think can be considered to be nonarchist. This might, at the end of the day, just be a question of semantics (and of course there are translation issues as well). But there too I am ecumenical in being open to nonoppressive forms of sovereignty (but not in terms of trying to work with existing forms of Northern sovereignty that, I feel pretty confident in saying, are terrible).

The Ontological Foundation of Being and Politics

RSR: I want to see if this part is able to bring a stronger ontological foundation to the problem of politics that overcomes the shortcomings you signaled in Arendt's construction as she finally falls prey to archism. Here is a firm political ontology that proves that the precondition of the world is that no being can be qualified in order to exist.

In *Decolonizing Democracy* (2016) I undertake a deep revision of Aristotle's concepts of potentiality (*dunamis*) and actuality, particularly the distinction between *Energeia* and *Entelecheia*, to challenge an unwavering Western interpretation of power that has become more stringent, but also Giorgio Agamben's interpretation of power and political action. This revision aims to demonstrate the fundamental contingency of politics, thereby establishing the logical primacy of democracy within any political framework. This is the philosophical backbone of the theory.

> In between potentia and actuality hinges not only the definition of power but the utter possibility of existence, of what is possible and impossible, logical, contingent, necessary and time. We have called the relation of potentiality and actuality the "dyad." (Sanín-Restrepo 2021, 14)

In essence, potentia represents potentiality, what can be the capacity for being, whereas actuality signifies existence, the manifestation of that potential.

Aristotle distinguishes between *Energeia* and *Entelecheia* to define actuality. *Energeia*[9] signifies activity or "being-at-work," emphasizing immanent action and the continuous maintenance of a substance. *Entelecheia*,[10] however, introduces the concept of "telos" (end or perfection), implying a final cause that dictates a thing's purpose. This distinction is vital for differentiating power as domination (potestas) from immanent, dynamic power.

I argue that by understanding *Energeia* as power without a transcendent finality, we can unlock the potential for contingency and "becoming-other," countering Agamben's and Negri's view that leads to political impotence as they understand actuality solely as *Entelecheia*, which is a final form that comes forth through a *telos*.

First, Aristotle is the great conjurer of contingency; as we will see below, he awards actuality primacy over potentia. Second, in building the idea of the political, within actuality, Aristotle awards primacy to *Entelecheia* through final causes, so things can only become actual if they fulfill a finality that is exterior to them. What is the primordial aim of the construction of the dyad? To transform nonbeing into a consequence of being, so that any being that comes to be, is the result of a prefigured actuality (transcendent model). The contingency of the future is then trapped in the necessity of the present actuality. For Aristotle, potentia is subjugated to actuality, but not any kind of actuality but one that incarnates a finality. Through this operation, Aristotle introduces necessity as the neutralizing force of contingency. Consequently, when speaking of the contingency of the potential, the notion here is not that potentiality itself is contingent, but rather that the realization of what is potential is contingent—it might or might not occur. Within the relationship of the dyad, contingency is carefully refined into a specific process. For example, a caterpillar might transform into a butterfly (where the process of becoming is contingent). However, once it has become this butterfly, its actuality is viewed as necessary, reflecting on the interplay that binds potentiality and actuality.

Agamben interprets the actualization of potentiality as the loss of contingency (the qualification of life into a certain *this*, bare life, *bios*, biopolitics), leading to political stagnation. He advocates a retreat into impotence, believing that potentiality is trapped within actuality (thus the conditions of belonging to a body politic are defined by finality, which equates to the death of politics).

However, I argue that Agamben's error lies in conflating actuality with *Entelecheia*, neglecting the liberating potential of *Energeia*.

To counter this, the analysis proposes "actualizing difference" through *Energeia*. Aristotle's theory of causes, particularly the final cause, reinforces the dominance of actuality. *Entelecheia*, with its emphasis on telos, imposes an external, transcendent goal, limiting immanent action (when a thing comes to be actual it can only be so because it developed the finality or perfection imposed by his theory of causes). *Energeia*, conversely, focuses on the "being-at-work" of a substance, where the process itself is the end.

Energeia is immanent, with the principle of generation contained within itself. For instance, a caterpillar becoming a butterfly is a process of *Energeia*, without external qualification. A boy becoming a woman, a man, or them is also a process of *Energeia*, not of *Entelecheia*.

Agamben is trapped by his understanding of actuality solely as *Entelecheia*, which he correctly equates with domination. *Entelecheia* implies that only those who achieve a predetermined perfection (virtue, to follow Aristotle's own example) are part of the political. This leads to divisions between the rational and irrational, the virtuous and the vile, and between life (*bios*) and bare life (*zoē*).

However, and this is our formidable twist, if politics is defined by *Energeia*, it encompasses all beings without qualification. *Energeia* emphasizes the continuous, immanent production of differences, where power is a synergistic, communicative process.

The condition for actualizing difference through *Energeia* is that actuality is not imposed as a finality. *Energeia* allows for transitions of power and supposes contingency and immanence. Politics, defined by *Energeia*, is not a qualified exercise but a common condition of being, where life itself is the sole criterion.

Energeia is its own immanent perfection, with no qualification or obedience to any transcendent model. *Energeia*'s immanent perfection is an open, unending infinity, where every difference contributes to the constitution of being. This perspective offers a way to break free from the constraints of *Entelecheia* that has marked potestas (archism) as inevitable in Western thought and practice while also overcoming Agamben's pessimistic view of political power, opening up an inclusive and dynamic political reality.

I think this approach supersedes Arendt's and Agamben's ontological foundation of politics.

JRM: I think this is absolutely great. I love your distinction between *Energeia* and *Entelecheia*, as well as your description of how contingency does not mean that nothing ever occurs but only that it is absolutely contingent until it happens. This reminds me of a quote from Arendt about John Duns Scotus, where he depicts a donkey who has two identical piles of hay to eat from. It is absolutely contingent which one the donkey eats but eventually they grow hungry and pick one.

I have always been very leery of Agamben's idea of inoperativity. It smacks too much for me of left melancholia. And I also think that the tendency to blame everything on Aristotle gives one thinker way too much power. Therefore, I'm glad that you have been able to find an argument within Aristotle to counter the sense that we are doomed to teleology unless we just completely give up (I don't think I'm being totally fair to Agamben here, but just for the sake of argument ...).

I love the way you have allowed for power to remain something that humans can engage with against tyranny and encryption. Thinking of *Energeia* "as power without a transcendent finality" does mean that the power inherent in contingency can occur without giving up on agency, resistance, and counterpower. To me that is very good news. I think this has something to do, as you also suggest above, with the nature of human ontology once again. In an interesting way, Aristotle's notion of a *zoon politikon* is a functional oxymoron. The fact that we have speech, for Aristotle, means that in a way we are a permanent wild card that acts against the very teleology that he often seems to prefer. Here again, I am also thinking of Arendt who values speech precisely because it takes us outside of ourselves and engages us in relations with others that neither of us get to absolutely control. No conversation ever goes the way you expect it, but things get done as a result and that is an example of *Energeia* in practice. I've long thought that language is a power that the people control; they get to determine the meaning and use of words, and the sovereign is forced to speak in *their* language. That is a big advantage for the hidden people. In fact, encryption itself lies, all must be spoken in language that comes from the people as such. There are many stories like in *1984* of attempts to conquer language and make it a tool of pure domination, but I think in practice this cannot ever take place because language is always changing, contingent, a form, once again, of *Energeia.*

Permanent Assembly

RSR: One of the key takeaways of your work is the vitality and complexity of the permanent assembly on which your latest book focuses on. As you say, a permanent assembly is life itself; it is a deeply ingrained practice of historical communities to keep archism at bay. And you identify that; in contrast, Western forms of resistance are too infested by archism and thus the principles of equality, inclusiveness, and especially immanence, of permanent assemblies become a difficult task to perform, like trying to talk in a foreign language you totally ignore.

As you have described it, permanent assemblies are

> evolved social practices that anticipate, recognize and contain the kinds of usurpation of power and authority that help lead to archism in the first place ... In this sense continuous assembly is an ultimate form of deep organizing; it turns a group of disparate individuals and families into a collective, one that thinks and

> acts in real time. This kind of collective self-knowledge, this extensive form of deep organization, is, I will argue further, both vital and precious because it allows a community to cohere under conditions of extreme duress. (Martel forthcoming)

Here I have a couple of questions and observations.

Regarding matters of subjectivity and praxis, one of the main tasks of encryption is to break being, shatter autonomy, and impede organization, leaving no option but to obey, consume, and through it feel free. "Personality" dangles between the State and the ego-consumer-little-me called the individual, enshrined as citizen, simulated as "the people" and atomized into commodification (the axis State corporations). There is no middle ground. Any sense of collectivity that is not corporative and obeys the thirst of the market is encrypted. Encryption captures, polarizes, fragments, and absorbs the social brain (see Sanín-Restrepo 2016). It tears us apart, reducing the other to a commoditized other. The power of encryption and neoliberalism as its showcase is to disenfranchise, to turn old allies (farmers, immigrants, students, feminists[11]) against each other.

Before this monumental hurdle, as you say, "those institutions had to be created from scratch" (Martel forthcoming). This puts us at a practical bind. How do we learn to assemble? Do we learn to assemble by assembling, through constant practice, until it becomes organic? In a way, even metaphorically, the first assemblers must die as they are tainted by the past; only the future assembleist can create the true free horizontal practice. The old are kind of usurpers, like the freed people from Egypt must die in the desert as they were slaves, and only their children, who were born free, must enter Israel.

In the societies described by the two Davids this discussion was nonexistent as permanent assembly is not an artificial institution added to the practices of the group, but was germane to the group; it was the group itself, as wind and air are not separate things but different manifestations of the same phenomena. Permanent assembly was ingrained; it was quotidian; it would be like discussing do we really breathe? The same goes for equality.

One thing is vital to highlight, and this was the spirit that informed "Decrypting Justice," the first book of this series. When we shift our perspective and construct reality, not through the registering tools of archism, we begin to see that resistance, disobedience, and new forms of collective imagination are always springing about; we need first the ways to register them and second a new way to connect them. As we recently put it:

> Maybe there are living experiences, sprouting all over, people in resistance, people creating through collective imagination and invisible threads of solidarity that can offer a way out. Invisible threads? Yes, that is the point. When we look for them with the registering tools of hegemonic institutions (law, constitutions, science, money, the state), we cannot see and feel but noise and turmoil, and so despair and rage set in. But, when we partake in those experiences, immanently, from what those experiences manifest, our registers are cleansed and transformed immediately, the

world opens up anew and shows us how abundant it really is, and maybe we can begin to talk about justice. (Sanín-Restrepo and Machado-Araujo 2025, 7)

JRM: You've asked what I think is the most important question of all! I think that the ability to form institutions of continuous assembly must occur not when a revolutionary moment begins but long before. This is what we can build while we await a revolutionary moment (I'd go further and say that the building of continuous assemblies in places where it is currently not practiced is a way to bring the revolution to pass). For this reason, and I think TEP really does this, there needs to be more dialogue between leftists in the Global North and Indigenous and Black Radical communities in order to trade knowledges. I think that the Indigenous, Black Radical, and other communities that have not been entirely reduced by archist encryption can demonstrate the form that we should all adopt, but the content is up to each community based on its own culture, history, needs, and so forth. But the Global North has something to add to the conversation too. I think: to achieve scale we need to learn from the *Communards* in France in the 1870s, the anarchists in Spain in the 1930s, the autonomists in Italy in the 1970s. These groups had big plans (some of which were put into execution) to scale up their revolutions. The problem was that without a really embedded institution of continuous assembly, they had to rely on what I think of as "archist supplements" like parties, unions, and even the State (in the case of Allende's revolution in Chile, for example). Those supplements could be counted on to turn against the revolutions and so the nascent organs of continuous assembly were not able to survive.

Yet the *ayllu* have been surviving for well over a thousand years. The experiment in collective farming in Haiti after the revolution lasted well over a hundred years (it took a twenty-year occupation by the United States to largely uproot it). Those groups show how not only can we resist but we can win! I think all of these groups need each other to collectively reconstitute the hidden people and take power back, decrypt the prison that holds us in its maw, and turn both archism and encryption into the awful, increasingly dim memories they need to become.

OK, now I have a question for you. Several related questions, really. I'm curious about the connection between potestas and encryption. It makes sense to me, on the one hand, that a power that doesn't have the ontological basis that it claims to have would need to encrypt that fact and maybe that is the basis for encryption in the first place. But, at the same time, it strikes me as creating a lot of vulnerability in the system to depend so utterly on a ruse. I'm curious about how vulnerable potestas is in your view in the sense that it could entirely collapse. Clearly, the system of encryption has survived many moments of exposure (essentially every revolutionary moment is one of those, and also, even in nonrevolutionary times, it seems to me that there are repeated and almost constant forms of exposure; the fact of the commune form's ongoing existence strikes me as an instance where the exposure is sustained and ongoing, for one example). Does encryption just reknit its web of lies immediately following an exposure of its ruse? I've always found the moment in Orwell's *1984*— where it says, "Oceania was at war with Eastasia, Oceania had always been at war with Eastasia" (1981, 150)—to be both a frightening thought and also a highly unlikely one. I know that there are flatearthers today and that these days denial of reality is a stock in trade for large segments of the US population, for one example, but I've always felt too that this is largely for instrumental reasons, like there is a payoff to think this and not that. That certainly could be true for the elites in the system of encryption, but what about the rest of us? How does encryption insinuate itself into our very inner psychic spaces so that we see it even when we don't want to? And what keeps it (this is my main question) from being a kind of all-for-nothing scheme where either all of us see it or all of us don't? That would be very dangerous for encryption, but I think in practice it works as a kind of network of lies rather than one big lie and so it can survive assaults on one section without wholly collapsing (unfortunately). So, is encryption more like a patchwork of false realities stitched over the world, or is it more of a constant with local applications?

RSR: These are great questions as they put everything in action and interrogate our place within this complex context we are dealing with. I'll try to weave an interconnected answer to them.

The major feature of potestas is that although it might appear monolithic, and thus rigid (and this is important for its own ideological projection) it is truly a highly movable structure, with fluid tactic deployments, and working through vast and ever-changing, ever-adapting networks. More of this below.

Now, for the names. As another chapter, written with Marinella Machado-Araujo, develops, the term *Potestas* is the anchor for a systemic history of the deactivation of democracy to favor forms of power exercised by minorities and the justification of hierarchies thereof. Thus, we find that the emergence of *potestas*, or power as domination, is the knot that resolves the fundamental tension within the concept of *politeia*. You see, as Agamben tells us, when Plato encountered *politeia*, he saw it as an aberration, origins without origin, the primordial anarchic void of the becoming of everything. Thus, his effort, in what we come to know as "The Republic," was to drown the raw, unbounded force of constituent power within the structured form of constituted power. Plato's efforts to transform *politeia* into a codified, controlled form of government, *politeuma*, reflect this fear. This division between constituent and constituted power creates an inherent ambiguity, a "foundational wound" that subsequent political thought seeks to heal. As language is indomitable, the term still revealed a primordial fracture in Western political thought. This fracture stems from the fear of contingency and the illimited power of the people.

Aristotle attempted to bridge this gap by defining *politeia* as governance for the common good, tying the amphibious creature (*politeia* and *politeiuma*) to the higher concept of sovereignty "kyrios" as a transcendent force that fuses the two aspects of power.

However, it is in the very pragmatic Rome, with the newfound spirit of the law, that the decisive shift toward *potestas* occurs. The *libertas* of the *Populus*, their constituent power, is subordinated to the *auctoritas* of the senate and the *potestas* of the magistrates. This marks a highly sophisticated closure of the fissure, where constituted power drives and controls constituent power. The definition of the *Res-publica*, "common good," is then monopolized by a privileged minority, those who exercise *potestas*. What is primordial to grasp here is that potestas is rich in meaning as it ties together patriarchy, private property, and the objectification of lesser beings. Thus, the term *potestas* emerges as the concrete manifestation of constituted power's dominance, where the potential for immanent, contingent political action is suppressed in favor of a controlled, hierarchical order.

This is clear for the Two Davids when they state:

> The Roman Law conception of natural freedom is essentially based on the power of the individual (by implication, a male head of household) to dispose of his property as he sees fit. In Roman Law property isn't even exactly a right, since rights are negotiated with others and involve mutual obligations; it's simply power … This formulation has some peculiarities that jurists have struggled with ever since, as it implies freedom is essentially a state of primordial exception to the legal order. It also implies that property is not a set of understandings between people over who gets to use or look after things, but rather a relation between a person and an object characterized by absolute power. (2021, 508–9)

Therefore, encryption (of power, of the people) is better understood not only as hiding and obscuring but also as separating, dividing, and impeding as well. What does it divide? In the strictest sense those who govern and those who are powerless. To accomplish this, power must be extracted from being. Power is then confined to megastructures (molar structures as Deleuze (2014) interprets Foucault) like the State, effectively arresting it from all other forms of being. This regime of truth creates a fundamental philosophical and ethical separation. What does it impede? That the lines are crossed, it impedes that potentia can be exercised without any particular finality, that the people can self-organize. Insofar, encryption hides the fact that it separates, divides, impedes; it hides the product of said acts when it hides and confounds *Energeia* as *Entelecheia*, constituent power within constituted structures, and immanence as eminence.

While *potestas* is always vulnerable to exposure, as demonstrated by revolutionary moments and persistent resistance, it exhibits remarkable resilience. It adapts, absorbs, and renarrates. This is not a singular, conscious deception, a unified ruse as you will, but a systemic process embedded in institutions and ideologies. The *1984* analogy highlights how *potestas* can redefine reality itself, rewriting history to maintain its narrative. We may simply remember Foucault's (1978) proof that resistance is integral to oppression.

Nevertheless, the concept of the "hidden people" is critical to this operation, and this is the novelty. Transcendent models are not a patchwork of isolated falsehoods, but a consistent underlying principle with localized applications. It is an ontological maneuver. The "hidden people" are the "excess" of the system; the excluded that are needed to sustain the illusion of the "people as a whole" means that encryption has achieved an unsuspected leap as the people hide the people within the people, sovereignty is hidden in plain sight.

In a chapter in *Decrypting Justice* (2025) Machado-Araujo and I delved deeply into the nature of transcendent models. To establish, first, that the work of potestas is done, ironically enough, in the form of networks that overlap, that are fluid and decentered when it comes to encrypting power. Second, our analysis revealed that modern AI architectures are fundamentally rooted in classic "second natures" (Adam Smith's concept of the economy, or Hobbes's idea of the modern State), which we define as elaborate, transcendent autopoietic systems. These systems exhibit sophisticated internal apparatuses and defense mechanisms, enabling them to actively program and safeguard their operational integrity against disruptive crises, notably by defining the very parameters of what constitutes a "crisis."

Systems, like States or laws, are intricate machines; their workings are a blend of self-preservation and imposed order. They don't simply exist; they actively construct their reality, a sophisticated form of encryption. This construction hinges on a clever illusion: the simulation of conflict. Real tensions—inequalities, injustices, exclusions, State terrorism—are absorbed and transformed, presented as manageable, docile; internal disputes and disruptions are taken care by experts dealing with esoteric languages and the hidden rules of the model. The core deception lies in the simulation of conflict. The system presents itself as a space for debate, for change, but the terms of engagement are carefully controlled. Real challenges are transformed into manageable disputes, ensuring that the fundamental power structure remains intact. The law, in this context, becomes a tool for regulating violence, not eliminating it, a cycle of force used to maintain control. It creates an "anti-community," where those deemed outside the norm are perpetually marginalized.

As we put it in another chapter for this book:

> The relationship between the "arché" and its manifestation is always a *post facto* construction. The transcendent model, essentially an empty signifier, is initially named and loosely characterized. Its concrete definition—its categories, functions, and pragmatic realm—is determined by qualified interpreters (the pontiff, the constitutional judge) who, based on the prevailing world conditions, fill in its content. This process allows experts or "encryptors" to impose domination *ex post facto*, utilizing the inherent openness and autopoietic fabric of the model to shape it according to rules ingrained within its structure.

Consequently, this vast network of transcendent models is a sophisticated autopoietic machine that (1) creates a complex realm of reality (ideology), (2) programs and anticipates threats, (3) is elastic enough to reaccommodate changes and conflicts as if they were part of the machine, (4) use a cluster of experts (constitutional judges, economists) dealing with esoteric languages who apply the rules ingrained in the model with plasticity and always imposing the principles of the model in an *ex post facto* manner.

Ultimately, this is a system built on myth, not genuine political engagement. It creates an illusion of contact, of participation, but it's a contact without substance, a transfer of information without genuine exchange. The "hidden people," those excluded from the system's core, represent the constant threat, the potential for true community the system must suppress. The system in order to survive must keep those people from realizing their own collective power.

How do we typically navigate these encrypted spaces? Primarily, encryption undermines the very possibility of genuine encounter, of seeing ourselves and others through the lens of alterity. It targets otherness, reducing it either to a commodity (as Marx observed) or to a State-defined abstraction, filtered through the reductive lenses of law and bureaucracy.

Encryption is a machine that creates precariousness, both in the sense of reducing life's abundance and color to scarcity and greyness, and in reducing the capacity we have to reach the other because encryption determines deficient tools to do so; we are deprived of life's abundance and the forms to name it, and to approximate the other. The reduction of beingness, authentic beingness, to the State, a few corporations, and the greedy individual, truly undermines our communication. Consequently, the systematic erosion of communicative and solidarity-based tools leaves us with a limited repertoire. When confronted with the other's suffering, we instinctively resort to the available tools of encryption—the encrypted legal apparatus, and all its paraphernalia of judges, legal processes, and so on, for instance—in an attempt to offer aid. However, through decryption and sustained collective action, we seek to demonstrate that alternative tools exist, they are permanently used and made effective by movements of resistance, while encrypted tools are being decrypted and turned useful through and for permanent assemblies. With this latter statement what I mean is that encryption is never able to suffocate imagination and creativity, although that is its main objective, hence political imagination also entails a struggle to liberate what encryption has ransacked and coopted. For example, the liberal claim that it has awarded rights and freedom utterly denies historical fact as it has been the struggles from below that have opened the tap of freedom. In this sense the fight is also to liberate the emancipatory potential of what seems deadly encrypted, as law.

In another chapter, Machado-Araujo and I will explore the effects the fusion of sovereignty and the people has in ideological and psychoanalytical terms, as well as the order of the spectacle and Baudrillard's simulacrum. We explore the Two Davids' concept of "charisma" tightly bound to Agamben's concept of "Glory," the necessary material adoration of power that hides God in the void of power.

The glorification of the self simply short-circuits order, ideology, freedom, and obedience in politics. When sovereignty was placed in God, monarchs, or nations, power's glorification was external. But when Glory and sovereignty fall on the people—both sovereign and subject—contradictions arise. The demand for absolute authority and its negation creates a feedback loop where the people internalize and perpetuate their subjugation. This narcissistic loop often results in displacement onto a strong bullyish leader promising to restore the people's greatness.

The people are walled into sovereignty as paradoxically "nothingness" and "everything," filling the void with a "liturgy of the self." Charismatic spectacle redirects power to a transcendent realm.

Psychoanalytically, as per Melanie Klein (1975) and Žižek (2001), this involves identifying with the aggressor, idealizing power, and defending against vulnerability through grandiosity. Propaganda, manipulation, and the threat of violence create a "foreclosure of dissent," denying the Real of oppression. In Baudrillard's terms (1988), people become "hyperreal" constructs, acting within a simulacrum where forced glorification is a ritual-reinforcing illusion.

JRM: A wonderful and illuminating answer! I have one final question that gets at what is happening around the world today. Do you think that encryption waxes and wanes along with cycles of liberalism and authoritarianism? During liberal times, we often speak of "dog whistles," nods to the hierarchies of race and gender and class that sustain archist encryption, but which are hidden (i.e., encrypted) through ideology and all of the systems that you have described. But sometimes the whistle becomes a trumpet (a tuba!). In such cases, are we seeing something like the "genuine face" of what is being encrypted in all of its ugly violent manifestation? Or is this too somehow part of encryption, a secondary way to hide what is being hidden through a kind of homeostatic process where no part of the cycle is more genuine or real than any other and the whole act, including its alterations, is itself basic to the nature of encryption as such? I could see how the cycling through itself could produce "relief" when the authoritarian or fascist phase ends, thus making the liberal phase seem benign and endurable by comparison. If that is the case, however, what does this mean about encryption itself? Is it, like the purloined letter in Poe's allegory, hiding in plain sight, hiding by not hiding?

RSR: We are at that crossroad. It would seem that the appeal to liberal laws and its sacred institutions such as the rule of law and legality is withering away through mega-macho, ultra-religious, and full-throttle capitalism that seems not to need to hide anywhere, that displays their intent in a straightforth manner, and that has no pudor to show us the pustules of power. It is all out there, in the raw, a bizarre form of *decryption*, racism as the true out-in-the-open virtue of politics, the hatred of the feminine as the very structure of the exercise of power. Nevertheless, we are certain, power has never been so encrypted (as Adorno and Horkheimer were also certain that the fascism of their time came cleanly out of the womb of liberalism). The two main keys of encryption are at play here, in a doublefold of sorts, while also being full-throttle. (1) The fusion of the people and sovereignty that liberalism achieved through constitutionalization is here transferred to the leader. As I anticipated, *Glorification*, which is an integral part of archism, goes awry when the people glorify themselves as sovereign, but as their image is fragmented, and the act is narcissist, the transference to a strong leader made in the mud of buffoonery is only logical. The leader promises to restore the loss grandeur of the people (here the people as synecdoche is evermore present) against that other fragment of the people (the hidden counterpart) that are identified as the negation (racial, gender) of the identity and uniformity of the "real" people (whiteness, masculinity). And (2) the sovereign, the absolute decision, although it seems fragmented, is still paramount to create the exception and through it legitimize submitting the greatest portion of the world's population to the precarity of capitalism. Now, what these processes of the hardening of exclusion lines produce is a permanent revindication of *who* the right people are (nationality, race), but it allows for a swifter *ex post facto* arranging of the conditions of belonging to it, and it allows for the revolving door between law and the market to be more efficient (the idea that law is in charge of protecting a fraction of the people while expelling the rest to be devoured by the market). Thus, for example, whiteness and holding a certain nationality do not render you immune anymore to being ejected (temporally, permanently) to the underbelly of the beast; anyone can be the hidden people, at any time. So, if anything, these processes accelerate encryption; they make it more mobile and stauncher.

In conclusion, and here is the fold, if the people are not enshrined in the constitution, if patriotism is not assured by solid legal mechanisms like borders, and if their core values (aberrant vision of themselves) are not executed through wars (conventional, commercial), the bond between the people and the leader would break; it would be inexistent. Hence, encryption, of the people, as transference of sovereignty (simulated), is still the beating heart of oppression; it is its lifeline.

Notes

1 This introduction establishes a dialogue between archism and the TEP, laying out the connections and exploring whether discrepancies are merely terminological or run deeper. The following section will detail the book's structure, presenting each chapter and the links between them.

2 Maybe every abyss is but a mirror.

3 The richness of our dialogue is assured by the diversity, adaptability, and force of our collective strategies for liberation. Indeed, contrary to the limitations imposed by rigid liberal disciplines that are the narrowing of imagination, it is this profusion of perspectives that guarantees precision. In a large collaborative model, no single conceptual apparatus can grasp the entire picture as it requires the synthesis of many findings. The extension of multiple lines of evidence, from different disciplines, is needed to build a comprehensive and accurate understanding where the combined knowledge is greater than the sum of its parts. And just as complex scientific phenomena, like climate change or the human genome, cannot be understood through a single perspective, power as domination, sovereignty, and especially liberation necessitates the overlap of many visions and the deployment of many tools at different intensities and forces.

4 What is cast in *Energeia* (unqualified beingness) is composition as perfection, with no further qualification, transcendence, or finalism than the composition of the common of politics. And what would this composition look like? As an open infinity, an open constitution of being where every difference is included as its own topic of enunciation. A decrypted space of language where language means the utter necessity of the common, furthermore, where the common and language become one and the same thing. In short, *Energeia* means that the future is yet to be decided.

5 See Benjamin (1999), especially, 66 (B2,4), 544 (S1,5), 548 (S2a,3), 842–3 (G17).

6 In the latter case Schürmann dislodges an-archy with concrete historical movements and very precise anarchist political struggles (Bakunin, Goldman, the Spanish Revolution). I know you do the same, but he posits the fact that at the origin of any form of power there is only a void and at that every metaphysical definition of being is simply epochal and thus relative. As such, any arché as the model that any being most conform to in order to be is built on false models or transcendent models—as we call them. Thus, arché as the origin of power and beingness is ontologically inauthentic.

In other words, given the impossibility of establishing any true origin of power or the authenticity of any being, a false model, a simulacrum is imposed in its place as glory and adoration, as the fulfilment of the void.

7 One of the affinities, I would go further and say axioms of both theories, is that politics cannot be teleological. As you put it: "This notion of dialectic is, above all, stripped of its teleological tendencies in order to deliver something that is quite the opposite, a sense of movement towards something that is absolutely unpredictable, which cannot exist until it does" (Martel forthcoming). This is precisely the point of TEP: we cannot anticipate something that does not yet exist, because doing so is a form of potestas.

8 Hence power rests not only in the magnificent structures (the State, the law, the economy) but palpitates in the potency of every being. Hence, any being (a neutrino, a baby, a star, a cell) exercises power as it exists. The potentiality of the condensation of water, a hug, a bomb, a law, a bullet are all expressions of power; they alter the world in its conditions of possibility and recognition. To exist is to be in a relation; to be in a relation is to give and receive power (Sanín-Restrepo and Machado-Araujo 2025).

9 Energeia whose root is *ergonó*, which can be translated as activity, action, and operation, from which derives the adjective *energon*, meaning active or working. The etymological compound brings us *energeia*, from *en* (in, within) + *ergon* (work). In this first approximation we have a first meaning not only of actuality but a very specific finality of actuality that is the work required to maintain the state of a substance through the *being at work* of the substance (Sanín-Restrepo 2016, 98).

10 We get "Entelecheia" by combining *entelēs* (ἐντελής, "complete, full-grown") with *echein* (*hexis*), which means to be a certain way by the continuing effort of holding on to that condition. But a third and defining block of significance is put into the composite when Aristotle plays with the more usual word *endelecheia* (ἐντελέχεια, "persistence") by inserting *telos* (τέλος, completion) as the definite component of the concept (Sachs 2005). Etymologically, Entelecheia is thus composed of *en* (within) + *telos* (end, perfection) + *ekhein* (to be in a certain state)" (Sanín-Restrepo 2016, 98–9).

11 I didn't even have to look far for this; I just found it reading the paper the very same day, a feminist movement that is identitary and anti-immigration. www.lefigaro.fr/actualite-france/feminisme-comment-la-manifestation-du-8-mars-vire-a-l-affrontement-entre-mouvements-feministes-20250308.

References

Arendt, Hannah. 1986. *On Revolution*. New York: Penguin Books.

Baudrillard, Jean. 1988. "Simulacra and Simulations." In *Selected Writings*, edited by Mark Poster. Stanford, CA: Stanford University Press, 166–84.

Benjamin, Walter. 1999. *The Arcades Project*. Cambridge, MA: Harvard University Press.

Butler, Octavia. 1993. *Parable of the Sower*. New York: Grand Central.

Deleuze, Gilles. 2014. *Michel Foucault y el poder. Viajes Iniciáticos*. Madrid: Errata Naturae.

Foucault, Michel. 1978. *The History of Sexuality Volume I: An Introduction*. New York: Pantheon Books.

Graeber, David, and David Wengrow. 2021. *The Dawn of Everything: A New History of Humanity*. New York: Farrar, Straus and Giroux. Kindle edition.

Horkheimer, Max, and Theodor W. Adorno. 2002. *Dialectic of Enlightenment: Philosophical Fragments*. Stanford, CA: Stanford University Press.
Klein, Melanie. 1975. *Envy and Gratitude and Other Works: 1946–1963*. London: Vintage.
Martel, James R. Forthcoming. *Continuous Assembly: The Power and Promise of Non Archism*. Durham, NC: Duke University Press.
Meillassoux, Quentin. 2008. *After Finitude. An Essay on the Necessity of Contingency*. Translated by Ray Brassier. London: Bloomsbury Academic.
Orwell, George. 1981. *1984*. New York: Signet Classics.
Rancière, Jacques. 2001. *Ten Theses on Politics*. Baltimore, MD: Johns Hopkins University Press.
Ross, Kristin. 2024. *The Commune Form: The Transformation of Everyday Life*. New York: Random House.
Sachs, Joe. 2005. "Aristotle: Motion and Its Place in Nature." *Internet Encyclopedia of Philosophy*. www.iep.utm.edu/aris-mot/#H2.
Sanín-Restrepo, Ricardo. 2016. *Decolonizing Democracy: Power in a Solid State*. London: Rowman and Littlefield.
Sanín-Restrepo, Ricardo. 2018. "The Meaning of the Encryption of Power as the Razor's Edge of Politics." In *Decrypting Power*. London: Rowman and Littlefield, ix–xxx.
Sanín-Restrepo, Ricardo. 2021. *Being and Contingency: Decrypting Heidegger's Terminology*. London: Rowman & Littlefield.
Sanín-Restrepo, Ricardo, and Marinella Machado-Araujo. 2020. "The Theory of Encryption of Power: Itinerary of an Idea." *Revista da Faculdade Mineira de Direito* 23(45): 1–17.
Sanín-Restrepo, Ricardo, and Marinella Machado Araujo. 2022. "Keys to Decrypt the Republic Against Democracy." *Law and Critique* 33(1): 41–62. https://doi.org/10.1007/s10978-020-09272-w.
Sanín-Restrepo, Ricardo, and Marinella Machado-Araujo. 2025. "A Prolific Paradox of Justice and Two Theses on the Encryption of the Hidden People." In *Decrypting Justice: From Epistemic Violence to Immanent Democracy*, edited by Ricardo Sanín-Restrepo, Marinella Machado-Araujo, and Sabelo Ndlovu-Gatsheni. Lanham, MD: Lexington Books and Bloomsbury Academic, 15–41.
Schürmann, Reiner. 1987. *Heidegger on Being and Acting: From Principles to Anarchy*. Bloomington: Indiana University Press.
Žižek, Slavoj. 2001. *Enjoy Your Symptom! Jacques Lacan in Hollywood and Out*. London: Routledge.

Presentation of the Book and Its Chapters

James R. Martel and Ricardo Sanín-Restrepo

Sovereignty is a tricky business, a slippery object with a protean nature, a ghost armed with claws. Thus, despite its apparent monolithic quality, it changes forms and seems to flow within and through language, epistemology, politics, ethics, and every form in which power appears. The question thus imposes itself: is sovereignty tantamount to power? Is it power's sole source? Or is it its closure? Is it the very form of power? Or is it its content? We breathe its heavy air; we see guided by its darkness; its emblems (hard and subtle) are everywhere while still it hides its hand. What, then, is the relation of sovereignty to power, democracy, law, politics, theology, and colonialism? Is this relation fleeting and secondary? Or rather, is it primordial, so primordial that we fail to account for every instance in which it exercises its monumental force? Are we granting far too much importance to a word? At the end of the day, it is simply a word, so how has this word been almost omnisciently present in determining the history of a world defined by the imperatives of a small group of people from a minor geographical zone holding onto a self-defined single race and auto-proclaimed civilization, and the dialectics of abiding by and resisting it by the majority of the rest of the world? Therefore, what announces itself is basically a tightly knit relation between sovereignty and resistance, which itself seems to signal a wider, more comprehensive dialectic of command and disobedience, of an appetite and a need for uniformity on one side and the need to break from it in order to survive and to be, on the other.

Consequently, this book explores the critical juncture of sovereignty, archism (hierarchical power), and the complex processes by which power is hidden against and in the name of democracy (encrypted) and how it may be revealed (decryption). While each chapter engages with these three core concepts, the book's central challenge is directed squarely at sovereignty while its driving force is to embrace and reveal radical democracy.

Archism and the theory of encryption of power (TEP) serve as essential conceptual tools through which we approach, dissect, and perhaps even seek to temper sovereignty, ultimately pointing toward alternative possibilities within and beyond its grasp. Through these two frameworks we are able to fathom new depths in sovereignty, as well as perceive new threads woven by people's acting from below in permanent resistance.

The perspectives within the book are not uniform. Some authors critically view sovereignty as a formidable barrier to genuine democracy, highlighting its negative aspects. Others, however, examine it differently, proposing positive or affirmative forms of sovereignty that are encrypted—and thus must be decrypted and fundamentally reshaped. This divergence is in keeping with a larger literature on sovereignty wherein, from the perspective of the Global North, sovereignty is the dominant and oppressive world system that most of our authors are addressing. At the same time, in Indigenous Studies, the term sovereignty has been reclaimed as a power to resist Northern and settler domination. Thus, for example, Zackary Taktuk Smith's essay embraces a different form of sovereignty even as it seeks to contest the sovereign form that emanates from the Global North.

What unites all contributors is the shared imperative to confront the sovereign phenomenon from diverse perspectives, recognizing that no single viewpoint can fully encapsulate its complexities. This collective effort seeks to cultivate forms of resistance capable of fostering a radical democracy that thrives on the anarchic, contingent, and unaccountable potential of the new. It is paramount to understand that the anarchic, contingent, and unaccountable potential of the new are, again, not the individual desires or goals of the authors of the book (it is not proselytism) but, as we will see, the very ontological condition of the world, thus *of what may become to be* through the exercise of power.

The chapters collectively underscore the importance of examining sovereignty through multiplicity, extracting forms of resistance that redefine democracy itself. Such resistance is not merely about opposition but about empowering ideas and actions to reveal their strength and guiding force. It is within this untamed and vibrant realm of collective imagination that the future can be reshaped, liberated from the confines of existing structures that appear to exist solely on the claim that they are necessary and insurmountable.[1]

In essence, the book aims to analyze sovereignty like a complex, multidimensional figure, examining its inner workings from all perspectives. By looking inside, outside, and around it, we seek to discover concrete ways to enhance political imagination both *from* its existing conditions and *against* its constraining power.

We have organized the book upon three thematic axes that are loose, allowing the reader a permanent conversation and remodeling of its order. The first two chapters introduce the topics of the history and conceptualization of sovereignty while unpacking the possibilities of decryption and the study of archism to produce new critiques and consequently new meanings to bear upon it.

The second part is composed of two chapters that dig deep into the philosophical entrails of sovereignty as it is sustained by political theology. These chapters are bound together by their shared critical engagement with the multifaceted nature of power within contemporary political landscapes. Each contribution underscores the paramount importance of a deep analysis of political theology in understanding how power operates, often through subtle and deeply embedded historical and conceptual frameworks. They delve into the often-obscured mechanisms through which power is legitimized and exercised, examining its implications for concepts such as democracy, identity, and sovereignty. By highlighting the enduring influence of theological concepts on political thought and practice, these analyses emphasize the necessity of a rigorous examination of this intersection to fully grasp the complexities of power and its impact on our understanding of political life.

The authors of this middle part share a common target and a means to attain it. Sovereignty, understood as a unified and foundational power (arché), encrypts the potential of radical democracy—and democracy as a social order capable of overcoming the idea of "the people" as a false subject of sovereignty. Through the TEP and archism the authors create a brand-new form of deeming sovereignty in its innerworkings with political theology, conceptualizing the constituent character of *an-archy*, contrasting it with the founding, archaic, and transcendent nature of sovereignty. In tandem, they debunk the liberal legal doctrine's falsifications of sovereignty and arrive at a common platform of decrypting archism.

The third part of chapters is grouped around what we have termed sovereignty in movement, decryption *in situ*, or—as one chapter happily names it—*nomadic sovereignty*. Henceforth the reader will encounter a rich analysis and critique of power's historical evolution and how it conceals itself, emphasizing resistance and sovereignty "from below," challenging State-centric views. They explore the plantation system's legacy, neoliberal complexities, and colonialism's ongoing impact, shaping power structures that operate by "encryption."

Resistance becomes "decryption," as movements like Marronage, Zapatismo, and Indigenous struggles reveal alternative powers and self-determination in utterly new forms of decrypting power. These enact "nomadic" or "an-archic" sovereignty, destabilizing State control and upending the foul power of potestas.

Drawing on diverse theories, the chapters argue that true liberation requires embracing resistance and its voices and creations. Rather than a single blueprint, they advocate unveiling power's hidden workings and furthering alternative social and political visions.

Chapter 1

In "The Not-So-Hidden People: One Path Out of Encryption and Archism," James R. Martel seeks to introduce a hybrid of the theory of encryption (TEP) and archism by speaking of archist encryption. Archist encryption is both the cause (encryption) and the result (archism) of 500 years of slavery, genocide, imperialism, white supremacy, and capitalism. Archist encryption has produced what Sanín-Restrepo and Machado-Araujo call "the hidden people," namely the occultation of people in their actual existence, only to be replaced by forms of pseudo-subjectivity and false identity. In this chapter Martel argues that not all people are equally well hidden. In two communities that it focus on, Indigenous communities as well as communities that partake in what Cedric Robinson calls the Black Radical Tradition, we see a form of resilience that stems from the fact that these communities have been battling and resisting archist encryption for centuries now. Whereas in the Global North the resilience of local communities has been worn down, leading to a near-total capture—and hence hiding—of the people (although one idea that Martel shares with Sanín-Restrepo and Machado-Araujo's thesis is that encryption can never be absolute and totalizing), in these other communities you find that decryption is, in some sense, embedded into their practices from the ground up.

A great deal of this resilience and resistance stems from the fact, in the author's view, that these communities have never abandoned a critical form of political self-organization, namely the practice of continuous political, economic, social, and cultural assembly (or just continuous assembly for short). These communities engage in what Kristen Ross calls the commune form, an organization whereby ordinary daily life doubles as a kind of ongoing assembly where people come to know and trust one another and, in that way, defy the kinds of lies and innuendos that are the stuff of archist encryption. Thus, the *ayllu*—to give just one example, the organizational form of Indigenous communities from the Andean highlands of present-day Peru and Bolivia—have been resisting domination for over a thousand years (and counting!).

The critical point about continuous assembly is that, insofar as collectively a people know everything they need to know, there is nevertheless a requirement for that information to be shared in order to actualize its potential. Archist encryption works to separate and isolate people from each other so that, rather than accessing collective forms of information and assessing, judging, and acting on them, communities are left under the aegis of managers, bosses, *gamonales*, patrons, elected officials, and other forms of hierarchical authority, leading to their own occlusion.

When the world is awash with lies (a situation that is very clear right now in many countries, but which has always been the case under conditions of archist encryption) we need forms of self-organization that allow a people to decide for themselves what to think and what to do. This chapter argues that the best defense against archist encryption is the commune form and the continuous assembly that it offers. This is not a panacea—such guarantees are the stuff of archist encryption itself. Instead it is only a chance, but in fact—whereas the left in the Global North has mainly only managed to pull off moments of resistance that have lasted for a short while (think of the three months of the Paris commune, the glorious anarchist summer of 1936 in Spain, the early years of the Soviets in the Russian Revolution)—the *ayllu* are entering into their second millennium. For this reason, models for how to engage in decryption are widely available to leftists in the Global North. In times between revolutions, such as our own, it would behoove such leftists to self-organize in forms of continuous assembly, not to copy Indigenous and Black Radical forms—since by definition each community must engage on its own terms with its own conditions—but rather to allow their own model of decryption to emerge and its hidden people to come out a bit further into the sun.

Chapter 2

In "The Narcissism of Sovereignty: A Pattern for Liberation Through the Hidden People," Sanín-Restrepo and Machado-Araujo argue that there is a distinctive feature that is the driving force of Western political theories and practices: the need to disenfranchise democracy, as the latter is understood in its uttermost ontological and practical dimension as the anarchic, contingent, and unpredictable potential of collective political imagination.

The core argument posits a dialectical struggle between sovereignty as the force of the necessity of domination and the privilege of the few, and democracy as the sole condition for there to be a world. The article demonstrates how methods of neutralizing democracy lead to a chronic narrowing of its definition, ultimately forcing it to align with the concept of sovereignty, understood as power based on oppression (*potestas*). Sovereignty achieves this by imposing rigid hierarchies as natural, establishing unquestionable narratives of origin as unique, and asserting its own unbreakable necessity, constantly preying on and feeding from democracy's inherent potential.

The intricate history of this conversion is drawn in clear lines. Therefore, sovereignty is presented as the organizing principle of Western and colonial history, dictating narratives, imposing epistemologies, bounding aesthetical possibilities, and suppressing alternatives. Challenging some interpretations, the text argues that sovereignty remains the dominant model of *potestas* in our days.

As the authors argue, a key mechanism, one that produces a quantum leap in the consideration of power, democracy, and sovereignty, is the sovereign creation of a "hidden people," through modern constitutions, which merges domination with legitimacy to justify violence and the social dissolution inherent in capitalism and epitomized in colonial liberalism. The conclusion is that the sovereign act of creating a "hidden people" is not a peripheral or secondary outcome of today's power but rather its fundamental core. Consequently, in contexts of coloniality, the constitutional definition of "the people" represents the ultimate expression of this sovereign function, of the replacing of democracy by sovereignty, and what keeps oppression healthy through a simulacrum of democracy.

The analysis proposes besieging sovereignty from the perspective of *Energeia* (unconditioned power of beingness), which historically outspreads and ontologically grounds Jacques Rancière's notion of democracy as characterized by the absence of qualifications for governing.

The chapter connects with Graeber and Wengrow's work (*The Dawn of Everything*) as the latter identifies three principles of *potestas* (control of violence/sovereignty, control of information/encryption, and individual charisma). Henceforth, the authors argue that late coloniality, through the fusion of the people and sovereignty, maximally reinforces these features. The TEP allows the reader to assess sovereignty as the encryption of the people's power maintained by experts, and charisma as built upon the simulated power/narcissistic self-image of the people as sovereign. The transformation of charisma is further explored through Agamben's notion of Glory, where the people simultaneously adore and represent this false sovereign glory, leading to lost agency and narcissistic authoritarian dynamics.

Finally, the essay emphasizes that the fundamental precondition of political existence is absolute contingency (*Energeia*), a truth obscured by the pervasive imposition of *Entelecheia* (finality, predetermined objectives) in Western political thought to neutralize contingency and build hierarchical structures. Power based on

Entelecheia is deemed a simulacrum of democracy, while resistance rooted in *Energeia* represents the true expression of the political, revealing modern Western power structures as sophisticated forms of masked domination.

Chapter 3

In "Constituent An-Archy: Marx, Castoriadis, and Sanín-Restrepo Against the Encryption of Constituent Power as Sovereignty," Andityas Matos looks at the idea of "constituent an-archy" as a form of power that avoids the traps of encryption even as it remains within the confines of *potentia*. For Matos, the an-archic is a rejection of all teleology; it is constituently empty and does not leave any determination in its wake. It is the antithesis (hence the name an-archy) of command and domination. Whereas some have made an argument for *destituent* power, Matos argues that an an-archic form of power is possible even when possessing the features of constituent authority more generally.

Thinking about this in terms of TEP, we could say that Matos is arguing that encryption can be reversed or undermined even by its own formations. Whereas constituent power is normally understood as being very much a part of archism, in this reading it can be archism's undoing. For Matos, the key point is that democracy itself is and has never been a liberal project. Liberalism has encrypted democracy in order to convince people that they somehow have a stake in archist forms of power. This does not mean, however, that we should abandon democracy. On the contrary, it is vital to recapture and decrypt democracy so that the false promises that liberalism offers are realized in an an-archist alternative form.

Matos reminds us that although constituent power is often connected to forms of sovereignty that encrypt and disempower the people, it is etymologically connected to collective forms of politics. Insofar as the word *constitute* means to build up institutions together (con-stitute). By unfettering the domesticated form of constituent power, which is mired in the authoritarianism of potestas, constituent power's true connection to potentia, to the open-ended and nondeterminant power of collective forms of authority, Matos shows a way for decryption to seize back the terrain of political power and authority.

Chapter 4

"Sovereignty, Anarchy, and Encryption of Power" by Simón Royo-Hernández presents a profound philosophical argument grounded in an-archic ontology, critically examining contemporary power structures. The author demonstrates how the TEP enriches and advances the anarchic tradition in political philosophy, providing a novel framework to better navigate the complexities of constituted power and its simulacra. The notion of simulacrum deepens and explains the clockwork of encrypted power and thus facilitates its overcoming through collective imagination.

The central thesis is rooted in the concept of *arché*—historical principles of domination, authority, and hierarchy that have shaped Western thought and politics. Contrasting this is *an-arché*, which proposes a philosophical and political paradigm defined by the absence of foundation, hierarchy, and governance. As anticipated, a crucial contribution of the essay is the deployment of the TEP. According to the author, TEP posits that modern sovereign power, especially in liberal democracies and globalized capitalism, operates by creating simulacra—institutional simulations such as representative democracy and constitutional rights—that disguise its inherently hierarchical nature. This "encryption" neutralizes political agency and fosters an illusion where servitude feels like freedom.

To counter this encrypted reality, the essay champions *biopotency*, an idea derived from Andityas Matos. Biopotency symbolizes an inexhaustible reserve of life and potential that resists absorption by totalitarian power. It is tied to TEP's concepts of *Potentia* and "the hidden people"—the marginalized and excluded individuals who hold the true potential for radical democracy. Following the TEP, the author drives a profound critique of liberal constitutionalism and modern sovereignty, exposing its paradox: while claiming "the people" as the (simulated) sovereign, it simultaneously excludes parts of the population, enabling oppression under the guise of liberation.

Drawing from thinkers such as Reiner Schürmann, Étienne de La Boétie, and the contributions of Ricardo Sanín-Restrepo and Andityas Matos on encryption and biopotency, the essay advocates for embracing *an-arché*. It emphasizes fostering communities based on equality and mutual aid, with communes and horizontal organizations representing tangible manifestations of anarchic potential—a "democracy to come" that resists the encrypted hierarchical order. Ultimately, the work delivers a powerful philosophical challenge to conventional notions of power and governance, offering anarchic ontology and the theory of encryption as essential tools to unveil concealed domination and envision a path toward authentic, nonhierarchical liberation rooted in the intrinsic potentiality of all beings.

Chapter 5

"The starting premise of this essay is that an analysis of power best comes from below." This is the opening line and the living spirit of the chapter entitled "Nomadic Sovereignty Opposed to the Archist Plantation System." In it Moysød and Faramelli undertake a critical analysis of power structures by examining them from the perspective of those excluded from systems of potestas—specifically through the lens of "lived resistance." A central aim of the chapter, which shifts the perspective and conceptually enhances the TEP, is to demonstrate how power is both "encrypted" and "decrypted" from this grounded position, arguing that a true understanding of power and therefore liberation can only emerge *from below and to the left, from inside and outside* of the State.

A key point in the chapter is the crucial need to understand the mechanisms that encrypt power. Power, particularly in its contemporary "archist" forms, operates by concealing its true nature and operations, creating a seemingly inevitable and natural order. The authors argue that this encryption process is deeply rooted in the historical development of the "plantation system."

To explore this, the authors focus on two key texts: *Subcomandante* Marcos's 1995 communique, "Power as a Mirror and an Image" (2004), and Russell Maroon Shoatz's 2006 work, *The Dragon and the Hydra: A Historical Study of Organizational Methods*. These texts provide insights into both the State's mechanisms of encryption of power and the forces that exist outside and are "existential" to the State, acting as agents of decryption.

Following the lead of the aforementioned texts and the spirit that decryption brings, the chapter is structured to build its argument progressively, a form of poetically unveiling (Aletheia!) what power conceals, but more importantly how the power from below unconceals as it creates and evolves, as it imagines new paths of liberation showing us what the world can be. It begins by developing a theory of the "plantation" as the *0-degree point* and a foundational "metamodel" for contemporary expressions of archism. This section is crucial for understanding the encryption of power, as it argues that the plantation establishes the fundamental extractive and control logics (the ugly blueprint, in Katherine McKittrick parlance) that are later encrypted and mystified by State structures in modernity and refined thoroughly by liberalism.

Following this, the chapter cleverly addresses the encryption of power in the "Neoliberal State." It examines how State power functions as a "mirror," creating a "simulacrum" that appears more real than reality. Drawing heavily on Marcos's powerfully written essay, this section illustrates the complex process by which the neoliberal State encrypts its power, particularly by folding the "War Machine" (crisis, instability) *into* its structure, presenting itself as the only solution to crises it inherently generates. What is uttermost relevant in their study is how it demonstrates how neoliberalism creates a much more complex and intricate form of encryption of power than classical historical models of the State that therefore require a more sophisticated response from any theoretical apparatus.

Finally, the chapter develops the powerful concept of "nomadic sovereignty." This concept is presented as the counterforce to the encryption of power—standing as the means by which power is "decrypted." Nomadic sovereignty, exemplified by movements like Marronage and Zapatismo, operates by existing both inside and outside of the State, blitzing and destabilizing its apparatuses of *capture* and *control*. It enacts sovereign positions that are not recognized by the State, one that refuses capture and expenditure for the dominant system. The discussion includes different conceptualizations of movement and Marronage (Glissant, Roberts, Wilder) and links them to Rancière's idea of micropolitical resistance and Wynter's concept of the "Plot" and "petit marronage" as sites of autonomous, an-archic becoming that resist enclosure and extraction. These acts of resistance, by asserting alternative forms of sociality and self-valorization, work to undo the encryption imposed by the plantation system and the State.

Utilizing a theoretical framework drawing from thinkers such as Rancière, Glissant, Wynter, Deleuze, and Guattari, and channeling them through Martel's archism and the TEP, the authors emphasize that these concepts are employed as analytical tools to illuminate insights already present in Marronage and Zapatismo, serving to articulate and intensify the processes of power encryption and decryption found in them.

While acknowledging the distinct historical and cultural contexts of Marronage and Zapatismo, the essay seeks to find a "rhyming scheme" between them, revealing a shared logic of resistance that emerges from below. The essay's polyphonic nature reflects this approach, embracing dissonance as generative. Ultimately, the essay does not offer a simple revolutionary blueprint but proposes a methodology for decrypting power by embracing the "polyvocality" of resistant theories and politics, seeking an "errant path" that reveals the hidden workings of power from the perspective of those who actively resist its capture and encryption.

Chapter 6

"Iñuggusiqput (Our Way of Life): Iñupiat (Re)vitalization as Decryption," by Zackary Taktuk Smith, offers that there are modes of prophetic insight and imagination that serve both to resist and unmake long entrenched modes of encryption. In his study of the Iñupiat community in the Alaskan Arctic, Smith focuses on the way the local Indigenous community has navigated the Alaska Native Claims Settlement Act of 1971 through the lens of their own culture and traditions. Rather than seeing the Iñupiat as a kind of remnant of the past who stubbornly cling to their culture in the face of neoliberal forms of encryption, Smith offers that the Iñupiat are in fact engaged in ongoing forms of self-expression, modes of being that serve to rival and compete with neoliberal forms of organization.

Part of the way this is organized is through alternative modes of temporality. The very past to which the Iñupiat would otherwise be consigned—that is, the encrypted mode of genocidal domination, which reduces them to a vanished, not-even-hidden, people—the people work through their own modes of temporality, one that combines theological and cosmological forms that are themselves constantly being updated by real-time conditions and experiences.

The prophetic tradition of the Iñupiat includes what Smith calls the *power of imagination*, not some phantasmic wishful thinking for conditions to be other than they are but rather a reading of material conditions through the lens and understandings that are provided by prophetic traditions that are themselves ongoing and ever changing. In this way, the community marshals its own cultural and political resources against the resources of archism that, although infinitely larger, do not have a cosmological basis of their own and thus are always vulnerable to be recast and reconceptualized by external traditions such as that of the Iñupiat themselves.

Thus, while the Alaska Native Claims Settlement Act may have been intended as a kind of wrapping up of Indigenous life in Alaska as far as its encrypting architects were concerned, it has instead been a vehicle that is only partially successful in neoliberalizing Indigenous claims and powers. As Smith shows, in the face of this attempt to relegate these communities once and for all to a historical oblivion, these communities organized themselves in response, using the form of encrypted modalities in order to resist them. This was possible, Smith argues, precisely because their own prophetic traditions allowed them to engage with dominant encrypting forms without entirely succumbing to them.

Indeed, one of the upshots of Smith's essay is that forms of resistance and prophetic traditions that constitute the Iñupiat power of imagination are not only capable of resisting and carving out space for Indigenous life in the face of ever-greater incursions of archist and encrypting power, but they also have the ability to create institutions and ways of life that are entirely unfettered by such power, allowing the Iñupiat to have not only a past that archism is happy to allow for but also a present and even a future of their own.

Chapter 7

In "Empire, Archipelago, and Abyss: Spaces of Power and Resistance in James Bond's Caribbean Imaginary," Jonnie Eriksson and Kalle Jonasson engage with the mythopoetry of the James Bond film franchise to think deeply about how even the most exploitative commercial depiction of a place (i.e., the ongoing theme of the Caribbean in many Bond films, as well as in the novels of Ian Fleming for whom the Caribbean loomed large as both a refuge and an object of fantasy) cannot escape from a more subversive aspect of a region that has long resisted encryption. What this suggests in turn is that even the most encrypted places and people—and the Caribbean may well be one of those places given its long history of slavery and genocide—this does not result in the complete victory of encryption, in which case there would be nothing left to encrypt. In fact, the ongoing fact of encryption always points to a community—the hidden people—who persist, and this essay helps us to interpret and read that persistence even in spaces where it seems most unlikely to appear.

For these authors, the Bond franchise offers both a vision of the *soft power* of US and British hegemony as well as a sign that something resists and persists in that demonstration of power. The so-called romance of the British Empire is expressed through literary and filmic depictions of a swashbuckling young Briton who appears to be irresistible both sexually and politically speaking. The fixation and connection between Bond's womanizing and adventurism is particularly legible when it comes to islands because the British Empire was, in the author's terms, an *archipelagic* empire, comprising of many islands and spaces that are interconnected over a vast territory of sea. Islands in general, and Caribbean islands perhaps most especially, convey both the power and vulnerability of that archipelagic imperial structure. It is powerful because of the vast reach and expanse, a power that is backed up by the might of the British navy. It is vulnerable because, in its infinite number, these islands can be a site of marronage and resistance as much as they are zones of acquiescence, and Caribbean history, with all of its revolts and uprisings—most critically marked by the successful Haitian Revolution at the turn of the nineteenth century—can never be entirely erased or ruled out. This patchwork of power and defeat is replicated, the authors argue, in the myriad Bond films themselves, which similarly has a sprawling and varied aspect that makes a simple statement of white supremacy or other archist modalities impossible to maintain.

As the authors point out, both Bond and Ian Fleming himself are haunted by the Caribbean. In other words, their assertions of mastery are also records of loss and defeat. The authors note that in *In Her Majesty's Secret Service*, although this is the one film that takes place entirely in Europe, we see—perhaps for that reason—an unexpectedly vulnerable side of Bond, culminating in his marriage and killing of his wife. Whereas, in the Caribbean and other zones of contestation, Bond may be on his guard; in Europe, it may be safer to show that Bond is a vulnerable human being after all.

What the Bond series shows in the end is the power of the hidden people, even when they are being sexually, politically, and commercially exploited. Even a figure as self-confident and lethal as James Bond cannot entirely eclipse their power or render them voiceless. If such films are able to convey the power of the hidden people, then we can see strategies for decryption that can be developed even in the very heart of the Global North and its tools of propaganda and self-image.

Chapter 8

"Decrypting the Mexican *Enforced Disappearance Apparatus* in the *Soft Dictatorship*" catalogues the ways that Mexico has managed to produce an image of "soft authoritarianism" (*dictablanda* in Spanish) even as it has historically been in fact a very violent and repressive regime. This air of being "soft" has allowed Mexico a kind of best of both worlds' form of power (from the perspective of its own leadership that is; from the perspective of its victims, it is precisely the opposite) wherein they can engage in a great deal of political and repressive violence even as they enjoy the benefits of appearing to be moderate, democratic, and benign in contrast to other regimes like Argentina, Brazil, and Chile that did not manage to soft-pedal their own murderous regimes.

More critically for this volume, Bacilio shows the way encryption functions in different forms in different places. The widespread experience in Latin America of dictatorships in the 1970s and 1980s made the connection between authoritarianism and global capitalism all too clear for people living under those regimes. It is the return to democracy that has allowed encryption to better insinuate itself into the lives of people in Latin American countries. In the United States, on the other hand, we are seeing a naked and open form of dictatorship emerging in the form of the Trump administration. By contrast, all the preceding years of democracy appear, in retrospect, to be far more benign. Bacilio's examination of *dictablanda* in Mexico exposes both ruses. By offering a vision of a soft authoritarianism we can see Mexico as a kind of bridge between different forms of encryption as they intensify and diversify over time. Bacilio allows us to see encryption in real time, as it hides its more authoritarian face without being any less violent or hierarchical. Here, we can see encryption in its dictatorial *and* democratic guise at the same exact time.

Bacilio shows how the illusion of soft authoritarianism serves, therefore, as a very highly effective example of encryption whereby the effects of State violence are felt but not acknowledged. When violence is more overt, it is a chance for people to fight back, but when they are not even acknowledged as victims, then the chances for the hidden people to strike back at their oppressors are much more difficult. Of course, the families of the murdered knew what the Mexican State was doing, but it was difficult to build up a kind of collective opposition due to the successful appearance of a *dictablanda* (even after Mario Vargas Llosa pointed this out on national television).

One terrible paradox of this mode of encryption is that even as Mexico has "returned to democracy" with the final defeat of the PRI after seventy-one years of power, the degree of violence has amplified considerably. This is in part because neoliberalism has farmed out State violence to many other actors, what Bacilio calls micropowers. Non-State actors like the drug cartels engage in a more open violence that, because it is functioning through State-like powers, often, in effective collusion with the PRI, continues to extend a form of State repression in a new guise.

This all adds up to what Bacilio calls the "Enforced Disappearance Apparatus," an entire network of State and State-like killings that are enclosed within a web of encryption that makes it both more deadly (especially in its later guise) and more difficult to get at. We can see how the mechanism of encryption is itself extremely adaptable and flexible and can create illusions as needed in a huge variety of spaces and times and in ways that always serve the demands of archist power even as they cover over those very same requirements. Even time itself, as Bacilio tells us, becomes distorted by these acts of encryption where the question of whether a particular killing even occurred (and, therefore, has some specific moment in time that it can be connected with) cannot be determined with full accuracy.

Looking at the work of Giorgio Agamben, Bacilio offers that here we see a very clear demonstration of the *homo sacer*, a form of bare life where people can not only be killed with impunity but where the very act of killing itself becomes obscured and overwritten, a state of being that Agamben himself did not necessarily anticipate.

Note

1 Our motivation for creating this book wasn't to position academics as simply aiding democratic practices through analysis, description, or critique. On the contrary, our engagement represents an act of solidarity and common cause with radical decolonial practices happening worldwide. The transformative results of these practices are too often obscured by the encryption of sovereignty in its various manifestations, particularly through archism. This obfuscation dictates a limited way of seeing and feeling, negating the capacity for multiplicity and the creation of the new. Instead, it entrenches forms of archism—the notion of power as necessarily hierarchical and

unchangeable—perpetuated through sovereignty's many outlets like law, economic systems, liberal myths of origin, political theology, and countless other forms that stifle collective political creativity.

Reference

Marcos, Subcomandante. 2004. "Power as a Mirror and an Image." In *Ya Basta! Ten Years of the Zapatista Uprising*, edited by Ziga Vodovnik. San Francisco, CA: AK Press, 153–9.

1

The Not-So-Hidden People: One Path Out of Encryption and Archism

James R. Martel

The (Not So) Hidden People

In their exposition of the theory of encryption, Ricardo Sanín-Restrepo and Marinella Machado-Araujo speak of "the hidden people," that is, a people whose oppression becomes occluded by the (false) concept of their own freedom and power. As they write:

> [Under conditions of encryption] the people become the transcendent and mystic model of their own exclusion, of the war to subdue and expropriate them. Injustice is naturalized as justice. The outside becomes the inside, as the exception becomes the (simulated) sovereign. An anthropophagic, narcissistic, and at the same time nihilistic political and legal design, that, nonetheless, is the open slit within the structure of power as domination through which resistance and transformation are possible. We are before a fundamental concept of the theory of encryption of power: "the hidden people." (2025, 16)

Here, the hidden people are the product of the lie of encryption itself; the idea of the people being "sovereign" serves as a way to disempower and rule over them all the more. This is in effect a colonial project, a kind of internal colonization of the self. For Sanín-Restrepo and Machado-Araujo, encryption—and the production of the hidden people that it entails—is a unique feature and product of the era of colonialism (2025, 15). Similar to my own view of archism as a unique form of hierarchical power, the theory of encryption sees the past 500 years, roughly speaking, as a time of unprecedented domination and occlusion of collective power. Against this force, they propose the practice of decryption as a way to return the hidden people to its own true power, a way to upend the lies of colonialism and the hierarchical structures that it brought into the world.

In my reading of things, one way that would help to facilitate decryption is to look to communities that have been relatively successful at avoiding being wholly absorbed into the pseudo-social forms of encryption, that is to say, people who are hidden, yes, but not entirely so. I think there are at least two groups who fit this description especially well. The first group are Indigenous people who have been fighting a more direct and genocidal form of colonialism for the past five centuries. Perhaps for this reason, but also due to the fact that those communities that have survived this genocide have retained (in many cases, not all) some aspects of their own nonarchist, nonencrypted political, social, and economic forms, I see them as offering a model to help us see what decryption might actually look like. The other group is one that emerges from what Cedric Robinson calls the Black Radical Tradition (2000). This tradition, too, has faced some of the most dire aggressions of colonial and imperial power, most particularly in the form of slavery, a form of domination that arguably has survived its formal end in the late nineteenth century and remains in practice to this day. Communities that take part in the Black Radical Tradition, too, have managed to retain some of their own nonencrypted political and economic forms as I will explain further.

In the case of both sets of communities, the form that I think is most pertinent to questions of resisting encryption, archism, and the state of being hidden is that of continuous political assembly (or just continuous assembly). That is to say, those communities that have managed to retain a political form that is inherently (as I will go on to argue further) resistant—if not perfectly so than largely—to the lies and distortions of archist encryption (for the sake of argument, I will treat these two theories as being complementary and thus merge the two effectively into one concept).

The main idea behind continuous assembly is that a community is in constant communication with itself. Machiavelli tells us that collectively the people are wiser than their leaders because, whereas the leader only has themselves and their advisors to consult with, the people collectively know everything (1950, 263). The problem is—and this is the basic method of encryption—that archism does everything in its power to prevent the people from assembling. Instead of real, purposeful assemblies, which are conscious of their political, economic, and social power, pseudo assemblies are set up. A good analogy to this is academic senates that proliferate at most universities in the United States and many other parts of the world as well. These senates have no real power. They have no financial control and are basically mainly consultative bodies to university administrations. Consultation only means that they get to complain to the administrator who then can do whatever they please. Yet, although toothless and thus harmless, in some way the existence of these academic senates is worse than if there were no such bodies at all, because the illusion that they are purposeful assemblies means that there is no perceived need to actually have one (see Martel and Missé 2024). This, then, becomes another example of encryption and the formation of the hidden people.

In many Indigenous communities and in many communities that reflect the Black Radical Tradition, organs of continual assembly remain an ongoing practice. One key example is the *ayllu* in the Andean Highlands. The *ayllu* function as a kind of ongoing form of political, economic, and social assembly, combining all three aspects into one. In the time of the Incan Empire, the *ayllu* were used as a way to organize work along the *mita* system of forced labor for the empire. This system was preserved after the Spanish conquest, and some version of it remains in effect to this day. Although this system served subsequent forms of domination, it also preserved in a sense the heart of Indigenous self-organization. The *ayllu* system has lasted over one thousand years (and counting!), and its form has historically allowed it to survive genocide, colonization, imperialism, liberalism, and now neoliberalism. When you compare its long history to the kinds of trajectories that you often find in Western leftist models, the three months of the Paris Commune, the brief (but glorious) anarchist summer of 1936, you can see the value of this nonarchist form of continuous assembly quite clearly.

In what follows, I will be making a case for the form of continuous assembly as the best political form to combat archist encryption. I will be arguing that this form fosters a kind of collective self-knowledge—an objective and collective form of trust—that defies, if imperfectly, the lies and seductions of archist encryption. The fact that the hidden people are not always entirely invisible is not only a sign that encryption is an imperfect and incomplete mode of domination. It also shows that encryption can be beaten back, that it can be contained and unraveled not necessarily only by entirely new forms of political, economic, and social organization but even by a form that has long predated the rise of archism and encryption alike, one that persists even into our own time.

The Commune Form

In her book *The Commune Form,* Kirstin Ross argues that this form is the basis for all forms of successful political resistance. She writes:

> The commune form is first and foremost about people living differently and changing their circumstances by working within the conditions available in the present. In this sense, the form as form was indistinguishable from the specific people who were changing their lives, living differently, at that moment in time and in the space—the neighborhoods—in which they were doing so. (2024, 4)

Here, Ross puts her finger on something critical; the commune form (akin to what I have been calling continuous assembly, but there is an important distinction that I will get to in a moment) is just an expression of ordinary life, but it's ordinary life—in the real sense of that term, breathing, eating, being together, and so forth—that is aware of itself as such. You could call it *organized* ordinary life, a way for the knowledges and powers of the people to become clear to themselves, a forum in which ideas could be worked out and decisions collectively made.

Ross goes on to write about the commune form as a historical event, a series of moments when the organization of ordinary life as such becomes visible to those participating in it. You could call this a form of class consciousness, although the notion of class has to be broadly expanded for reasons that I will make clearer soon.

Specifically focusing on Kropotkin's own analysis of revolutions in nineteenth-century Europe, Ross writes:

> The name "Commune," as such, stands in for and encompasses what Kropotkin (and most historians) understand to be the most radically democratic force at

> work in the French Revolution. But Kropotkin is saying something more than this. Revolution, in his view, is nothing more than the conflict between the state on the one hand and the communes on the other. The contradiction is not between the state and anarchy but between the state and another organization of political life, an alternative kind of political intelligence, a different kind of community. To the extent that the state recedes, the communes and their way of life flourish. (2024, 5)

Here, Ross is showing us that the commune form is not about ideology, at least not the way that we usually understand that term. The commune form is a form of resistance unto itself. It does not need any outside or external support. It is simply a vehicle by which a community can and does come to terms with its own forms of power and authority. By definition, any politics based on such a model will be extremely varied in the way that it expresses itself. Each commune will have its own voice and own decisions, and so there can be no one-size-fits-all model—or even a precise name—for what is produced out of these forms. My own general term for it would be nonarchism insofar as I see anarchism and left communism—two forms of leftist politics that I strongly identify with—as being in some sense a subset of the vast variety of nonarchist political models. My hope is that the term nonarchism is capacious enough to contain all of the many myriad political forms that can be generated from the people themselves.

Clearly this includes the hidden people. Ross's examples—the Paris Commune, the ZAD anti-airport movement in France, among others—are all generated from within the context of deep archist encryption. In that sense, the communities that Ross engages with could be considered to be the most hidden of all. Even so, although she speaks neither of archism nor of encryption, Ross emphasizes that no takeover of power can ever be complete because the commune form is always available as a key form of resistance. The question here becomes: if it is possible for such moments of resistance to occur even in the maw of archist encryption, how can such moments be sustained and expanded, leading not just to breaks in the fabric of encryption but also real and sustained victories?

Intermittent Versus Continuous Assembly

It is here that I would offer a distinction, however, between what Ross calls the commune form and what I have been calling continuous assembly. The key difference here is that whereas Ross's moments of the commune form occur intermittently—as is to be expected in the West where the invasion of archist encryption is once again the most thoroughgoing, where the hidden people are the *most* hidden of all—with forms of continuous assembly there is, as the name implies, more of an ongoing collective process. Both cases are instances of the commune form, but in cases where that form is continuous rather than intermittent and disjointed, the power of that model to resist archism and encryption is far more significant.

This comes back to the question of trust mentioned earlier. Whereas we tend to think of trust as a subjective and individual phenomenon (as in "I trust her. I do not trust him," etc.), as previously mentioned the trust that is generated by forms of continuous assembly is objective and collective. Archist encryption has specialized in making people not able to trust themselves. In academia, which is my own world, you can see this in what I like to call the "faculty deficit model," namely the idea that faculty are lazy and shiftless and, if left to their own devices, would never teach or do anything that didn't promote their own career. If you talk to college and university administrators, you will readily find examples of this way of thinking. How else to justify the ever-burgeoning number of administrators who serve as a necessary counterweight to this feckless but unfortunately necessary (at least for now) sector in the academic economy?

You see the same attitude in all forms of business where workers are similarly seen as lazy and incapable of managing themselves. This justifies the entire field of management, as well as the huge salaries paid to CEOs. You also see this attitude more generally in liberal democracy where representatives are seen as necessary to screen the passion of the people into a safe and modified political form (although in our current moment it is especially clear that things work the other way around).

If we cannot trust ourselves, then we certainly should not have recourse to the commune form whether it is continuous or not. We should obey our superiors and shut up and do our work. Our workplace itself, then, instead of doubling as a political forum, as it does in the case of the commune form, becomes a depoliticized space, one marked by surveillance, discipline, and small incentives to get us to cooperate. It is also a space deeply impacted by racial, gender, and other forms of hierarchy culminating in a form of class rule.

All of that is familiar to anyone versed in the theory of encryption, and indeed, one of the key benefits of Sanín-Restrepo and Machado-Araujo's work is that by naming something you give a way to render it vulnerable and subject to attack (I think calling this phenomenon archism does much the same thing). But for all of this, an intermittent or occasional expression of the commune form will be far more vulnerable to the poisonous lack of self-trust that archist encryption promotes than a community that has been in continuous assembly for the span of years, decades, and even centuries.

In communities that do not take part in cultural and social formations like the Black Radical Tradition or Indigenous communities, that is to say, communities that do not practice continuous assembly, it is much more difficult to sustain and preempt encryption largely because the collective self-knowledge and objective forms of trust that can only be produced over long periods of time have to begin, effectively, from scratch.

This is not because the commune form is only practiced by Indigenous or Black radical groups. All truly revolutionary moments are marked by a turn to the commune form. Hannah Arendt testifies to this in *On Revolution*, where she notes how the French, German, and Russian Revolutions were all marked by the creation of clubs, *räte,* and soviets, respectively (Arendt 1986). Yet, as Arendt also notes seemingly inevitably, these "organs of action" are superseded by "organs of representation," that is to say, the formation of parties and other archist structures that come with their own forms of encryption (1986, 273). By being forced to rely on archist structures—unions and even states are other examples of what might be called an "archist supplement"—these communities do not have the time or space to fully develop the radical potential of the commune form without interference from archist forces.[1] In this way they could be said to be engaged in forms of discontinuous assembly and thus unable to sustain a revolutionary tradition.

To give one notable example of what I'm talking about, one of the key mistakes that Spanish anarchists made in the 1930s was to rely overmuch on their union. The CNT (the National Worker's Confederation, in English) was a vast anarchist-dominated union, and it did indeed perform miracles in that it coordinated a vast anarchist uprising (in response to Franco's attempted military coup in 1936). The CNT organized and led a resistance that brought the advance of the fascists to a halt. While the liberal government in Madrid was ready to give up and cede power (as liberals are wont to do in the face of authoritarian challenges from the procapitalist right), the CNT, based in Barcelona, held a great deal of power.

The leaders of the CNT were all devout anarchists, perhaps most especially Buenaventura Durruti, a mechanic who went on to become one of the most important figures in anarchist Spain. The paradox that there were anarchist leaders at all was not lost on Durruti, and he feared greatly that his own fame would compromise his resolutely bottom-up political model. More generally, the Spanish anarchists feared what they called "leaderism," namely the way that leadership would emerge, and corrupt, the anarchist movement (Mintz 2013, 56). Durruti himself famously put down a formula that he hoped would guard against this eventuality. He said:

> No anarchists in the union committees except at the ground level. In these committees, in case of conflict with the boss, the militant is forced to compromise to arrive at an agreement. The contacts and activities which come from being in this position, push the militant towards bureaucracy. Conscious of this risk, we do not wish to run it. Our role is to analyze from the bottom the different dangers which can beset a union organization like ours. No militant should prolong his job in committees, beyond the time allotted to him. No permanent and indispensable people. (Cited in Paz 1976, 183)

The Spanish anarchist took countless other steps to avoid leaderism (as well as its twin disease "followerism") (Mintz 2013, 56). The CNT was matched by an affinity group, the FAI (Iberian Anarchist Federation, in English), which was kind of an anarchist watchdog. There were no standing committees, no bargaining team, no salaried employees. All union activists had to be full-time workers. And yet, for all of this, the leadership did eventually sell out the movement. In November 1936, four of the anarchist leaders agreed to join the liberal government even after they had effectively won full power. This was tantamount to betraying the entire anti-representational (and anti-communal) principle of the anarchist movement. Far from being immune to "leaderism," then, the CNT and the anarchist movement more generally showed itself to be rife with it. As Vernon Richards tells us:

> What is certain is that within the CNT there have always been strong personalities who, as is always the case with those who would ride roughshod over basic principles, declared themselves to be practical men, the realists of the movement. (2019, 22)

Most tellingly perhaps, for the purposes of this essay, is the fact that, after long periods of remarkable candor, the anarchist leadership started to sound very much like other leaders in that they "sold" the decision in ways that seemed to augur further encryption. For example, *Solidaridad Obrera*, the main media organ of the CNT, declared:

> The government has stopped being an oppressive force against the working class in its regulation of the organs of the state. The state no longer serves to separate society into classes. With the participation of the C.N.T., the state and government no longer oppress the people. (Casas 1986, 202)

These kinds of innuendos are very familiar to those of us who live amidst encryption. For the anarchist rank-and-file, such falsities represented the literal end of a world.

The upshot of this is that if the Spanish anarchists were unable to use their archist supplement without it turning against them, I don't think anyone else can either. At the very least, if an archist supplement is needed, it should be engaged with as quickly as possible, while the true "organs of action" (to quote Arendt once again) must be built up and set to replace the archist supplement as soon as it can. It is true, once again, that there is a great temptation to stick to the archist supplement because it makes up for the lack of objective trust. Archist encryption teaches us, as already mentioned, to trust it rather than ourselves, and so we do trust unions and parties and states, and they, unfortunately, in turn betray that trust and further our encryption, precisely because they trust themselves far too much.

One reason I think that Arendt seems so gloomy about the prospects of overcoming the failure of revolutions is that she is primarily only interested in European and settler colonial revolutions, and for this reason, her sense of the inevitability of revolutionary failure may reflect her exclusion of so many revolutionary forces that effectively represent the Global South. When you take a wider scope of viewing, the prospects for resisting archist encryption become much more evident. When we turn to movements within the Black Radical Tradition and Indigenous movements, we see a much more promising field in terms of resisting and even undoing archist encryption.

The Black Radical Tradition

Let me begin with the Black Radical Tradition because in some ways it often manifests itself in situations that are deeply entangled with archist domination. Despite her own focus on European radical movements, Ross herself does recognize the value of both

Indigenous models and those generated by the Black Radical Tradition. Speaking of the latter, for example, she writes:

> Perhaps the most fitting comparison to the 1968 Nantes Commune lies far away, but occurring at the same time, in the streets of Detroit, Oakland, and other large cities in the United States, as members of the Black Panther Party for Self-Defense went about taking charge of the management of Black neighborhoods. With their school breakfasts, bakeries, and other grassroots community organizations, the Panthers, for all intents and purposes, as former Panther Lorenzo Kom'boa Ervin suggests, turned their communities and neighborhoods into dual-power communes. Both in Nantes and in Oakland, revolution was anchored in everyday life. Ideological purity mattered less than a transformation at the level of daily rhythms, everyday needs and pleasures. By taking collective responsibility for meeting people's daily needs, by reclaiming the everyday by and through political struggle, they were making revolution on a scale that people could recognize. (2024, 7–8)

The one distinction I would make here is that I don't think the Nantes Commune and the Black Panthers were quite as similar as Ross suggests. The Black Radical Tradition, something the Black Panthers are definitely an expression of, has a long history with the commune form that, while not as literally continuous as, say, the *ayllu* example, represents a kind of political culture that lends itself to different—and less hidden—forms of collective self-expression than other examples in the Global North.

In part this is a question of geopolitical location. In *Disembodiment*, Banu Bargu encourages us to think of the North and the South (terms she favors over the West and non-West) as mutually intermingled so that you have pockets of the North in the Global South (local political elites, expat communities, etc.) and you also have pockets of the South in the Global North (the urban and poor Black community in the United States being one such example; Bargu 2025). It's not, however, only a matter of being in the Global South that distinguishes, say, the ZAD movement from the Black Panthers. It is also the nature of the Black Radical Tradition itself.

In *Black Marxism*, Cedric Robinson details the nature of this tradition and the way that it allows for forms of continuity that are not as readily available to white leftist movements. He writes, for example, that

> Black radicalism … cannot be understood within the particular context of its genesis. It is not a variant of Western radicalism whose proponents happen to be Black. Rather, it is a specifically African response to an oppression emergent from the immediate determinants of European development in the modern era and framed by orders of human exploitation woven into the interstices of European social life from the inception of Western civilization. (2000, 73)

Here, Robinson is describing the way the Black Radical Tradition is independent from the trajectory of much of the rest of the Global North. While it is undeniably true that this tradition was forged through the gamut of slavery and white supremacy, it reflects its own organic and African origins and is not simply, therefore, a product or effect of white supremacy.

For Robinson, the Black Radical Tradition is also reinforced from the very fact that Blackness is so ostracized and held apart under conditions of white supremacy. He writes:

> The Black Radical Tradition cast doubt on the extent to which capitalism penetrated and re-formed social life and on its ability to create entirely new categories of human experience stripped bare of the historical consciousness embedded in culture. It gave them cause to question the authority of a radical intelligentsia drawn by its own analyses from marginal and ambiguous social strata to construct an adequate manifestation of proletariat power. And it drew them more and more toward the actual discourse of the revolutionary masses, the impulse to make history in their own terms. And finally, the Black radical tradition forced them to reevaluate the nature and historical roles of ideology and consciousness. After all it had been as an emergent African people and not as slaves that Black men and women had opposed enslavement. (2000, 170).

Here, the question of trust becomes much clearer. Although not all Black people are going to be trustworthy, the forged collective consciousness ("as an emergent African people and not as slaves") of the Black experience produces a kind of community sense that readily lends itself to the commune form. Although this form is, in some sense, intermittent insofar as circumstances can be more or less favorable to its full expression, there is, via the Black Radical Tradition itself, a form of continuity that helps to ensure that when the commune form is adopted, as it was for the Black Panthers, there is a kind of collective tradition ready to receive it and, as it were, hit the ground running.

We can see something of the presence of the Black Radical Tradition in the revolutionary organizing of DRUM (the Dodge Revolutionary Union Movement) that began in Detroit in 1968. The main organizers of DRUM were all themselves Black workers on the Dodge assembly line. Given the degree of overt racism that Black workers experienced, not only from their employers but also from the UAW, it was not hard to convince many of them to engage in a wildcat strike to oppose their poor treatment. This initial act then led to an enormous amount of collective organizing wherein the DRUM model produced many other related movements across Detroit. These offshoots, generally (but not always) at auto plants across the Detroit metropolitan area, included ELRUM (the Eldon Avenue Revolutionary Union Movement) and FRUM (the Ford Revolutionary Union Movement). These RUMs were soon loosely merged into the League of Black Revolutionary Workers (LBRW).

In their study of DRUM and the subsequent LBRW, entitled *Detroit, I Do Mind Dying,* Georgakas and Surkin note that as opposed to more ordinary forms of union organizing,

> DRUM was something else. It bypassed the UAW to organize workers directly into a structure dedicated to principles which went far beyond simple trade unionism.

> DRUM's earliest leaflets stated its goals of gaining direct representation of black workers. More like the IWW of an earlier generation of radicals than like a trade union, DRUM had many aspects of a popular revolutionary movement that could go in many directions. Although not always clear about its tactical methods or all of its strategic goals, DRUM was an illustration of what James Boggs had written in 1963 in The American Revolution: "Historically workers move ahead by the new. That is, they bypass existing organizations and form new ones uncorrupted by past habits and customs." (2012, 44)

DRUM was successful, the authors argue, because the organizers were able to act in ways that stemmed directly from the daily working life of Black workers at the plant. One of their initial successes, for example, involved two bars just beyond the limits of the Dodge plant. Black workers frequently went to these bars to drink but were never hired by the bars and were always treated badly. A boycott organized by DRUM quickly settled that problem (Georgakas and Surkin 2012, 46). While this example may seem trivial, it speaks precisely to the way the commune form in general—and continuous assembly in particular—allows for issues in ordinary life to be dealt with directly by the community itself without any interference from some outside or "higher" authority. The more daily life becomes a basis for collective self-organization as opposed to merely a basis for archist predation, the more the ability to resist encryption and archism more generally.

Indigenous Organization

As previously noted, in addition to the Black Radical Tradition, another vital group that engages in continuous assembly can be found with Indigenous communities. Not all Indigenous communities engage in literally continuous forms of assembly, of course. Many have been severely degraded by centuries of genocide and destruction. Like those communities that are part of the Black Radical Tradition, then, their participation in the commune form may not always be a constant, but they too have cultural and social resources to draw upon. Furthermore, some communities, like the previously mentioned *ayllu* in the Andean Highlands of Peru and Bolivia, *do* practice a quite literal form of continuous assembly. In such cases, the resources that are provided by such a form have allowed the *ayllu* not only to survive many onslaughts, including a genocide that reduced their population by 90 percent, but at times to even beat back various forms of archist predation.

In the late 1700s, the Tupac Amaru II rebellion (in Bolivia it was called the Tupac Katari rebellion) came close in places to driving the Spanish out of the Andes. The *ayllu* was a key component of how this movement worked (see Serulnikov 2003). In the early 2000s, the *ayllu* was key to two major victories in urban Bolivia against state neoliberalism. In the so-called Gas and Water Wars in Cochabamba and El Alto, respectively, urban communities were able to force the government to back off various forms of neoliberal deregulation of water and gas. This also led to the fall of the president, leading to new elections (see Zibechi 2010).

This last example is important because, even though the *ayllu* was and largely remains an agricultural form, uniting families who work together on common projects, it can be—and in the case of the Gas and Water Wars it actually was—transferred to an urban context. These examples are also important because non-Indigenous communities were also involved in these forms of resistance, and they were able to adopt the *ayllu* structure as a way to engage in continuous assembly as well (including in ways that involved military formations to resist the national army). These are critical points that I will pick up on in more detail shortly.

In their magnum opus *The Dawn of Everything*, David Graeber and David Wengrow (henceforth the two Davids) give countless examples of Indigenous forms of self-organization that serve, initially, to prevent the rise of archist encryption in the first place and then, when it does appear, to serve to resist it as best as they can. They go deep into human prehistory, looking at both archaeological and anthropological records to reverse-engineer a story of human progress and development. Rather than seeing the rise of the modern state and what I've been describing as archist encryption as either inevitable or desirable, they show that it is in fact a terrible historical accident, one that has led to centuries of needless suffering and death.

The two Davids offer myriad examples of communities that effectively staved off the development of the kinds of hierarchies that would lead to the archist state. This includes the *ayllu* itself. In this case they write that the *ayllu* practiced a kind of bureaucracy. Yet in this case, rather than leading to more centralized control and power, this form of bureaucracy produced less. They write:

> *Ayllu* too were based on a strong principle of equality; their members literally wore uniforms, with each valley having its own traditional designs of cloth. One of the *ayllu's* main functions was to redistribute agricultural land as families grew larger or smaller, to ensure none grew richer than any other. (Graeber and Wengrow 2021, 642)

They also mention that, in cases where top-down state-like entities were in fact developed, the response was often a revolution that overturned that proto-archist power and/or widespread abandonment by the local community that simply moved elsewhere. For example, they argue that the ancient city of Cahokia, located on the Mississippi floodplain, was overthrown by its own subjects (Graeber and Wengrow 2021, 467). They also speculate that the reason the Mayan cities were largely abandoned was also possibly due to an eventual refusal to submit to hierarchical forms of rule (2021, 377–8).

In countless examples (in a sense, the heft of this large book is itself *the* argument insofar as the vast variety of cases speak to the absence of archist forms of homogenization in and of itself), the two Davids describe how many of these Indigenous communities practiced a form of continuous assembly. One striking example they offer involves Indigenous communities that were encountered by French colonizers in North America. Speaking specifically of Brother Gabriel Sagard, a French priest who sought to learn Indigenous languages in order to convert these communities to Christianity, the two Davids note how, in his attempt,

> Sagard was surprised and impressed by his hosts' eloquence and powers of reasoned argument, skills honed by near-daily public discussions of communal affair; his hosts, in contrast, when they did get to see a group of Frenchmen gathered together, often remarked on the way that they seemed to be continually scrambling over each other and cutting each other off in conversation. People who tried to grab the stage, denying others the means to present their arguments, were acting in much the same way as those who grabbed the material means of subsistence and refused to share it. (Graeber and Wengrow 2021, 39)

In France, there were no opportunities for poor and local people to have any kind of meaningful political speech, and as a result, those people did not develop rhetorical skills. In these Indigenous communities, on the other hand, such skills were developed precisely because the social and political formation of these communities presupposed political agency on everyone's part.

Being able to speak to and with your own community is a critical way by which encryption can be resisted (or prevented from developing in the first place, as many examples provided by the two Davids suggest). If only some voices are heard, the nature of communication itself changes from one of collective expression to domination and control. Words are all effectively lies when only some people are able to speak them because in such cases it is individual or subgroup beliefs that are imposed on everyone else. When all speech is done publicly and collectively, on the other hand, the community itself gets to decide what is, and what is not, true. This, then, is a key basis for resisting encryption.

Without this ability, we are given false choices, say between the benign face of liberalism and the more hostile and overtly racist and violent face of fascism and other forms of authoritarianism. This false choice produces a form of capitalist homeostasis where we move between these bogus poles so as to give a sense of choice and freedom when we have nothing of the kind (although, as Jodi Dean has recently suggested, even capitalism itself may have succumbed to its own hype, and we are entering a stage of neofeudalism, which is something even worse and more predatory; Dean 2025).

A great contemporary example of an Indigenous-based movement that has effectively battled against encryption is the Zapatistas in Chiapas, Mexico. The Zapatistas began as a largely Indigenous movement, but it has reclassified itself somewhat as a peasant movement or a "right to land movement," allowing it greater purchase in multiracial Mexico (Collier and Lowery 2005, 7). The right to land is a concept that is also articulated by José Carlos Mariátegui in his own study of the *ayllu* (1988, 31). This is a right that is not up to the state to give or take, that is to say, it is not a liberal right but rather a right based on a community's own self-assertion and power. By expanding from indigeneity to a larger peasant movement, the Zapatistas are showing how it is possible to include more and more people within the category of those who are less hidden.

The Commune Form and the Paysan

This connection to agriculture is, therefore, not exclusive to Indigenous communities. In *The Commune Form*, Kristin Ross makes much of the fact that the European-based movements she is interested in (particularly the ZAD) were a kind of back-to-the-land movements based on farmers (she uses the French term "paysan" to reflect on these roots). For Ross, being a peasant is not in and of itself a revolutionary act. Yet, when the peasant (or paysan) recognizes themselves as being organized through their collective work on the land, they take on a far more radical role and perspective. Citing the literary scholar Erag Ramizi, Ross writes:

> In Ramizi's analysis, the transformation occurs when paysans are not merely inert figures of anachronism (Marx's "sacks of potatoes") but when they become instead actively, even impudently anachronistic, when they use their conflict with the present to become, like the Larzac farmers, active flies in the ointment, or sand in the gears of army tanks. They transform the situation whenever they stand in the way or refuse to allow their own quite distinct temporal rhythms to be determined or subsumed by the uniform labor time of the modern capitalist economy. After all, individual profit and competition are foreign to the subsistence economy and to peasant culture generally. Elements of practical communism and organic solidarity are known to persist in Indigenous agriculture and peasant practices. The small, autonomous grower maintains productivity by conforming both to tradition and to the natural conditions such as he or she found them. The principle of production in the peasant economy is that of satisfying the immediate needs of the family and thus developing and preserving the family's autonomy. As a repository of use values, as well as of knowledge of the land and its usages, the paysan is a source of memory and history. (Exchange, on the other hand, has no history.) Capitalist agriculture, whose only perspective is valuation and profit, dissolves the age-old practices of regenerative peasant farming and completely reorganizes the process of production, its material and technological conditions, as well as its temporality. (2024, 13–14)

Here, once again, ordinary life can become the basis for radical resistance. For Ross, the French paysan is akin to an Indigenous farmer and, perhaps in that way, allows for a kind of local culture of continuous assembly to exist even in the Global North. Also, she notes further, nonfarmers can adopt these methods in order to themselves become transformed by their own productive processes.

In my own reading of things I don't think that the connection to land per se is what makes the commune form work as it does. As the example of the Gas and Water Wars already shows, this model is transferable to urban settings (Ross understands that and gives examples of urban farming as well). The "right to land" is itself transferable to any right that is self-created rather than granted (or not granted) by the state. What I think is key to Ross's insight is less the nature of production (i.e., agricultural, or urban, or what have you) but rather the way that production lends itself to being folded into the commune form itself. Workers under capitalism have this potential, merely by being placed together in tight quarters (Marx 1978, 483). Yet, this has not in and of itself led to the production of the commune form. Indeed, precisely as with the example of academic senates, under conditions of archist encryption, the workplace has become a zone where the commune form is resisted most utterly, replaced by pseudo relations, and monitored and controlled at all time. The struggle for decryption, then, is as much cultural and experiential as it is ideological. Above all, what is required is a connection to materiality, wherein working life doubles, once again, as political life, and collectives are able to access one another in ways both mundane and extraordinary.

Conclusion

In thinking about ways to push back on archist encryption, then, we can see that there are some communities (Indigenous, those partaking in the Black Radical Tradition) who are relatively less hidden than others (settler colonialists, the Global North more generally). This shows that the quality of the hidden people is more of a patchwork than a homogenous field. Yet, in practice, this variation of hiddenness does not in and of itself push back on encryption as a whole insofar as most of the communities that are less hidden are also far more repressed and subject to ongoing forms of genocide and immiseration. To better combat encryption, it seems to me that what is needed is more of an alliance between communities that are less hidden and those that are more hidden.

Each set of communities has something to offer. Indigenous communities and those that take part in the Black Radical Tradition have the power of decryption itself as their greatest contribution. They can benefit from either perfect or at least ongoing forms of continuous assembly, and in that way, they serve as their own arbiters of truth and decision-making. This is a model that more hidden communities would do well to take on as their own. And, as the case with the Gas and Water Wars suggests, this model can be shared and, in that way, potentially overcome the need for treacherous archist supplements.

For their part the more hidden communities have their own assets to offer. Being based within archist encryption, they know the enemy and can impart vast amounts of knowledge about the ways and strategies of these power systems. Furthermore, they often have access to much more resources and privileges and can, therefore, do much more damage to archist power than those who live at its periphery.

There are, of course, many dangers and reasons to be cautious about calling for this alliance. The case of DRUM helps us to understand why. DRUM tended to work only with Black workers, although they made alliances with Arab workers and even with white workers at times. But they found that all too often the white workers were more susceptible to racist claims by employers and unions and could, therefore, not be trusted as solid and permanent allies.

These are not insurmountable problems, but it is true that when you are dealing with relationships between people with vastly different levels of privilege, there is always a danger that this privilege will reinsert encrypted narratives in the guise of overcoming them. For this reason, I think the model you saw in the Gas and Water Wars is helpful wherein non-Indigenous people were folded in the *ayllu* system rather than the other way around. In organizations like Black Lives Matter, too, Black life and leadership is prioritized even as all are welcome to participate in the movement. Similarly in the encampment movement that swept the United States in the spring of 2024, the more successful campaigns were those that centered on Palestinian activists and their concerns.

The insidious nature of encryption means that a great deal of care and attention will always have to be paid to how and under what circumstances resistance is organized, but centering the commune form and giving priority to those forms that have longer and more continuous histories will help overcome some of the many pernicious and seemingly intractable obstacles archist encryption puts in the way of those who would escape its clutches.

As previously mentioned, these kinds of partnerships between the more and less hidden people require a rethinking of many of the most basic elements of a leftist vocabulary. The notion of class, for example, needs to be expanded beyond the nature of production per se to a larger question of self-conscious organization. Similarly, the notion of revolution will not always look like the way leftists in the Global North imagine it. Sometimes revolutions can involve traditions that have lasted over one thousand years. Anything that resists archist encryption is revolutionary no matter what it looks like. More generally, to commit to the commune form, especially as it approaches the practice of continuous assembly, is to commit to a huge variety of different outcomes and local cultures. Homogeneity is itself an outcome of archist encryption. To embrace nonarchism is to embrace the vast diversity of human history and experience.

Perhaps the most important point to keep in mind is that archist encryption is in fact highly vulnerable. It is based, after all, on empty lies and deceit only. It has no ontological fixity, no absolute truth that it is based upon. In fact, the first and most important lie encryption tells us is that it is real, that it based on irrefutable and incontrovertible truths. When this ruse of ruses is uncovered and exposed, and when it is confronted with the real organization of human life along the lines of continuous assembly, then encryption might just begin to melt away back into the nothingness from which it issues, allowing the hidden people to finally come back out into the sunlight.

Note

1 I make this argument at length in a new book project tentatively entitled "Continuous Assembly: The Power and Promise of Non-Archism."

References

Arendt, Hannah. 1986. *On Revolution*. New York: Penguin Books.

Bargu, Banu. 2025. *Disembodiment: Corporeal Politics of Radical Refusal*. New York: Oxford Books.

Casas, Juan Gómez. 1986. *Anarchist Organization: The History of the FAI*. Montreal: Black Rose Books.
Collier, George A., and Elizabeth Lowery Quaratiello. 2005. *Basta! Land and the Zapatista Rebellion in Chiapas*. Oakland, CA: Food First Books.
Dean, Jodi. 2025. *Capital's Grave: Neofeudalism and the New Class Struggle*. New York: Penguin Books.
Georgakas, Dan, and Marvin Surkin. 2012. *Detroit: I Do Mind Dying: A Study in Urban Revolution*. Chicago, IL: Haymarket Books.
Graeber, David, and David Wengrow. 2021. *The Dawn of Everything: A New History of Humanity*. New York: Macmillan.
Machiavelli, Niccolò. 1950. *The Prince and the Discourses*. New York: Modern Library.
Mariátegui, José Carlos. 1988. "The Problem of Land." In *Seven Interpretive Essays on Peruvian Reality*. Austin: University of Texas Press, 31–76.
Martel, James, and Blanca Missé. 2024. "For Democratic Governance of Universities: The Case for Administrative Abolition." *Theory & Event*, 27(1): 5–29.
Mintz, Frank. 2013. *Anarchist and Worker's Self-Management in Revolutionary Spain*. Oakland, CA: AK Press.
Marx, Karl. 1978. "Manifesto of the Communist Party." In Karl Marx and Friedrich Engels, *The Marx-Engels Reader*, edited by Robert C. Tucker. New York: W.W. Norton, 469–500.
Paz, Abel. 1976. *Durruti: The People Armed*. Montreal: Black Rose Press.
Richards, Vernon. 2019. *Lessons of the Spanish Revolution, 1936–1939*. Oakland, CA: PM Press.
Robinson, Cedric. 2000. *Black Marxism: The Making of the Black Radical Tradition*. Chapel Hill: University of North Carolina Press.
Ross, Kristin 2024. *The Commune Form: The Transformation of Everyday Life*. New York: Verso.
Sanín-Restrepo, Ricardo, and Marinella Machado-Araujo. 2025 "A Prolific Paradox of Justice and Two Theses on the Encryption of the Hidden People." In *Decrypting Justice: From Epistemic Violence to Immanent Democracy*, edited by Ricardo Sanín-Restrepo, Marinella Machado-Araujo, and Sabelo J. Ndlovu-Gatsheni. New York: Lexington Books, 15–42.
Serulnikov, Serge. 2013. *Revolt in the Andes: the Age of Túpac Amaru*. Durham, NC: Duke University Press.
Zibechi, Raúl. 2010. *Dispersing Power: Social Movements as Anti-State Forces*. Oakland, CA: AK Press.

2

The Narcissism of Sovereignty: A Pattern for Liberation Through the Hidden People

Ricardo Sanín-Restrepo and Marinella Machado-Araujo

Introduction. The Problem. The Target

This analysis will trace a pattern, describe a tendency, and identify a form present throughout Western political theories and praxis that will see sovereignty chronically and steadfastly taking the place of democracy until the latter seamlessly aligns with the former (as power as oppression). An organic substitution, of life and limb that is the result of the primordial hate of democracy[1] (Rancière 2006), which can be phrased as the need of the privileged few—in power as a result of violence—to build systems that are immune to democracy and evermore in need of legitimizing themselves in democracy's name (and more doggedly in the name of the people). A history marked by the persistent countering and massive refinement of oppressive mechanisms aimed at subduing democracy. When we speak of democracy, we mean radical democracy, conceived as the anarchic, contingent, and unaccountable potentiality of the new emerging from an unpredictable void of collective political imagination.

This tracing of a pattern, description of a tendency, and identification of a form of the sovereign substitution will focus on answering a fundamental question of our bizarre times: are today's sadistic forms of oppression and their historical tendency toward apocalypticism still based on this substitution?

Allow us to set the table for an answer.

Like any substitution, the neutralizing force always replaces what it possesses with something else, in this case sovereignty implies imposing rigid hierarchies as natural, a tale of origins as unquestionable, and, above all, its own unbreakable necessity as the pinnacle of power.

The dialectical struggle between sovereignty and democracy is the center stage. We will examine the historical contortions of sovereignty, how it stifles at some points, how it becomes fluid at others, always praying on one thing alone, the core of democracy. This core is expressed in the capacity of people to self-organize and create a novel world without a preexisting model, which renders hierarchy not merely an anathema, but a logical impossibility.

Sovereignty is the organizing principle of Western and thus colonial history. It not only governs something abstract called government or State but also dictates the narrative, order, and placement of events. Its autopoietic nature enables it to enforce its own *necessity*, hegemonize its internal dominant principles, and suppress alternatives. As we will prove, against a more mainstream interpretation such as Hardt's and Negri's, this process still constitutes the overdetermining model of *potestas* (oppression), shaping both today's physical and intellectual landscapes, and ultimately solidifying sovereignty as the unquestionable arbiter of truth and power. As we will also show, the creation of a "hidden people" through sovereign action is not a mere side effect of power, it is its nucleus. The "hidden people" merges domination with legitimacy, justifying the violence and social dissolution inherent to capitalism. In coloniality, the constitutional creation of a people represents the epitome of the sovereign machine.

Our aim is also to discover if sovereignty is still the operating system of today's new and uncanny strands of potestas that are throwing every known philosophical category into disarray and thus creating sharp and engaging neologisms. We are referring to *technofeudalism* (Varoufakis 2023), the *end times of fascism* (Klein 2023) or *neofeudalism* (Dean 2025).

We will besiege sovereignty from two flanks, first, *Energeia*, as unconditioned power of beingness, and second, sheer *Meillassouxian* contingency (Meillassoux 2008) as the anarchic possibility of the new coming forth form no preestablished model. Through it, we will flesh out and ontologically and historically complement and extend what Jacques Rancière's *Ten Theses on Politics* condenses in the following quote:

> What thus characterizes a democracy is pure chance or the complete absence of qualifications for governing. Democracy is that state of exception where no oppositions can function, where there is no pre-determined principle of role allocation … Democracy is the specific situation in which there is an absence of qualifications that, in turn, becomes the qualification for the exercise of a democratic arche. What is destroyed in this logic is the particular quality of arche. (2001, 33)

As the Two Davids (Graeber and Wengrow) understand it, "One of the most pernicious aspects of standard world-historical narratives is precisely that they dry everything up" (2021, 21). Exactly, sovereignty imposes the epistemological model through which these narratives scorch the earth and flatten the alternate histories and social experiments, packing everything into a prefigured identity, its own identity.

As an illustrative pallet we invite the reader to consider how this chapter aligns with and provides philosophical depth to two sets of integrated arguments presented in David Graeber and David Wengrow's (the Two Davids) *The Dawn of Everything*. As some know, one of the main features of the book is that it debunks a series of truisms of necessity of human nature showing how they have no real grounding, they are not even mythical in the sense of elevating an idea of forms and of building structures of life, but are simply bad science, bad theory, spreading and covering every single space of visibility of the world.

One of the central conclusions of *The Dawn of Everything* is that three principles consistently manifest, in varying forms, whenever *potestas* (archism) governs a society. They term them control of violence (sovereignty), control of information (we would say encryption in *latu sensu*), and individual charisma. "Usually, all three coexist to some degree ... What really concerns us about these three principles is that each has become the basis for institutions now seen as foundational to the modern state" (Graeber and Wengrow 2021, 365–6).

As they put it, "Sovereignty, bureaucracy and politics are magnifications of elementary types of domination, grounded respectively in the use of violence, knowledge and charisma" (2021, 508).

Through the theory of encryption of power (TEP), our analysis aims to demonstrate how late coloniality, as the final fusion of the people and sovereignty, maximally reinforces these three features. Sovereignty is the encryption of the power of the people maintained through the simulacra of transcendent models (capital, the constitution) that are kept alive and mobile by a set of experts dealing in secrecy and concealment. Glory or charisma has been cemented on the simulated power of the people, the narcissistic self-image of people as sovereign.

Henceforth, we will investigate the significant transformation of the third feature, "charisma," which resonates strongly with Agamben's notion of *Glory*. Our analysis will focus on the profound implications of glorification of power, where the people are both those that need to fulfill the role of adoration and at the same time represent glory (as faux sovereign, glorifying their own glory). This leads to a collapse of the distinction between subject and object, resulting in a loss of individual agency and a narcissistic investment in a false self. Psychoanalytically, this suggests dynamics of identification with the aggressor, introjection of an idealized power figure, as well as a potential defense against underlying feelings of vulnerability through grandiose identification.[2]

The development of our arguments will also underpin the other side of the spectrum of the Two Davids findings, as they put it:

> Over the course of these chapters we have instead talked about basic forms of social liberty which one might actually put into practice: (1) the freedom to move away or relocate from one's surroundings; (2) the freedom to ignore or disobey commands issued by others; and (3) the freedom to shape entirely new social realities, or shift back and forth between different ones. (2021, 503)

We believe that, even though they are all integral to freedom, the third one is vital for the TEP, especially when we demonstrate contingency and the anarchic principle of democracy.

Arché-Transcendent Model, Definitions

Historically, philosophically, but more importantly, legally, when the unsettling, the uncanny, the novelty, manifests itself out of nowhere, it must be contained, driven to normality, to a predictive matrix. The uncanny must be represented by the known. As it is something, by principle, uncanny, the known is always an approximation, a shot in the dark. Representation tempers, explains, and drives back to an origin that is malleable, but also by this very same token, false. Representation, as that which can be said of a thing in a relation to a stable source, is thus necessary to establish a sense of reality and order (hierarchies), asserting that things exist for a reason rather than by chance, by necessity and not by contingency, that they do not come out of a monstrous void but that they can and will be aligned and tamed, ordered and reduced to the knowable.

Nevertheless, something else is lacking, the relation between the uncanny and representation requires a triangulation to a higher term. Therefore, a foundational, unrepresentable principle is necessary to regulate and stabilize them, to legitimize and give form to the representation. This principle is a fundamental, self-existent entity that provides the basis for all order and structure. The *inception*[3] in Heidegger's terms (2000) creates a State where a supreme, unrepresentable assumption is needed to control and shape all representations, ensuring that events are perceived as necessary rather than random, that they are of this world. "Of this world" comes to mean "through another world that represents it." How can representation be anything other than the matching of unfounded events to a supposed origin that is itself equally unfounded? This assumption that precedes any direct observation, the heavenly vault and bedrock of Western philosophy, is provided in the form of a transcendent model (*arché*).

Philosophers have historically attempted to resolve the conflict between representations and presuppositions by formulating a comprehensive but unrepresentable assumption that would enable all representations. Without this foundational assumption, for them, the entire world would become unstable and meaningless, even worse, anarchic. And here we tackle the sheer force of the word. *Arché* is both bottom and ceiling, origin and end. From the ancient Greek word ἀρχή (arkhē), which literally means "beginning, origin." In early Greek philosophy, it referred to the "first principle" or the fundamental substance from which everything else is derived.

As stated previously, this is the purpose behind Plato's *Forms*, Descartes's *mind*, Kant's *judgment*, and Hegel's *concept of absolute time* (Sanín-Restrepo 2018). These concepts aim to provide an ultimate presupposition that stands as the foundational element that maintains the coherence and architecture of everything uncanny, of a world of the manifold, of a time of multidirectionality, and of the problem called *the people*.

The process begins with the appearance of the uncanny, *presenting* (Schürmann 1987), which demands representation. However, these representations are inherently limited, they are self-referential, and lack intrinsic stability or connection, making them essentially isolated and incommunicable. Let us put it bluntly, they are the result of pure violent imposition. This necessitates the creation of a presupposition that is independent of representation, treating it as a secondary, nonessential element, a presupposition that transcends representation, a fundamental principle that governs representation itself. This principle, referred to as validity, goodness, correctness, ideality, beingness, or logic, serves as a meta-entity that manages, directs, places, and explains all other entities. It is a transcendent model that establishes the form of every existence. The presupposition acts as an external, unknowable force that dictates everything within the realm of the observable.

It is the transcendent that allows things to be named, while remaining itself beyond naming, allowing things to be touched and handled while being itself retrieved from the senses. It is the theological spirit of Western thought engraved in the heart of the fear of nothingness, of what becomes self from itself.

As Andityas Matos clearly states, "Indeed, political theology may be the most prominent example of the encryption of power, a metaphysical process that substitutes immanence for transcendence, multiplicity for unity, and potentia for potestas, resulting in centralized and self-contained political institutions" (Matos 2025). As we will demonstrate, through the creation of *the people as a synecdoche*, the latter comes full circle, the closing of the gap of sovereignty, politics, and theology.

What about political agency? The issue is simplified into a self-evident statement: existence is defined as opposition to nonexistence, and existence is always expressed through some form of power that is connected to a fundamental presupposition, whether it is termed idea, substance, logos, nature, society, man, epistemology, mind, judgment, or concept (Sanín-Restrepo 2018, 12), or even apparently stable institutions such as the nation State, homeland, constitution, money.

Now, is "to be" equivalent to the exercise of power? It becomes clear that all efforts are primarily focused on restricting the exercise of power through strict normative boundaries, where *being* and power and their immanent mutuality, (more than mutuality, their sameness) are severed, and an eminent bridge is built where "to be" is to exercise power "only in obedience of the model that dictates being and power." Accordingly, every nonbeing is always invoked by a being that already exists even if as a mere presupposition of presence (Heidegger 2001).

Is the transcendent model universal, timeless, in a word, metaphysical? According to Reiner Schürmann, reading Heidegger, the division of theory and practice rests on epochal schemata, rendering all practice "an-archic/an-*arché*." As he puts it, "In the age of metaphysics' closure, this procession from or legitimation by a first science proves to be epochal—regional, dated, finite, and 'finished' in both senses of the word: complete as well as terminated" (1987, 5). The conclusion is within reach. If it is epochal, it cannot be metaphysical. Indeed, if it is epochal, every principle is a product of power within a specific timeframe. These models, such as the "ideal city" or "happiness of the greatest number," are epochal, finite, and "finished." Consequently, they are not and cannot be absolute, autonomous universals when setting the standard for all becoming.

The aforementioned leads us to another important insight. The relationship between the *arché* and its manifestation is always a *post facto* construction. The transcendent model, essentially an empty signifier (Laclau 2005), is initially named and loosely characterized. Its concrete definition—its categories, functions, and pragmatic realm—is determined by qualified interpreters (the pontiff, the constitutional judge) who, based on the prevailing world conditions, fill in its content. This process allows experts or "encryptors" to impose domination *ex post facto*, utilizing the inherent openness and autopoietic fabric of the model[4] to shape it according to rules embedded within its structure.

The epochal nature of the *arché* resides in its specific practical application. While its constant feature is its status as an empty signifier, its function is to encrypt and maintain hierarchies. Popular sovereignty is the ultimate form of this encryption. The *arché* acts as both origin and zenith, dividing the body politic. Ultimately, the position of the *arché* is secured through the violence of the law.

The TEP begins with the understanding that "an-archy," as Schürmann clarifies, isn't a program or a dialectical counterpoint to "archism," but rather a fundamental condition of the abundancy of life. It represents the "withering away" of the metaphysical drive to establish a foundational "principle," a "principle without principle." This anarchy, the presupposition(less) of any system, is revealed when Heidegger's notion of *presencing* is considered: the imposition of an *arché* disrupts this pure presencing, demonstrating that all systems are epochal and thus anarchic. As Schürmann observes, "In the most hidden ground of his being, man truly is only if in his way he is like the rose—without why" (1987, 38). This "without why" signifies a life without telos, a life of pure potentiality, where "possibilities of becoming" replace the need for a preordained reason. These epochal enclosures, or transcendent models, attempt to impose a teleological structure, a "straight line" for human development, the blind obedience of mimesis, the gray ticking of a time of repetition, but ultimately, they are fragile constructs, the imposition of truth through violence.

Poetics,[5] by revealing the "empty substratum" beneath these models, allows us to go beyond epochal limitations, exposing the inherent contingency of power. As Schürmann articulates, "All entities convey a 'why' … But higher than actuality stands possibility" (1987, 16). This possibility, unbound by *arché* and "telos," exists beyond the coordinates of causality, a realm of pure potential, a space where no specific imposition can hold.

To understand power's encryption, we need a new thinking that unleashes *Energeia*: embracing the anarchic potential Schürmann reveals, a "principle without principle," where "possibilities of becoming" thrive. In our view, this requires an agile, nonconstructive thought, perpetually returning upon itself, engaging with the empty substratum of power's imposed "arché." This dynamic thinking, beyond static forms, allows us to discern and navigate power's fluid mechanisms, reclaiming agency by understanding how the empty signifier is filled, and thus, we move beyond passive acceptance to active participation in shaping meaning. A thought that does not end thinking, that is, always standing on the tip of its toes on the abyss of the contingent, never resting on what is or what appears to be but always embracing what can be. Never satisfied with curling back to a cause but always extending the probability of all causes into the infinite.

We need to break from political thought that can only think in hierarchies and submission to higher orders, of original causes and the assigning of categories to predefined niches. Politics has not only been conditioned by this way of doing, but this conditioning and doing is deeply political, it is a way to force being into rigid forms of power (existence, change). We call these rigid forms of exercise of power, *potestas*.

As I put earlier:

> The perseverance of models of identity means two interconnected things: first, politics has served as a harsh demarcation line of life, and second, that to belong to a body politic, any agent (before becoming a subject, before exercising difference) must conform to the qualifications of identity set forth by an invisible (transcendent) model. The apparent perfect circularity collapses when we acknowledge that the model that serves as a frontier for existence is arranged from within by those who already belong to the body politic. Henceforth, the model is not an absolute and universal principle but simply the rules of the necessity of power that the mighty fix through violence to garner a criterion of certainty for inclusion and exclusion. (Sanín-Restrepo 2018, xiii)

What is the position of a transcendent model? "To dictate, from a vanishing point of invisibility, outside language and any relation, the conditions to which every and any form of beingness must abide in order to be" (Sanín-Restrepo and Machado-Araujo 2020, 22).

It is the transcendent model that captures multiplicity, harnesses contingency, and ultimately defines "beingness" and through it captures or solidifies and monopolizes power.

In the words of Andityas Matos:

> Here, we must again ask what encryption encrypts, what it hides and, in doing so, what it distorts. The answer can only be: the an-archic and collective experience of constructing social meaning, which occurs immanently and is conditioned by difference. Yet, this experience ultimately becomes encrypted and codified in the form of universal apparatuses—sovereignty, Constitution, representation, etc.—that solidify power. (2025, 46)

Putting a something in the place of nothing, and archism in the place of an-archy is the history of Western power. What consequences does it have when this something is the people? Let us explore further.

Politeia and Potestas

As we advanced recently (Sanín-Restrepo and Machado-Araujo 2022), Giorgio Agamben (2005, 2) illustrates that the Greek term *politeia* is the linchpin for understanding the very essence of the political, it encapsulates a foundational paradox, serving as the very locus of political thought. *Politeia* simultaneously came to signify the act of foundation, the raw, unbridled force of *constituent power*, and the structured, formalized expression of that power in the form *of government* or *constituted power*.

How could this contradiction have happened? And, more importantly, why did Plato and Aristotle, self-proclaimed beacons of the fight against the muddling of logic facilitate it? The answer is simple, the fear of contingency, potentiality, and the power of the people.

In his "Introductory Note on the Concept of Democracy," Agamben highlights the duality within "democracy" by examining the Greek terms *politeia* and *politeuma*. *Politeia* signifies "political activity" or "constituent power," entailing the foundational "juridico-political rationality" of a political community. Conversely, *politeuma* represents the outcome, the product, or "constituted power" as well as the "technique of government." He notes a fundamental ambiguity where *politeia* is sometimes translated as "constitution" and sometimes as "government."

The implicit tension of *Politeia* represents the primordial fracture within Western political philosophy (Agamben 2005, 2011b). *Politeia* implies, on one hand, a *constituent power* that is immanent, self-generating, and unbound, in other words anarchic, that recognizes no external limitations or grounding. It is the pure potentiality of political being, contingency in its purest form.

The enduring legacy of this duality is most vividly illustrated in Plato's eponymous dialogue, conventionally rendered as *Republic* (Plato 2000). Which, in its original Greek title, *Politeia*, immediately highlights that there is a fundamental nothingness at the origin of power, this inherent tension produces the need to cover the crack of utter contingency that breathes through it.

Hence, Plato's efforts are directed into turning *politeia* into a hedged form of power, a legally constituted organization, where its form (*morphology*) and its operational procedures (*praxis*) are subject to formal codification. This bifurcated nature of *politeia* gives rise to the conceptual distinction between *constituent power* and *constitution*, or *politeia* and *politeuma*, respectively (Agamben 2005, 2011b). This amphibology, this inherent ambiguity, marks the very origin of Western reflection on power, encapsulating the central paradox of *constituent power and* the fear for the anarchic, the immanent, the unbound.

The internal fissure must be sealed. All subsequent Western political thought and action is a sustained violent attempt to heal this foundational wound (Sanín-Restrepo and Machado-Araujo 2022). This endeavor invariably culminates in the absorption of *constituent power* into the *constituted power*, leading to the naturalization and subsequent legitimization of the latter's dominance over the former. This process, however, does not eliminate the underlying tension, but rather masks it, represses it, as the foundational act of political creation is perpetually obscured by established structures. This naturalization, then, is not a resolution, but a suppression of the inherent paradox, leaving the potential for its reemergence perpetually latent. The very question of how a self-limiting constituted power *can emerge from and then dominate* an unlimited constituent power remains a monumental philosophical muddling that should not challenge the very foundations of political legitimacy.

Aristotle, in Book III of his *Politics* (2015c), drawing on insights from the *Nichomachean Ethics* (2015b), initiated an attempt to mend the primordial fissure inherent in *politeia*. He did so by emphasizing *politeia* primarily as a *form of government*, specifically one where governance is conducted for the *common good* of all the governed (*to koinon onoma pasōn tōn politeiōn*). The common good will eventually derive in the Commonwealth (Res-public) a precise seizure of constituent power by the constituted that will define Western sovereignty.

As Jacques Rancière puts it brilliantly dismantling Aristotle's pretense of imposing a rule for politics:

> It is enough to see the manner in which Aristotle characterizes the three possible classes of rule within a polis, each one possessing a particular title: "virtue" for the aristoi, "wealth" for the oligoi, and "freedom" for the demos. In this division, "freedom" appears as the paradoxical part of the demos about whom the Homeric hero tells us (in no uncertain terms) that it had only one thing to do: to keep quiet and bow down. (2001, 28)

Agamben (2011b) has pointed out the importance of the *Kyrios* within Aristotle's writings (2015c). This *Kyrios* is the sovereign power, which holds together and fuses the *politeia* and the *politeuma*. In this way, Agamben shows how the constituent power and the constituted power are held together through a higher instance, a transcendent model called sovereignty.

In Rome, the sealing of the fissure attains a new constraining and everlasting dimension. The *libertas* of the *Populus* is circumscribed and diminished, becoming subject to the direction of the senatorial *auctoritas* and the *potestas* of the magistrates. Thus, the complex and problematic fissure between *politeia* and *politeuma* culminates in a closure of meanings, where *constituent power* disappears and is thus subordinated and driven by *constituted power* or the res-public (*the republic*, the common good). Again, the definition of what is *good* and *common* is left to that privileged minority who detent power, in Roman terms, those who exercise *potestas* (see Sanín-Restrepo and Machado-Araujo 2022).

Consequently, the inherent tension of *constituent power*, rooted in infinite difference and multiplicity, is effectively reduced to a concrete notion of legal consensus. The concept of *mixed government*, systematized by Polybius in Rome and later amplified by Machiavelli, represents a further, decisive step in transforming the republic into a guardian of an inherently undemocratic spirit (Sanín-Restrepo and Machado-Araujo 2022).

This preemptive definition and control render the public sphere not a space of open, emergent political action, of fierce and productive agonism, but a domesticated legal domain managed and dictated by established authorities, effectively closing the space for the original constituent power to be and to act.

Classic Sovereignty—Constituent Power

The dawn of modernity is defined by the emergence of sovereignty as the unbreakable essence of power. Sovereignty is depicted in two key manners. Jean Bodin defines it as the "absolute and perpetual power of a Commonwealth" ([1596] 1980, Bk. I ch. 8). As the Two Davids say it, "Our term 'the state' only came into common usage in the late sixteenth century, when it was coined by a French lawyer named Jean Bodin, who also wrote, among many other things, an influential treatise on witchcraft, werewolves and the history of sorcerers" (Graeber and Wengrow 2021, 359).

As I have ascertained, "It is Hobbes, however, who organizes sovereignty into a precise category of political and legal philosophy, boosting its overwhelming presence, not only in the apparent balance of European affairs, but as the clotting element of power" (Sanín-Restrepo 2016, 162).

In *De Cive*, he outlines a system where "from the vertue of the Covenant whereby each Subject is tyed to the other to perform absolute and universall obedience to the City … there is an obligation derived to observe each one of the civill Lawes" (Hobbes [1651] 2000, XX, 73).

Hobbes's profound innovation lies in adding a rational contract to absolute power, thus legalizing voluntary servitude. What is engraved deeply in sovereignty is not only servitude but servitude as a necessary outcome. As the Two Davids put it:

> Hobbes's Leviathan, published in 1651, is in many ways the founding text of modern political theory. It held that, humans being the selfish creatures they are, life in an original State of Nature was in no sense innocent; it must instead have been "solitary, poor, nasty, brutish, and short"—basically, a state of war, with everybody fighting against everybody else. (2021, 4)

The imposition of violence as necessary, logically derives from a foul human nature that legitimizes the need for the univocal violence of sovereignty that itself implies logical hierarchies. The subjugation to sovereignty becomes not only preferable, but necessary. Hobbes's strategy proves devastatingly effective: by reducing the people to mere subjects of law and subordinating them to absolute sovereignty, he forecloses the very possibility of an immanent constituent power, effectively severing autonomy from the populace and enshrining it within the sovereign.

Hannah Arendt argues that Hobbes's construction of sovereignty lays the groundwork for totalitarian regimes. A fundamental point of contention lies in Arendt's distinction between power and violence, a distinction she finds Hobbes fatally blurs (Arendt 2004). In our frame, Hobbes turns power as existence (beingness) into a concentrated form of power where the sovereign absorbs and monopolizes it and thus inhibits beingness as such. In Hobbes's formulation, sovereignty rests on the ability to enforce obedience, effectively conflating power with the threat of violence, leading to a concept of sovereignty based on utter domination.[6]

In Hobbes's own words:

> The sovereignty is the soul of the Commonwealth; which, once departed from the body, the members do no more receive their motion from it. The end of obedience is protection; which, wheresoever a man seeth it, either in his own or in another's sword, nature applieth his obedience to it, and his endeavour to maintain it." ([1651] 1999, II, 49)

What sovereignty negates is nothing else than immanent *constituent power*.

While Hobbes lays the groundwork for the total submission of the people to the sovereign, it was John Locke who introduced a deep "metaphysical" shift to sovereignty, focusing on subjectivity and political agency through a novel configuration of private property. Locke's *treatises* ([1689] 1980) represent a pivotal "turn" in political philosophy. As we previously established, it was a shift akin to Plato's contribution to metaphysics and later, Kant's to epistemology (Sanín-Restrepo and Machado-Araujo 2022). This turn established the foundation for a new form of power, global capitalism, operating within the framework of colonialism.

But what is the core of Locke's philosophical maneuver? Grounding subjectivity in private property. Antonio Negri and Michael Hardt (2009) have termed this shift "The Republic of Property." This process legitimized Western State dispossession and labor commodification, while empowering the new "citizen-proprietor" to accumulate further property, thereby reinforcing the State's legitimacy and perpetuating the cycle of dispossession.

In Locke's own words, "The great and chief end, therefore, of men's uniting into commonwealths, and putting themselves under government, is the preservation of their property" ([1689] 1980, chapter IX, §124).

In *The Racial Contract*, Charles Mills argues that Locke's liberalism, while seemingly universal, is actually based on a "racial contract" that excludes nonwhite people from full participation in society. Mills (1997) argues that Locke's theories were used to justify the creation of a white supremacist social order.

Consequently, property transitions from a mere external predefined object of commerce to a constitutive attribute of being. Individuals interact with the external world and with others solely through the medium of property. To be is to have, to have is to exercise power, without property there is no beingness. This results in a system where the *republic of property* utilizes civic virtue, patriotism (as racism), and the rule of law to justify unlimited expropriation and the establishment of rigid racial hierarchies, often rendered invisible to legal scrutiny as legality in turn is based on the republic of property.

As Hardt and Negri articulate:

> Property, which is taken to be intrinsic to human thought and action, serves as the regulative idea of the constitutional state and the rule of law. This is not really a historical foundation but rather an ethical obligation, a constitutive form of the moral order. The concept of the individual is not defined by being but having. (2009, 7)

Locke's elevation of property to the central axis of politics also transforms it into the central axis of law and economics. It parallels Plato's division of labor between those capable of political participation (intellectuals, aristocrats) and those excluded (manual laborers). Property becomes the driving force of the world, an ontological measure of freedom, reducing freedom to the exchange of commodities and transforming human beings into objects. In Locke's framework, the transition from nature to culture is equated with the transition from a divine order to an individual defined by their ownership of themselves and the world ([1689] 1980, 123–6, §25–51; Sanín-Restrepo and Machado-Araujo 2022).

Even though Hobbes and Locke's contributions to the neutralization of constituent power are fundamental,[7] several other historical and theoretical steps are needed to get to the ultraneutralization by modern constitutions.

Sovereignty becomes the form of what Aníbal Quijano's (2000) translators serendipitously coined as the *colonial matrix of power*.[8] As such, it serves multiple purposes: it establishes a legal framework and a practical blueprint for European colonization, it facilitates the façade of secularization of power while maintaining its theological underpinnings, it controls vast populations within European territories while undermining differences (witch-hunts, for example), and it creates a legal and epistemological (never mind aesthetical) hierarchical division between "civilized" Europe and the "uncivilized" rest.

The Nation State

The allocation of sovereignty to the nation State is the previous phase to closing the gap of the constituent power whose final stage is assigning it to the people through modern constitutions.

The nation State is the pipeline of encryption for modernity and colonialism. Firstly, it consolidates the State as a monolithic legal structure and thus the only legitimate monopoly of violence. Secondly, as the gateway to full throttle colonialism, nationalism facilitates the calculated and organized territorial acquisition by select European nations, establishing clear boundaries through a legal framework of warfare that ensures parity and stability within Western Europe (the rules of warfare). Simultaneously, it acts as a tool to compress the enormous diversity of the colonial world as the bizarre image of Europe's singular legal framework of the nation State, a harsh dividing line of "us" and "them." This manipulation extends beyond mere legal constructs. It dictates that the nation State embodies the definitive model of humanity (Castro-Gómez 2005; Ndlovu-Gatsheni 2024), compelling the colonial world to mirror it, thereby validating its cultural, social, economic, and political worth.

National identity is constructed through the expulsion of absolute difference. Difference, therefore, becomes negation: those who deviate from the prescribed national identity are excluded. The law serves as the instrument by which the nation contains, reduces, eliminates, and suppresses any deviation from its model. In colonial terms, the nation State, through sovereignty, establishes a universal, Western/European model of culture and humanity, defining the boundaries of political truth in the law, epistemology, the economy and aesthetics. This demands the eradication of difference and the passive submission of (non)humanity to the meanings imposed by European nation States (Sanín-Restrepo 2016). The sovereign nation is elevated to the essence and driving force of history, conceived as the product of a rational historical spirit, where all history is reduced to European history, and all human perfection to the nation's ideal (Hardt and Negri 2005, 146).

The nation, as the complete figure of sovereignty, precedes its historical development, shaping history by eliminating threats of difference and multiplicity. It establishes the European citizen as the archetypal human, elevating it to a universal standard to be emulated or, if necessary, forcibly imposed through law. The citizen, milked from the nation State, becomes the checkpoint of legality, policing the borders to maintain national cohesion and preventing any deviation from the system. The creation of a rigid racial divide is crucial for the formation of a unified national identity (Mignolo 2003), this is the core of colonial power.

The nation State, a "two-headed hydra," along with its inseparable components, spreads its influence through postcolonial projects. The model of nationality is replicated in movements of (pseudo) independence, becoming their central organizing principle. Consequently, decolonization struggles often merely perpetuate patterns of exclusion. The newly formed independent elites simply replicate the structures of colonial power, maintaining the geopolitical client system and the internal legal and political exclusions of women, Black and Indigenous people, and the poor (Quijano 2000; Mignolo 2003; Sanín-Restrepo 2016; Ndlovu-Gatsheni 2024). The colonial ideal of the enlightened European man is seamlessly adopted by the Creole elites.

The proposed resolution to modernity's inherent crisis rests on the conception that nationalism is an unavoidable and ultimate phase of historical progression, a culmination that effectively dissolves all existing contradictions into a singular, flawless synthesis. The nation State solidifies a specific vision of a dominant modern society, and the ascendance of the bourgeoisie transforms from a localized narrative into the universally accepted truth of history (Said 1978), glorified immediately within the constitution. The West not only has history but predestination, their history is of a heroic overcoming of obstacles by nations and individuals in the name of a greater good (Fanon 1986), while non-Westerns swim in a muddy mythic circle of emptiness.

Western historical experience is then projected as the universal historical trajectory for all. Economic activity is elevated to a quasi-sacred, ethnic entity perceived as a patriotic duty contributing to national grandeur (Quijano 2000; Castro-Gómez 2005). Not a blade can fit between the nation and the State, between the citizen and *his* identity that embodies the model. Modern international law is a continuation of this project, enabling European nations to impose their model globally (Ndlovu-Gatsheni 2024).

From the Nation to the People. Constitutional Transformation

The nation State serves to concentrate power, impose ideology as rationality, classify races, and divide peoples, yet it remains abstract and exterior to sovereignty. The table is easily set for the final assault against democracy. Modernity, as Negri argues, is a conflict between democracy and sovereignty, stating, "the opposite of democracy is not totalitarianism but the concept of sovereignty itself" (1999, 28). The people as a creation of sovereignty, begin to coalesce around Hobbes's definition. The final stage of sovereignty's neutralization involves its complete interiorization, where democracy is deactivated in its own name. This process is simple: turning the paradox into a rule. It culminates in the creation of a simulated sovereign, exemplified by the US Constitution, which conceals constituent power and elevates private property as the central element of power.

As I have expressed:

> Since the migration of political philosophy to liberal constitutionalism, when we name the people we invoke nothing less than the origin and legitimacy of modernity and its structure. The concept of the people is not just a component of this whole, but its coagulating element, its nuclei of meaning. However, and this is the basic simulacrum of democracy, coloniality/modernity as an idea, as an organization of meanings that gives itself the airs of a system, can only function under one unescapable condition: the stringent neutralization of the people through the false universal recognition of liberalism. (Sanín-Restrepo 2016, 39)

The most sophisticated encryption machine in coloniality is the constitutional idea. It creates social hierarchies based on race, gender, and nationality; it converts *the commons* into private property, and establishes capitalism as the dominant global ideology. The constitution is a masterpiece of design, perfectly welding the people and democracy—their agency and structure—into a formidable and flawlessly functioning system of oppression.

The hidden people, the "all but one," exist in a liminal space, neither fully inside nor outside the legal framework, suspended in a "state of exception." They are the "excess," the "excrement" of the political body, the very element excluded to preserve the transcendent, yet unattainable, model of liberal order. While the "people" as a totality are presented as the norm, the hidden people are the exception, the site where law is suspended, rendering them vulnerable to unchecked power, especially the heinous power of the market. This absence, this incompleteness, is the very foundation of the modern political-constitutional order.

The concept of "the people" becomes a deceptive symbol, a "synecdoche," where a limited part—the included—falsely represents an infinite whole—the excluded. This *pars pro toto* synecdoche masks the hidden people, the unrepresentable excess of liberal democracies, who exist beyond the boundaries of representation.

The fundamental tension lies between the "principle of immanence of difference"—linked to "constituent power"—and "potestas," embodied in "sovereignty." While philosophical traditions emphasize absolute immanence as the foundation of ethics and ontology (Deleuze and Guattari 1983; Derrida 1997) they often overlook the historical subjugation of difference to potestas. Consequently, a necessary "mediation" is required, a means for difference to engage and overcome the structures of potestas. We cannot simply reject sovereignty as if it was dependent on wishful thinking, it would be tantamount to relinquishing the possibility of political action.

Mediation becomes the central challenge for any analysis of power. True democracy can only emerge when the hidden people, as the active force of difference, confront the artificial separation between sovereignty and constituent power. This requires a veritable synthesis of sovereignty and the people, a reunification that modernity has fractured through the state of exception and the simulated fusion. Only when those rendered inert and vulnerable claim the power to determine their own lives can genuine democracy exist (Sanín-Restrepo 2016; Sanín-Restrepo and Machado-Araujo 2025). This synthesis would eliminate the need for an excluded, vulnerable "outside," thereby transforming the very nature of politics and the world. When the exceptional seizes the exception, sovereignty as potestas dissolves, and politics is fundamentally redefined.

Sovereignty, Neofeudalism, Empire?

Nevertheless, the central question persists: in our days of turmoil, of hardcore fascism and neofeudalism, of ethnostates and endless destruction, does sovereignty remain the definitive marker of power, the creator of worlds? In other words, is it still worth our attention, specifically, does it retain the power to decide on the exception from the exception? (Schmitt 2006; Agamben 2005).

As Hardt and Negri argue that Westphalian sovereignty has separated from the nation State, they also assert that law is no longer the sole matrix of power. Insofar, they criticize the conventional focus on sovereignty by highlighting a significant transformation where the characteristics of classical sovereignty have either disappeared or become fragmented. Accordingly, for them, the emergence of *Empire* exemplifies this shift, transcending the territorial confines and centralized control of traditional nation State sovereignty. *Empire*, is a decentralized and deterritorialized form of power, operating through a network of national and transnational institutions, corporations, and technologies. This transformation renders the traditional concept of sovereign decision-making, especially the emphasis on exceptions, increasingly obsolete.[9] They complement their critique by asserting that an obsessive focus on sovereignty leads to "Apocalypticism" (a jab against Agamben). This emphasis, they claim, elevates sovereignty to a quasi-theological position, placing it above society.

Nevertheless, the speed of the transformations of our *global disorder* hint at the fact that Hardt and Negri are speaking of an old world. So, let us actualize the discussion. For example, Jodi Dean (2025) argues that neofeudalism fragments sovereignty by merging political and economic power. Henceforth, global financial institutions and giant tech platforms gain enormous power alongside and even beyond nation States, forcing countries to abide by their rules. This blurring of economic and political spheres, Dean argues, where economic actors wield tremendous political power and vice versa, erodes the classic bourgeois State's legal fictions and thus supposes a deep transformation of its sovereignty. Insofar, offshore tax havens exemplify this challenge to traditional law, highlighting a hierarchical system of dependence that undermines unified sovereignty. This neofeudal structure creates fresh forms of hierarchy and dependence that is reminiscent of a feudal system of lords and peasants, which challenges to its core the idea of a unified and universally applied sovereignty (Dean 2025).

However, as we had previously argued (Sanín-Restrepo 2016; Sanín-Restrepo and Méndez-Hincapíe 2018), while sovereignty has adapted to changing conditions, its fundamental role in coloniality remains undisturbed: the creation of an exception through the exceptional, the construction of a regime where inclusion and exclusion are programmed from.

Though power morphs through mechanisms such as control societies, post-Fordist flexibilization, and cognitive capitalism—manifesting as pervasive surveillance, decentralized labor exploitation in global supply chains, and the monopolization of knowledge through intellectual property—these shifts don't erase sovereignty's anchoring role within coloniality, on the contrary, they affirm it.

Massive privatizations that are imposed at gunpoint (or chokepoints by the World Bank or the IMF servicing the massive networks of corporations), algorithmic biases perpetuating racial profiling, the extraction of data for AI development, and the control of essential patents by multinational corporations all illustrate how these "new" power forms are deeply intertwined with, and perpetuate, colonial legacies. The focal point is this, they all necessitate an abyssal decision of normality and exception from the exception, they necessitate a sovereign decision that parts the waters of normality and exception, of who is called to live and who must die to feed the monster of extraction.

We might not see the classic emblems of sovereignty acting the way they did, but be warned, it is not because sovereignty has disappeared but because its capacity and means have morphed. The decentralized and deterritorialized form of power operating through transnational corporations, international trade agreements, and the exploitation of crises—disaster capitalism (Klein 2023), for instance, thrives in moments where national sovereignty becomes vaporous or is somehow suspended, allowing for the imposition of free-market policies. Nevertheless, the point we would badly miss is that getting to such a state of things still depends on the sovereign decision, which is not only exceptional, but hierarchical and highly centralized. The focus on sovereignty in its classic form as a singular sovereignty can indeed obscure the more insidious ways in which sovereignty operates through diffuse networks. The networks have changed, the principle of exception and potestas remains.

Yanis Varoufakis argues that "technofeudalism" fundamentally alters sovereignty by shifting its root from nation States to newfangled digital "lords," possessing and transforming life in a seemingly illimited manner. These tech corporations, as they control vital digital infrastructure and data, establish a "platform sovereignty," setting rules well beyond national regulations, well beyond any capacity of the old liberal State to predict its outcomes. This undermines traditional State authority as these entities operate with increasing autonomy, creating new dependencies and challenging the very concept of market-based governance (Varoufakis 2023).

The points from Dean, Klein, and Varoufakis are not only well taken but their fresh visions and diagnosis are vital to keep up the pace of this neodestruction. Nevertheless, they do not alter the kernel of sovereignty that, as we will see, is still the creation of normality and exception from the exception that is tantamount to the necessity of the creation and sustenance of the hidden people.

Despite the fluidity and adaptability of power, coloniality, as a persistent matrix (Quijano 2000), relies on sovereignty as its core mechanism. Defined as the power to exclude and include, sovereignty remains the common thread linking diverse forms of power, from biopower to the outsourcing of war to crisis capitalism. It is through sovereignty that coloniality maintains the division of a people into a false totality and its excluded counterpart, effectively making sovereignty the active, enduring machine of power in coloniality.

The creation of a "hidden people" through sovereign action is not a side effect, but its core. This "hidden people" is central to sovereignty, merging domination with legitimacy and justifying the violence and social dissolution inherent in capitalism. The constitutional creation of a people, and its hidden counterpart as the exception, epitomizes the sovereign machine, shielding sovereignty from critique by making the people sovereign, sovereignty become more entrenched, hiding under the guise of globalization.

Sovereignty is still the exercise of potestas and potestas relies on a permanent revolving door where some need substantial protection by the law and the police: financial systems, pharmaceuticals (in the form of either unregulated activities or direct protection); while others are either policed heavily (walls, prisons) or abandoned by law so they can be devoured by the market. No matter what the case, sovereignty is not only the common thread but the inevitable origin of potestas. When the billionaire tech bros cuddled around the president, they were purchasing the sovereign exception.

There is no circumventing sovereignty and its exceptionality.

The *hidden people* embody this exception, residing within the *state of exception* that demarcates the legal inside and outside. They serve as the element preventing the totality from being a true totality, while simultaneously enabling its operational function within the established norms. However, because they represent the exception, the *hidden people* are perpetually vulnerable to annihilation.

Allow us to recapitulate. Modern sovereignty, shaped by encryption and the "hidden people," employs a "simulacrum," a blend of coloniality and liberalism that paradoxically positions these groups as both sovereign and exception. This creates a perfect domination machine, relying on universal recognition of their vulnerability, where their destruction is perpetually justified. The simulacrum functions as an anhypothetical principle, rendering it unchallengeable, with any attack on it paradoxically reinforcing its power.

Hence, every institution or aspiration is mired by the trick of sovereignty, for example, as the Two Davids put it, "'equality before the law', … is ultimately equality before the sovereign" (2021, 44). Equality in servitude, the maintenance and perpetuation of hierarchies.

Decrypting power reveals that democracy in coloniality is a vast simulation, allowing a microminority to control political, economic, and legal language. In this simulation, the concept of totality plays a key role. Decisions are based on the totality of the people, but who counts is predetermined by those that program economic and legal values from the inside.

If dominant systems rely on excluding difference and enforcing uniformity, then the hidden people, by their very existence, redefine politics as a constant struggle for the recognition of difference (Rancière 2001). Henceforth, even if it is true that the sovereign decision has been decentered and has achieved a novel protean nature outside of its classical center, the decision of the exception through the exception remains paramount to the configuration of power.

Consider another example. AI algorithms predicting future demand for rare earth minerals, leading to a surge in mining operations in the Third World (allowed by the lack of regulation of these activities in the host nation). This results in environmental devastation and the displacement of Indigenous communities in South America. Part of the profits generated from these mining activities are funneled into luxurious real estate developments in urban centers like New York or London. This drives up property prices, gentrifies massive areas, and pushes people out of urban centers into vulnerable conditions, many of whom migrated South American countries due to extractive practices of foreign investment in the first place. Now, another part of these foreign investments is rolled back into making a specific first world country an example of universal health coverage and so and so. The chain of exploitation is truly an Ouroboros. The first world country in this example does not even need to have a corporation to its name, as Canada does, it can be simply an investment, like Norway has. The extractive practices create local devastation, forced migration while the money goes back to the investor country making it an example of happiness and social wellbeing, and this, of course also operates as an ideological standard to prove the country's superiority in the global scale of development.[10]

Sovereignty, as the power to declare an "exception" to established law, is a fundamental tool of domination that intensifies precariousness and amplifies wealth concentration. This power allows a sovereign to operate within and outside normal legal frameworks, defining and suspending laws. Even with fragmented power structures, the ability to declare exceptions remains central.

Transcendent models quell the people through enforced unanimity, molding them into compliant segments. Conversely, the hidden people embody resistance—the suffering and their struggle, dissent and its manifestations, the unrestrained being. This resistance is not sporadic, but a continuous exertion of power against the established form, preventing the colonial law of identity and unity from masquerading as the flawless outcome of reason and human endeavor. Difference as resistance is not a predefined expression; it unfolds within a plane of consistency, a dialectical confrontation with an oppressive model that necessitates the suppression of difference. The resistance of the hidden people is intrinsic, independent of legal, philosophical, or institutional, external validation. This resistance fundamentally rejects any imposed finality from unseen, elite-driven models operating through a simulated totality. This rejection is decryption. Democracy, defying historical hierarchies, is the relentless exercise of difference as the unconstrained origin; resistance is the enactment of potentia, and the constant pursuit of a new legality that distributes difference as the absolute law of truth production.

As we recently put it:

> Even if it is true that the hidden people are created as the negativity of sovereignty and its law, their permanent exercise of power is not a utopian or idealistic fantasy, but a realistic and pragmatic truth that emerges from the concrete struggles and movements of social transformation. More than a pragmatic possibility, they are twofold: They are the people in permanent resistance to traditional forms of domination, but within this struggle, they announce what is to come, the world that must be, as the exercise of difference. (Sanín-Restrepo and Machado-Araujo 2025, 20)

An-*arché*

In *Le Jardin d'Épicure*, Anatole France (1895) tells us: "Les cieux, qu'on croyait incorruptibles, ne connaissent d'éternel que l'éternel écoulement des choses."[11]

The Greek term "ἀρχή" (archē) translates to beginning, origin, first cause, or principle, and signifies the fundamental source or primary principle, especially in philosophical and theological contexts, such as the cosmos's origin in ancient Greek cosmology.

For Schürmann:

> The word ἀϱχή seems to have entered philosophical language only with Plato and Aristotle. Aristotle is the one who explicitly joins the more ancient sense of inception with that of domination. From the time of Homer, the common meaning of the verb ἄϱχειν had been "to lead," "to ` come first," "to open," for instance, a battle or a discourse. In the epic tradition, ἀϱχή designates what is at the beginning, either in an order of succession in time, like childhood, or in an order of constitutive elements, as flour is the basis of dough or as the organs are the elementary parts of the body. The other meaning, that of command, of power, of domination, although absent from Homer, is found in Herodotus and Pindar. (1987, 97)

Schürmann uses an-archy instead of anarchy. As Andityas Matos describes: "An-archy is far more demanding than classical anarchism, as it aims to bring power to the surface as potentia, rather than separating, hierarchizing, and glorifying it as a natural and given entity. An-archy is the name of decrypted democracy" (2025, 60).

The TEP, through its revision of Aristotle's (2015a) *Energeia* and *Entelecheia* (Sanín-Restrepo 2016; see also the introduction to this book), understands anarchy as the immanent and continuous expression of *Energeia*, a "being-in-work" without predetermined ends. It rejects *Entelecheia*'s telos-driven, exclusionary structures, which define power as domination (potestas) and limit political participation. Anarchy, in this context, embodies the radical contingency of becoming, where no being is qualified before existing (as Rancière has proven through other means), and politics is a dynamic, inclusive process of difference-making, contradicting any fixed, transcendent model of power. This proves that the State, capitalism, and constitutions are simulacra of power, as they impose *Entelecheia* and deny the fundamental contingency and immanence of political being, which *Energeia* represents.

Telos (the end or purpose) and *arché* (the origin or principle) are inherently interconnected—each implies the existence of the other. A telos assumes an *arché* that must be realized or fulfilled, while an *arché* presupposes a telos to provide it with direction and purpose. This mutual presupposition limits *potentia* (pure potential), as it binds any activity to a preordained trajectory or outcome. By imposing a telos on an activity, the potential for open-ended becoming is constrained, thereby consolidating power into fixed structures and predetermined pathways. In essence, the dynamic potential of *potentia* is curtailed when an activity is locked within the boundaries of a telos that derives its authority from a preexisting *arché*.

How, then, does *arché* dominate? In anticipating telos.

Power resides within all beings, not above them, making politics inherently contingent and thus discarding fixed, imposed necessities. We reject the notion that the world is ruled by necessity, particularly in its foundational philosophical understanding, such as Leibniz's concept of *the best of all possible worlds*, which precludes change (Leibniz 1989). This stance is crucial because Western philosophy has integrated necessity into its core tenets, alongside Aristotle's principle of noncontradiction, thereby shaping logic, ethics, and epistemology, a point underscored by Kant (1992) when saying that in logic not a single step has been taken beyond Aristotle's principle of noncontradiction.

Think of being and becoming, think of democracy as constituent and unfounded power within the pincers of contingency and necessity. Difference, by its nature, is contingent, consequently, any attempt to fix it within the realm of necessity constitutes its fundamental logical negation (as difference is imposed by the internal regime of necessity).

Upon discovering politics as an exercise of predefined and thus necessary models, Rancière brilliantly counters:

> In short, politics is explained as the accomplishment of a way of life that is proper to those who are destined for it. This partition—which is actually the object of politics—is posited as its basis. What is proper to politics is thus lost at the outset if politics is thought of as a specific way of living. Politics cannot be defined on the basis of any pre-existing subject. The political "difference" that makes it possible to think its subject must be sought in the form of its relation. (2001, 25)

Following Rancière, the TEP aims to demonstrate that any claim of absolute necessity is fundamentally false. Such a claim would signify the death of politics itself, a catastrophic suppression of beings' potential to transform, to become something else, the crippling of our political imagination, and the absolute impossibility of social change.

The "encryption of power" is, fundamentally, the institutionalized process of excluding beings through the imposition of stringent qualifications for belonging to transcendent models. Power as domination depends on its capacity to encrypt itself, to obscure its mechanisms and render them invisible, with the constitution serving as the most sophisticated and effective encryption machine, creating a false totality that masks the inherent divisions and exclusions within the political body.

As beautifully put by Jacques Rancière:

> Democracy is not a form of state. It is not a form of social life. It is a form of the constitution of the political subject. It is the institution of politics as such, as the power of those who have no more entitlements to govern than to be governed. (2006, 36)

Glory and Charisma, the Narcissism of the People

Here we will develop a crucial consideration in the relationship between *Arché* and the people as sovereign, particularly in terms of "Glory." In *The Kingdom and the Glory* (2011) Agamben argues that modern power is not solely based on "government" (the administration of things), but also on "Glory" (the ceremonial, liturgical, and acclamatory aspects). "Glory" is the apparatus that generates and sustains consent, legitimizing power through spectacle and acclamation.

Following Matos (2025, 32):

> According to the rigorous philosophical archaeology that Agamben presents in the eighth chapter of *The Kingdom and the Glory*, glory corresponds exactly to the theological-economic-political apparatus that serves, with all its ceremonial and liturgical machinery, to remove power from the Earth and redirect it to Heaven.

The inherent void of *Arché*, the pursuit of an origin that implies something unknown, suggests a transcendent quality—a nonmateriality that generates materiality, the unseen that creates the seen. Consequently, when the fiction of the people ascends to sovereignty, they also incarnate a void, not an anarchic void but a divine one, one that must be cherished and glorified permanently in order to enact itself. A self-reference, a mirror image of nothingness. The liturgy of receiving the body of Christ necessarily becomes cannibalistic, and not in the profound sense of consuming as the assimilation of otherness as in Juan José Saer's powerful novel *The Witness* (1983), but in the sense of destruction of otherness as a way to maintain the libidinal link of oppression intact.

The concept of people as simulated sovereign carries with it an inherent contradiction: it demands both absolute authority and its simultaneous negation (in Adorno's 2004 sense), as sovereignty is grounded in a void that cannot be fully realized. Absolute power and absolute submission are bound to produce a tear at the heart of ideology that will resound in ontology.

This tension between presence and absence is encapsulated in the symbolic force of "Glory." Glory acts as both a veil and a conduit for power, encrypting the emptiness that lies at the foundation of sovereign authority. It constructs a framework in which sovereignty appears self-sufficient, yet it relies on a continuous process of glorification to sustain itself. This dynamic establishes a feedback loop, where sovereignty is not just performed but consumed (the body of Christ), internalized, and perpetuated by the people it governs. But then, with the elevation of the people as sovereign, something unsuspected happens, as the people that carried and executed glorification, must be glorified themselves … by themselves.

Within this framework, "the people" serve as both the object and subject of sovereignty, a paradoxical duality that underscores the instability of the entire construct.

This elevation of the people as sovereign introduces a profound deception, suffocating the potential for a new humanity to emerge, as Nietzsche (1974, S125) envisioned after the "death of God." Here humanity, after the death of God is severed from its origin, resulting in a bizarre constitution of beingness where humanity is simultaneously "nothingness" and "everything." This creates a paradox, a state where there is "nothing else" beyond the sovereign people, even as they are themselves defined by a void they must glorify.

It is the creation of hierarchy through the liturgy of the self, which is the charisma of a nonworld. Whatever is glorified is instantiated as charismatic.[12] As Matos (2025, 45) notes, "In this way, we definitively transition from the Greek epistemic-ontological encryption to the true encryption of power. With the advent of glory, politics (kingdom) is reduced to mere 'economy' (ὀιχονομία), that is, administration (government)." The transcendent models are the architecture, they define shape, functions, and hedges; thus politics is reduced to the management or execution of the said architecture (a mere economy). Nevertheless, going beyond Matos, what becomes clear is that what is glorified and becomes charismatic is the void itself. Not an anarchic void of possibilities and sheer contingency, but the void as the negation, as the impossibility to create anew, the void as the blind command of sovereignty that contains no order in itself beyond adoration. What the people find in glorification is not the voice of God speaking in divine mysteries that must be interpreted by the pontiff. It is not the word of the monarch that is absolute and clear. What they find is their own voice, trampled in the inability to speak, monstrous, shut down in a hysteric form of narcissism.

Consequently, the concept of the sovereign people, elevated to a "divine void," fuels a spectacle of power, a sacrament of violence against others and themselves. This faux deity is built on charismatic power, leading to a fetishization of the abstract self and the creation of the hidden people. Agamben argues that "Glory" legitimizes this power through spectacle, echoing divine presence. This nexus between theology and politics is further reinforced by encryption, the glorification of lack.

In this late colonial theater, the simulated sovereign becomes the ultimate spectacle, a distorted mirror reflecting the people's alienated desires, faults, and guilt. The control of violence, information, and enforced glorification coalesce into a hyperreal simulacrum of power, a spectacle that demands constant affirmation. As Debord (1994, §1) warned, "All that once was directly lived has become mere representation." Lived reality is subsumed by the image, the distorted image that must be endlessly glorified, endlessly kept in suspension, taken as the truth without mediation, the horror of the direct revelation of God's words[13] that would bring forth annihilation.

This double fold, the direct glory of God in the absence of the word made flesh as a revelation, this bind upon itself, can only lead to narcissistic identification and grandiosity, where individuals merge their sense of self with a fabricated image of authority, driven by a narcissistic investment in a false self as a defense against inadequacy (Klein 1975). The mediation will be filled by a strong leader, the king buffoon that in the absence of God and knowing it so, will mimic the glory of the people as farce.

Nevertheless, the opposite cohabits as a sense of utter frustration and impotence. The collapse of the distinction between subject and object produces psychic suffering, loss of agency, objectification, and ultimately the shattering of beingness. Furthermore, the forced glorification of power shows idealization and introjection of the oppressor, leading to psychic dependence (Carmona and Jayantiari 2023). This compulsion can also be interpreted as an expression of a fragmented superego, driven by internalized guilt and shame. The scenario strongly resembles mass psychology and identification with the aggressor, where individuals are forced to identify with their oppressor (McLeod 2025). In this form of psychotic splitting, the "good" is attributed to the sovereign, and the "bad" is projected onto the self, but as both are equal, they cancel each other out as an odd form of interior splitting closer to hysteria than anything else.

A Žižekian (2001) analysis of ideology illuminates the psychic mechanisms at work. This odd form of glorification isn't merely external or procedural; it's a psychic imperative, a "symptom" of the ideological structure. The people, compelled to enjoy their symptom, internalize the power dynamic, becoming both the victim and the enforcer of their own subjugation, caressing true forms of psychosis. This is the Lacanian Real of power: not a tangible force, but a traumatic void around which our desires and fantasies orbit. As Žižek (1989, 45) states, "ideology is not simply a 'false consciousness,' an illusion offered to us by the ruling elite; rather, it is a fundamental level of our social reality itself—a reality that structures our very sense of what is possible and thinkable." This "symptom" reflects the way subjects cope with the Real, finding a perverse satisfaction in the very structure of their oppression (Žižek 2001).

We have before us a monumental short-circuit inside the machine of ideology that bleeds into ontology, the self-glorification of the powerless as all-powerful without mediator, no God, or Nation, simply the people themselves as the anointed. Nevertheless, there is no wholeness, no bearings to hold on to; simply a strange fragmentation of the self that leads to mass psychosis. As the mirror, when looked upon the order and the need of obedience reflects nothingness; but when looked through desire is split into infinite images.

The people, trapped in a narcissistic loop, seek validation through the glorification of this image, mistaking it for their own collective identity, for their own grandeur. This is the *objet petit a*, the cause of desire, that which "is not an object in the ordinary sense, but rather a gap, a lack, around which desire circulates" (Lacan 1977, 103). So, we come to a sort of aberrant redundancy, "the gap is the gap!," the "Big other is me as an aberrant self." The irruption of the Real stumping and fragmenting the Symbolic is at hand.

The "big Other"—the symbolic order embodied by the sovereign—demands this performance, this ritualistic affirmation of its power. Nevertheless, the sovereign presents a double and disconcerting facet; on one side it is them, their own desire that commands the pleasure principle; on the other side, it is total submission to the rule of desire of the sovereign. This duality reflects the inherent instability of the Symbolic order, where the big Other is both omnipotent and fundamentally lacking.

Psychoanalytically, this aberrant and pseudonarcissistic glorification generates profound dissonance. The Real of oppression clashes with the symbolic fiction of popular sovereignty. This dissonance manifests as a psychic "knot," involving conscious belief and unconscious knowledge.

The constant barrage of propaganda, the manipulation of information, the elevation of a chosen people (as the ultimate commodity!), and the threat of violence create a foreclosure of dissent, a psychic defense mechanism that denies the Real of oppression. The spectacle becomes a screen, masking the underlying power dynamics and creating a false sense of unity. In this "society of the spectacle," the people are not merely passive observers but active participants in their own ideological enslavement, compelled to perform their roles in the grand theater of power. This is the ultimate triumph of ideology: to make us love our chains, to glorify the very forces that oppress us.

In this scenario, the glorification of the people transcends mere propaganda; it becomes a hyperreal simulacrum, a copy without an original. The people as a unified sovereign entity cease to exist. Instead, they are replaced by a series of sign-values, a floating signifier manipulated by the spectacle of power. This is Baudrillard's (1988) realm of the third-order simulacra[14]: the people are not a representation of a preexisting reality, but a simulation that generates its own reality. They are a model of sovereignty, a preprogrammed image that auto-dictates their behavior and beliefs, that regurgitates power as a contradictory soup where the order to kill and die are enmeshed.

As Baudrillard (1988, 166) states, "Simulation is no longer that of a territory, a referential being or a substance. It is the generation by models of a real without origin or reality: a hyperreal." Consequently, the people are no longer real in the traditional sense; they are a simulated version of themselves, a "hyperreal" construct.

Within this hyperreal context, the simulation functions as the operative reality. The people's actions, expressions of loyalty, and perceived sovereignty are all real within the context of the simulacrum, even if they lack a basis in any preexisting reality. The enforced glorification is not a deception but an action within the simulated reality. As Baudrillard (1988, 177) notes, "It is no longer a question of imitation, nor duplication, nor even parody. It is a question of substituting the signs of the real for the real."

The lines between representation and reality are utterly blurred (Abensour 2007), trapping the people in a self-referential loop that glorifies their fabricated image. This glorification is not about power being exercised over them, but about the power of the simulacrum itself. The people, no longer subjects of power but their effects, surrender their capacity for critical thought and independent action. Imploded into the simulacrum, they respond to a distorted image—a code that dictates their behavior through preprogrammed responses. Acting not out of genuine autarky but in alignment with the simulacrum, they fulfill their roles in the spectacle of power. In this Baudrillardian landscape, the glorification of the people is not a celebration of their power but a testament to their complete absorption into the simulacrum, their transformation into a sign-value in the spectacle of power.

The inherent frustration of the impossible glorification of the people as sovereign leads to a displacement, manifesting as the rise of strong charismatic leaders. This surge in strong leaders and radical politics stems from a confluence of factors. Leaders project a hyperreal simulacrum of strength, appealing to a constructed people (as synecdoche) whose greatness they vow to restore, whose splitting wound they swear to heal. The fusion (of the leader and people) creates a spectacle of sovereignty, distorting representation and represented, justifying radical action via a perpetual "state of exception." The people's glorification, a performative act, reinforces this spectacle, it reinforces and necessitates sovereignty.

In this hyperreal environment, radical politics thrive on emotional appeals and manufactured enemies, exploiting the anxieties of a populace immersed in the spectacle of power, where the leader becomes the embodiment of a simulated collective will.

As Wendy Brown (2010, 127) observes, "the erosion of democratic subjects fuels ressentiment-driven politics." Applied to this context, it exploits the manufactured "people" (used as a synecdoche) and their fabricated glory—a simulacrum of sovereignty that bypasses democracy. This glory transcends mere propaganda, "creating God and theological-political power out of a void, an 'an-archic Nothingness that must be encrypted at any cost' " (Matos 2025). In this sense, "glory conceals God." Within late modernity, glory becomes intertwined with bureaucracy, with charisma as the core of what is hidden. It manifests as "a self-celebrating spectacle that encrypts the emptiness upon which it rests" (Matos 2025).

This glorification transforms into narcissistic self-acclamation through the construct of "the people." Such projection leads individuals to perceive themselves as embodying the collective will, thereby reinforcing ideological legitimacy. When individuals project their personal desires and fantasies onto this ideological construct, they develop a form of narcissism that fosters exclusionary politics, dismissing dissenting voices.

In this framework, the body of the people are transubstantiated into a Big Mac, a gun, a MAGA hat, or a Smartphone, as Glory, an embodiment of ideology sustained by the spectacle of manufactured glory encrypts the void of sovereignty through the necessary use of sovereignty itself.

Conclusion

Either the world is the result of radical democracy, or it is a violent simulacrum of the world. We have rigorously traced the persistent pattern of a primal fear of radical democracy throughout Western political thought and practice, more than fear it is a necessity for those who rule to install fear over those ruled so as to solidify potestas as the necessary outcome of interaction. This fear manifests as a relentless, refined deployment of oppressive mechanisms designed to subdue the anarchic, contingent, and transformative potential of constituent power. We have demonstrated how the systematic neutralization of democracy leads to its progressive redefinition, ultimately merging it with the concept of sovereignty—a power predicated on oppression. This process involves the imposition of rigid hierarchies, the construction of unquestionable narratives of origin, and the assertion of sovereignty's own unbreakable necessity.

The dialectical struggle between sovereignty and democracy forms the core of our examination. We have unveiled the historical manipulations of sovereignty—its fluctuating rigidity and fluidity—all directed toward the singular aim of suppressing the inherent anarchy, contingency, and potentiality of democracy.

After exploring the protean nature of sovereignty and resistance, passing from the Greek *inception* to the Roman construction of the *Republic* and from there to the nation State as the vehicle for coloniality, we arrive at modern constitutions. The latter expresses the ultimate sophistication of this dynamic, constructing a simulated sovereignty that fuses "the people" with the sovereign, masking inherent divisions and suppressing democracy. This transformation is not simply quantitative or qualitative; it is quantic, it is a game changer.

Confronting the disarray of our present times, that is smack in the middle of 2025, we try to demonstrate how despite the transformations of global power through neo and technofeudalism and the rise of *Empire*, sovereignty persists as the fundamental mechanism of domination, particularly within coloniality. Its core function remains the power to create an "exception," incarnated by the "hidden people," who are essential for defining the dominant "totality." We prove that the symbiosis of sovereignty and the hidden people is not an accidental feature of domination of our times, but, rather well, it is its core and therefore any attempt at liberation must emerge from it.

Hence, while power operates through new networks and technologies, these adaptations do not erase sovereignty's central role in establishing inclusion and exclusion. Ultimately, the ability to define the exception, even in decentralized forms, remains the critical element of power, perpetuating hierarchies and obscuring the underlying mechanisms of control.

Through transcendent models, aberrant forms of charismatic glorification, and the creation of "hidden people," sovereignty sustains its dominance while exploiting vulnerabilities and reinforcing global precarities.

Ultimately, this analysis provides an ontological and historical expansion of Jacques Rancière's solid proof that democracy is characterized by the absence of qualifications for governing. We have shown how the destruction of the particular quality of *arché,* is the very essence of radical democracy, a condition that sovereignty relentlessly seeks to extinguish.

In a deepening of the consequences of the fusion of "the people" as a simulated sovereign we examined what the "glorification" of the people as sovereign—by the people as victims of said sovereignty—would imply for ideology and ontology. This process not only reinforces narcissistic self-glorification but also generates a hyperreal simulacrum.

In all encompassing drives we demonstrate how the fundamental precondition of political existence is absolute contingency, a truth obscured by the pervasive imposition of *Entelecheia*—finality—upon our understanding of power. By reexamining Aristotle's (2015a) concepts of potentia, actuality, *Energeia*, and *Entelecheia*, we reveal how Western political thought has historically prioritized a predetermined teleological view of power, thereby neutralizing the inherent contingency of being. We have shown that *Entelecheia*, with its emphasis on external objectives and transcendent models, has served as a tool for domination, defining inclusion and exclusion based on preestablished criteria, such as "virtue," "nation," or "citizenship." This has led to the construction of hierarchical political structures that suppress the transformative potential of radical democracy. Conversely, by emphasizing *Energeia*—the continuous, immanent process of "being-in-work"—we unlock the possibility of a politics grounded in contingency and immanence. This approach recognizes that political existence is not about achieving a predetermined end but about the ongoing creation and negotiation of differences, where life itself is the sole criterion. Ultimately, this reinterpretation necessitates a radical reversal of our understanding of Western political history. Any form of power that imposes *Entelecheia*—a finality—is a simulacrum of democracy, inclusion, and difference, while any resistance rooted in *Energeia*—the unqualified existence of being—represents the true expression of the political. The modern construction of Western power, embodied in the State, capitalism, and constitutions, is revealed as a sophisticated form of domination, masking its true nature through the illusion of democratic processes.

Notes

1 Ruling powers fundamentally need to instill fear in the masses to secure their dominance (potestas) and neutralize the majority's potential power, making their control seem inevitable.

2 We will analyze this with some degree of depth; nevertheless, we leave it to the Zizekian troop to go deeper in this tunnel.

3 Martin Heidegger's notion of the "Greek inception" highlights the early Greek philosophers—figures like Heraclitus, Parmenides, and Anaximander—as the originators of Western philosophical thought. According to Heidegger, these thinkers possessed a profound and unique grasp of being (Sein), which has since been eclipsed by subsequent philosophical traditions. Heidegger views this era as a pivotal moment when fundamental questions about existence, nature, and reality were intimately tied to the lived experience of being itself. He interprets their understanding of being as dynamic and evolving, not fixed or immutable. In his later writings, Heidegger advocates for a return to this primordial Greek experience of being to transcend the constraints of modern, technological modes of thinking. He argues that reconnecting with the insights of the early Greek philosophers can foster a deeper and more genuine relationship with the world.

4 For a complete study of transcendent models as autopoietic see Sanín-Restrepo and Machado-Araujo (2025).

5 In the sense explained in Sanín-Restrepo (2018).

6 In the midst of the tectonic forces that will shape the future British Empire, a work stemming from the radical forces, James Harrington's *The Commonwealth of Oceana* ([1656] 1977), presents a radical proposition: a republic, unlike an empire or aristocracy, necessitates an egalitarian distribution of land. Harrington, writing in 1656, persuasively argues, drawing from the Western theoretical tradition (Aristotle, Machiavelli), that a true State can only exist when land is divided into equal portions among all men, without exception. This equal distribution of land logically leads to an equal distribution of State power, which is a clever way to state that logically the State is superfluous. As Harrington states in *Oceana*, "Government … is founded upon the distribution of land." Hence, *Oceana* advocates for rotating governments chosen by lottery, a heresy in Hobbes's hegemonical terms. As we saw above, the cure for this radical position came in the form of Locke's enshrining private property as the essence of being that simply neatly ties up Hobbes's sovereign move to drown popular power (Sanín-Restrepo and Machado-Araujo 2022).

7 As the two Davids remind us, modernity only left another possible alternative:

> Rousseau's story about how humankind descended into inequality from an original state of egalitarian innocence seems more optimistic (at least there was somewhere better to fall from), but nowadays it's mostly deployed to convince us that while the system we live under might be unjust, the most we can realistically aim for is a bit of modest tinkering. (2021, 7)

8 Aníbal Quijano's "coloniality of power" reveals how colonial structures persist beyond formal rule, embedding racial and cultural hierarchies into global power. Scholars later synthesized this into "colonial matrix of power," emphasizing the pervasive, interconnected nature of these lingering colonial patterns across economic, cultural, and knowledge domains.

9 For instance, they evoke biopower, and how a mutation of sovereignty demonstrates this adaptation. Foucault's analysis reveals how the confluence of social sciences and population control gave rise to technologies of power that transcend classical sovereignty. Through mechanisms like statistics, medicine, and disciplinary institutions, biopower controls the docile body, extending beyond the reach of State and law. This power, symbolized by the panopticon, targets bodies, behaviors, and knowledge, reinforcing the axiom that bodies constitute the biopolitical fabric of being.

10 Norway's record of universal social security—the envy of the world and proof that socialism works, a dreamed paradise for retirees—depends on the country financing extractive foreign companies through its Government Pension Fund (the Oil Fund). Examples include Norwegian investments in extractive projects that threatened UNESCO World Heritage Sites in 2017 (WWF Sight).

11 "The heavens, which were believed to be incorruptible, know nothing of eternity except the eternal flow of things."

12 "Charisma," originating from the Greek χάρισμα (chárisma), meaning "gift of grace," initially a religious term for divine gifts, evolved notably through Max Weber (1978, 252) to describe a leadership style based on extraordinary personal appeal.

13 "Even if man had remained free from all stain, his condition would have been too lowly for him to reach God without a Mediator" (Calvin 1960, 465).

14 Our use of simulacra and simulacrum within the theory of encryption of power is different from Baudrillard's. See Sanín-Restrepo (2016).

References

Abensour, Miguel. 2007. *Para una Filosofía Política Crítica*. Barcelona: Anthropos Editorial—UAM.

Adorno, Theodor W. 2004. *Negative Dialectics*. London: Routledge.

Agamben, Giorgio. 2005. *State of Exception*. Chicago: University of Chicago Press.

Agamben, Giorgio. 2011a. *The Kingdom and the Glory: For a Theological Genealogy of Economy and Government*. Translated by Lorenzo Chiesa and Matteo Mandarini. Stanford, CA: Stanford University Press.

Agamben, Giorgio. 2011b. "Introductory Note on the Concept of Democracy." In *Democracy in What State?*, edited by Giorgio Agamben, Alain Badiou, Daniel Bensaid, Wendy Brown, Jean-Luc Nancy, Jacques Rancière, Kristin Ross, and Slavoj Žižek, translated by William McCuaig. New York: Columbia University Press, 1–5.

Arendt, Hannah. 2004. *The Origins of Totalitarianism*. New York: Houghton Mifflin Harcourt.

Aristotle. 2015a. *Metaphysics*. Perseus Digital Library. www.perseus.tufts.edu/ hopper/.

Aristotle. 2015b. *Nicomachean Ethics*. Perseus Digital Library. www.perseus. tufts.edu/ hopper/.

Aristotle. 2015c. *Politics*. Perseus Digital Library. www.perseus.tufts.edu/hopper/

Baudrillard, Jean. 1988. "Simulacra and Simulations." In *Selected Writings*, edited by Mark Poster. Stanford, CA: Stanford University Press.

Bodin, Jean. [1596] 1980. *Selected Writings on Philosophy, Religion and Politics*. Queensland: Librairie Droz in association with James Cook University of North Queensland.

Brown, Wendy. 2010. *Walled States, Waning Sovereignty*. New York: Zone Books.

Calvin, John. 1960. *Institutiones II.xii.1; Quoted According to the Institutes of the Christian Religion*, vol. 1. Edited by John T. McNeill. Translated by Ford Lewis Battles. Philadelphia, PA: Westminster Press, 465.

Carmona, Alfonso, and I Gusti Agung Mas Rwa Jayantiari. 2023. "Regulating the Prohibition of Glorification as an Effort Not to Normalize Sexual Harassment." *International Journal of Criminal, Common and Statutory Law* 3(2): 19–22.

Castro-Gómez, Santiago. 2005. *La Hybris del Punto Cero*. Bogotá: Editorial Universidad Javeriana.

Dean, Jodi. 2025. *Capital's Grave: Neofeudalism and the New Class Struggle*. London: Verso Books.

Debord, Guy. 1994. *The Society of the Spectacle*. Translated by Donald Nicholson-Smith. New York: Zone Books.

Deleuze, Gilles, and Felix Guattari. 1983. *A Thousand Plateaus: Capitalism and Schizophrenia*. Minneapolis: University of Minnesota Press.

Derrida, Jacques. 1997. *Of Grammatology*. Translated by Gayatri Chakravorty Spivak. Baltimore, MD: Johns Hopkins University Press.

Fanon, Franz. 1986. *Black Skin, White Masks*. London: Pluto Press.

France, Anatole. 1895. *Le Jardin d'Épicure*. Paris: Calmann Lévy.

Graeber David, and David Wengrow. 2021. *The Dawn of Everything: A New History of Humanity*. New York: Farrar, Straus and Giroux. Kindle edition.

Hardt, Michael, and Antonio Negri. 2005. *Imperio*. Buenos Aires: Editorial Paidós.

Hardt, Michael, and Antonio Negri. 2009. *Commonwealth*. Cambridge, MA: Harvard University Press.
Harrington, James. 1977. *Commonwealth of Oceana*. Cambridge: Cambridge University Press.
Heidegger, Martin. 2000. *Introduction to Metaphysics*. New Haven, CT: Yale Nota Bene.
Heidegger, Martin. 2001. *Being and Time*. Oxford: Blackwell.
Hobbes, Thomas. [1651] 1999. *The Leviathan*. Eugene: University of Oregon Press.
Hobbes, Thomas. [1651] 2000. *De Cive*. London: Blackmask.
Kant, Immanuel. 1992. *Lectures on Logic*. Translated by J. Michael Young. Cambridge: Cambridge University Press.
Klein, Melanie. 1975. *Envy and Gratitude and Other Works: 1946–1963*. London: Vintage.
Klein, Naomi. 2023. *Doppelganger: A Trip into the Mirror World*. New York: Farrar, Straus and Giroux.
Lacan, Jacques.1977. *The Four Fundamental Concepts of Psychoanalysis*. London: Hogarth Press.
Laclau, Ernesto. 2005. *On Populist Reason*. London: Verso.
Leibniz, G. W. 1989. *Philosophical Essays*. Edited by R. Ariew and D. Garber. Indianapolis, IN: Hackett.
Locke, John. [1689] 1980. "Second Treatise." In *John Locke Second Treatise of Government*, edited, with an introduction by C. B. McPherson. Indianapolis, IN: Hackett, 1–141.
Matos, Andityas. 2025. *Decrypting Political Theology: Genealogy, Tendencies, Antagonisms*. London: Bloomsbury Academic.
McLeod, Saul. 2025. "Identification with the Aggressor." *Simply Psychology*, February 26.
Meillassoux, Quentin. 2008. *After Finitude. An Essay on the Necessity of Contingency*. Translated by Ray Brassier. London: Bloomsbury Academic.
Mignolo, Walter. 2003. *The Darker Side of the Renaissance: Literacy, Territoriality, and Colonization*. Ann Arbor: University of Michigan Press.
Mills, Charls. W. 1997. *The Racial Contract*. New York: Cornell University Press.
Ndlovu-Gatsheni, Sabelo J. 2024. *Beyond the Coloniality of Internationalism: Reworlding the World from the Global South*. Dakar: Codesria.
Negri, Antonio. 1999. *Insurgencies*. Minneapolis: University of Minnesota Press.
Nietzsche, Friedrich. 1974. *The Gay Science: With a Prelude in Rhymes and an Appendix of Songs*. Translated by Walter Kaufman. New York: Vintage Books.
Plato. 2000. *Republic*. Translated by Benjamin Jowett. Mineola, NY: Dover.
Quijano, Aníbal. 2000. "Coloniality of Power, Eurocentrism, and Latin America." *Nepantla: Views from South* 1(3): 533–80.
Rancière, Jacques. 2001. *Ten Theses on Politics*. Baltimore, MD: Johns Hopkins University Press.
Rancière, Jacques. 2006. *Hatred of Democracy*. Translated by Steve Corcoran. London: Verso.
Saer, Juan José. 1983. *El Entenado*. Buenos Aires: Seix Barral.
Said, Edward W. 1978. *Orientalism*. New York: Pantheon Books.
Sanín-Restrepo, Ricardo. 2016. *Decolonizing Democracy: Power in a Solid State*. London: Rowman and Littlefield.
Sanín-Restrepo, Ricardo. 2018. "The Meaning of the Encryption of Power as the Razor´s Edge of Politics." In *Decrypting Power*. London: Rowman and Littlefield, ix–xxx.
Sanín-Restrepo, Ricardo, and Marinella Machado-Araujo. 2020. "The Theory of Encryption of Power: Itinerary of an Idea." *Revista da Faculdade Mineira de Direito* 23(45): 1–17.

Sanín-Restrepo, Ricardo, and Marinella Machado-Araujo. 2022. "Keys to Decrypt the Republic Against Democracy." *Law and Critique* 33(1): 41–62. https://doi.org/10.1007/s10978-020-09272-w.
Sanín-Restrepo, Ricardo, and Marinella Machado-Araujo. 2025. "A Prolific Paradox of Justice and Two Theses on the Encryption of the Hidden People." In *Decrypting Justice: From Epistemic Violence to Immanent Democracy*, edited by Ricardo Sanín-Restrepo, Marinella Machado-Araujo, and Sabelo Ndlovu-Gatsheni. Lanham, MD: Lexington Books and Bloomsbury Academic, 15–41.
Sanín-Restrepo, Ricardo, and Gabriel Méndez-Hincapíe. 2018. "The Encrypted Constitution: New Ways of Emancipation from Global Power." In *Decrypting Power*, edited by R. Sanín-Restrepo. London: Rowman & Littlefield, 1–22.
Schmitt, Carl. 2006. *The Nomos of the Earth in the International Law of the Jus Publicum Europaeum*. Translated and annotated by G. L. Ulmen. New York: Telos Press.
Schürmann, Reiner.1987. *Heidegger on Being and Acting: From Principles to Anarchy*. Bloomington: Indiana University Press.
Varoufakis, Yanis. 2023. *Technofeudalism: What Killed Capitalism*. London: Bodley Head.
Weber, Max. 1978. *Economy and Society: An Outline of Interpretive Sociology*. Edited by Guenther Roth and Claus Wittich. Berkeley: University of California Press, 1978.
Žižek, Slavoj. 1989. *The Sublime Object of Ideology*. London: Verso.
Žižek, Slavoj. 2001. *Enjoy Your Symptom! Jacques Lacan in Hollywood and Out*. London: Routledge.

Other Sources

Norges Bank Investment Fund. www.nbim.no/en/about-us/about-the-fund/
WWF Sight. "Norwegian Investments in Extractives Projects Threatening UNESCO World Heritage Sites in 2017." https://wwf-sight.org/norwegian-investments-in-extractives-projects-threatening-unesco-world-heritage-sites-in-2017/.

3

Constituent *An-archy*: Marx, Castoriadis, and Sanín-Restrepo Against the Encryption of Constituent Power as Sovereignty

Andityas Soares de Moura Costa Matos

Introduction

In this essay I pursue a critique of the idea of sovereignty by approaching Carl Schmitt's theory of constituent power in a democratic-radical key. I avail myself of young Marx's 1843 critique of Hegel's theory of the State, along with the notions of novelty and self-institution of society of Cornelius Castoriadis. The guiding thread of this argument is to oppose the idea of sovereignty, understood as a unified and foundational power (*arkhé*), to the possibility of a constituent *an-archy* (as proposed by Reiner Schürmann), that is, a social order without foundation, capable of overcoming the encryption of the people as a false subject of sovereignty, insofar as it is nothing more than its object. This last point has been recently explored by Sanín-Restrepo's theory of encryption of power. Accordingly, as I unfold this reading of Carl Schmitt by way of Marx and Castoriadis, I address the *an-archical* possibilities of the theory of encryption of power.

"[...] *aus einem Nichts geboren*," "born from a Nothing" (Schmitt 2021, 38). Since Carl Schmitt wrote these words more than a hundred years ago to evoke the obvious, namely, that sovereign decision is normatively based on nothing, there has been weeping and gnashing of teeth as they announced, with the apocalyptic and synthetic style peculiar to him, that the world had entered the age of *an-archy*. In effect, the fulfillment of metaphysics in the twentieth century, through a long technical-nihilistic drift, revealed its emptiness, so that every principle—in the sense of both beginning and command—collapsed. However, contrary to what traditionalists and conservatives think, this not only means unbridled relativism, individualist hedonism and the end of emancipatory struggles; it can also open space for an abandonment of the metaphysical apparatuses that shaped the history of the West, thereby urging for the construction of new ways of life no longer centered around the sovereign *arkhé*. I have been developing this idea in my research on *an-archy*, which I intend, in this text, to mix with the theoretical constructions of Sanín-Restrepo (theory of encryption of power), Marx ("disinversion" of the State theory of Hegel) and Castoriadis (auto-constitution of society).

My objective is to think about the constituent character—and not the founding, archaic, principial, metaphysical-transcendent—of *an-archy*. I present this notion in the first section ("*An-archy*"), bringing it closer to the concept of constituent power. From the standpoint of *an-archy*, the idea of sovereignty appears as the encryption of constituent power. In the second section ("Encryption"), I proceed to debunk this problematic construct, considering the conceptual and historical falsifications that the liberal legal doctrine has imposed thereupon. To do so, I rely on the theory of encryption of power developed by Ricardo Sanín-Restrepo. Next, in the third section ("Disinversion"), still concerned with the *pars destruens* of this chapter, I explore some brilliant intuitions of the young Karl Marx in his critique of Hegel's theory of the State, which "disinverts" the relationship between State (*potestas*) and democracy (*potentia*). I finally arrive at the *pars construens* in the fourth section ("Self-Institution"), presenting *an-archy* as social self-institution, wherein I draw from the philosophy of Cornelius Castoriadis. At the conclusion, by extracting the consequences of these theoretical constructions, I explore the meanings of what I dub as *constituent an-archy*.

An-archy

In a dense book titled *Le principe d'anarchie: Heidegger et la question de l'agir*, Reiner Schürmann—an ex-Dominican priest who died of AIDS in 1993, and who befriended Hannah Arendt and Hans Jonas—famously argues that it is impossible to derive a political philosophy from Martin Heidegger's work. In Schürmann's reading, this impossibility pivots on the corresponding unfeasibility of passing from Being into acting. This occurs, however, not because they are two diverse and irreconcilable dimensions, but because, after the anti-metaphysical disinfection that Western thought has been reputedly subjected to by Heidegger, there is no principle that supervenes Being, since acting is always already present in it, considering that Being is, ontologically speaking, that which comes into presence. In this way, Being and acting—life and politics—make up a single dimension lacking foundations, which is why Schürmann could see in Heidegger a thinker of the *an-archy*, that is, of the radical absence of origin or fundamental principle, so that the *There* (the *Da* of *Dasein* of the first Heidegger) of the human is exactly his lack of There, shaping abandonment (the *Gelassenheit* of the last Heidegger) as a structural condition of everything that cannot count on solid ground beneath it. In the world of technique and machination (*Gestell*) in which we live, no act, thought or action can be derived from a first cause, which means that *an-archy* constitutes the ultimate and insurmountable human horizon (Schürmann 1982).

As Roberto Esposito notes, the question that Schürmann asks concerns the possibility of an anarchic politics, that is, a politics that does not accept any of the traditional titles of legitimation that have accompanied the thought and practice of power for centuries, including therein those practices of power pursued under the names of anarchy and democracy. Now what is at stake is not simply a politics as usual, with its taxonomies and more or less reasonable arguments, but the extreme experience of an absence of legitimation, of convincing, and of reason, a true *an-archy*, in the sense I have been giving this word for the past ten years or so (Matos 2015, 2022).

Even though Schürmann does not outline, nor wants to outline, a concept of *an-archic* politics, he points out five characteristics of what he calls "the anarchic," that is, an action without foundation. They are: the abolition of all teleological order; the rejection of the idea of responsibility; the protest against the administered technical world; a certain degree of disinterest in the future of humanity; and the overlap between thought and action. Esposito highlights the evident paradox in Schürmann's construction, since in order to think about the unfounded, these five criteria are necessary, which end up functioning as principles of what is principleless (2020, 65–7). Schürmann is fully aware of the problem, but tends to ignore it, as he maintains that we are in a transition phase between the epoch of metaphysics and the anarchic epoch that will succeed it. Accordingly, it would be inevitable to adopt the language of the former, of a clearly "principial" nature. Thus, Schürmann reduces the paradox to a mere linguistic-epochal question.

But what would happen if we took this paradox seriously and understood that *an-archy*—and not any rationalist anarchist politics, such as those of Proudhon and Bakunin—refers to something that exceeds it? What could be the nonprinciple that poses *an-archy*? What if such principle would be not at the beginning, contrary to popular belief, but at the end? Here the theory of *an-archy* touches on the theory of encryption of constituent power, as discussed in the next section. Indeed, both theoretical positions converge in their treatment of power—particularly sovereign political power—not as a substantial Being, but rather as an apparatus that conceals the absence of an ontological foundation for the separation between subjects and objects of power, thereby encrypting the contingency and potentiality that continuously (de) found the world.

Still on Schürmann's book, Giorgio Agamben argues that its limit is clear, since the author tries to separate, without success, the two meanings of *arkhé* that our culture has always intertwined: origin and command, *principium* and *princeps*. According to the anthropogenetic economy that Agamben masterfully unveiled in *L'Uso dei Corpi*, they are the two poles of the same exclusive-inclusive machine that always has as its secret foundation—its principle, its *arkhé*—the element that is apparently denied. Thus, origin and command make up one of the dyads analyzed by Agamben—such as *zoē* and *bíos*, animal and human, law and anomie, constituted power and constituent power, kingdom and glory, and so on—which cannot simply be reversed or destroyed, but deactivated, that is, stopped from functioning by exposing the constitutively empty—*an-archic*, in the proper sense—core of the anthropological machine that, simultaneously and continuously, merges command and origin, justifying abstract ideas such as those exposed here and others that appear more natural, like the notion that children must obey their parents. Consequently, Agamben concludes that anarchy can never be in a position of principle—as in the paradoxical title of Schürmann's book—but only free itself through contact, "where both *arkhé* as origin and *arkhé* as command are both exposed in their non-relationship and neutralized" (2014, 348–9). Otherwise, the dyad would be reconstituted under new and terrible guises. Indeed, this gives us insight on why one of the four fascist tetrarchs of *Salò* affirms that true anarchy is the anarchy of power.

However, beyond the criticisms of Esposito and Agamben, what seems beyond doubt to me is that the dominance of principles—of all principles, not of one principle in particular—has reached exhaustion. Schürmann claims that all the principles of Western metaphysics have operated under the modalities of *pros hên* ("towards the One," that is, a command) or *aph'hênos* ("from the One," i.e., an origin), which means that they are directed toward the One or arise from of the One, forming, in both cases, the illusion of a univocal origin that is also a command. But, in fact, it is a model aimed at the enslavement of thought, as it is faced with the necessity of converting itself into "truth," and ultimately, of mere quantitative knowledge. This integrative and participatory principial movement, proposed by Plato and Aristotle, reinforced by the medievals and universalized by Cartesianism, can no longer function in contemporary times, the epoch of technique in which thinking became disembodied and deanthropologized, pointing to the need to think a form-of-life that is always de/cons/tituting, a nonprincipial principle, an *an-archic* principle that negates any and all attempts to immobilize immanence. However, to achieve this goal, it is indispensable to free *an-archy* from its captive state, subjected by the machine of sovereignty. This is where the theory of the encryption of power comes into the picture.

Encryption

According to Ricardo Sanín-Restrepo, encryption is "the imposition of institutional simulations of difference which condition, neutralize or prohibit political agency (action), reducing it (the difference) to static and solid models of identity that present themselves as the only form of power" (2018, 2). It is a metaphysical process which replaces immanence with transcendence, multiplicity with the One and power as potency with *potestas* translated into centralized political institutions. In this sense, encryption can be described, in a more clearly political sense, as such: "Encrypting (power) is simulating power (democratic, constituent) and prohibiting or conditioning Being while collapsing political agency (constituent power, resistance) within fixed, final, transcendent and solid structures (constituted power, law)" (Sanín-Restrepo 2018, 2).

First of all, it is necessary to recognize that, in general, encryption is not in itself negative or positive, given that every linguistic process requires, to a certain extent, linguistic dynamics in which encryption and decryption take place on the part of the subjects who participate in it, since they deal with symbols. However, when we are dealing with the *encryption of power* and not just of language, the situation is quite diverse. Indeed, the encryption of power makes it impossible to communicate social meanings that are not present a priori as transcendent models. Instead of language, its transmission, means of distribution, and, consequently, the reality it refers to—considering that every reality can only be linguistically accessed—are masked

(Sanín-Restrepo 2018, xviii). Ultimately, encryption can be framed as a process of "dictionarizing" of politics, as I explained in another text:

> [...] the dictionary is the apparatus that aims to capture in a closed whole the multiplicity of language; transposed to politics, this scheme indicates the attempt to define, once and for all, what politics is and what its procedures are, with the result that everything that is left out comes to be seen as anti-politics or an irresponsible utopia. The lexicographers of politics, committed to closing their field, are those instances that personalize power, which not only exercise it, but impose it upon others as a burden, controlling and determining what choices we can make, all of them fixed and labeled in the dictionary of institutionality. (Matos 2022, 13)

As such, the process of political encryption/dictionarizing serves to negate agency and difference to the Being that, in the last instance, does not *exercise* power, but *is* power itself. In other words, such Being is the highly problematic entity that is routinely called "the people" and that, as we shall see ahead, divides itself into a sovereign people and an encrypted or hidden people. In this regard, I stress that power and Being do not constitute themselves as diverse realities. Rather, they are historically comprehended to be separate precisely due to the process of encryption.

This is an old ontological question. Ignorance regarding this question underpins, for instance, a well-known criticism of Deleuze, according to which his work would not have a specific political valence. On the contrary, for Deleuze the total politicization of life requires the total vital immanentization of politics, given that this does not constitute something that may or may not be added to Being, but rather it is its most intimate and authentic dimension, an always de/cons/tituent process of itself. Thus, politics is understood as an *an-archic* form-of-life and not as some attribute that can subsequently qualify and specify Being. Therefore, for Deleuze—and for Sanín-Restrepo—"Being itself is political" (1990, 119).

In this sense, the task of the theory of encryption of power consists of revealing this political-existential reality, making difference sayable—and therefore experienceable—and creating strategies for decryption, considering the originally Spinozian ontological thesis according to which the Being is power, because Being is potency. In effect,

> one thing is power as *potentia*, which belongs to and is exercised by all beings of difference, with absolutely no distinction and finality. Another thing entirely different is power as *potestas*, as operation of absorbing the multiplicity of potency, their abundance and horizontal modes of production, in uniform structures that solidify it, conditioning and qualifying life as its main source of sustenance. (Sanín-Restrepo 2018, 4)

The contribution I bring to the theory of encryption of power, originally proposed by Sanín-Restrepo, consists in demonstrating that *an-archy*, understood as multiple and differential potency of Being and of acting without foundation, has been triply encrypted. In a first moment, the *an-archic* potency was encrypted under the form of *potestas*, receiving the name of sovereignty, and then, in a second moment of encryption, it began to be read through the unsustainable dualism that opposes constituted power to constituent power, in an operation analogous to the one that separates a sovereign people from a hidden people. Thus, it is a process that disempowers *an-archy* by encrypting it as sovereignty and then practically nullifying it by dividing sovereignty into two dimensions, one constituted and effectively expressed through the institutions of centralized and transcendental politics, and a constituent one, totally emptied and domesticated. One could finally speak of a third moment of encryption, when constituent power, according to liberal constitutionalist doctrine, is divided into original constituent power and derived constituent power, the latter being the only one allowed to "exist," as the former would have ended with the founding act of the constitution of a given State.

However, the people, even if encrypted in the form of "sovereign people," carry within themselves an index of irreducibility regarding constituent power, which can never be regulated and emptied by the determining measures of the State and capital. If it is accepted that it is up to the constituent power to create order, it would be contradictory to claim that this same order can regulate it, presenting itself as a structure immune to the flow and inexhaustibility of the creative power of mutant subjectivities and forms-of-life. This is the reason why the process of establishing democracy is a paradox, which indicates that it can only be *lived*, not theorized and controlled by constituted (encrypted) power. As it separates rulers (sovereign people) and ruled (hidden people), this encryption ends up defining the political in relation to the juridical, the dynamic in relation to the passive, the multiple in relation to the One, always to the detriment of the first element of these dyads. In fact, since its origins, legal-constitutional discourse has attempted to restrict constituent power to the representational space of constituted power, given that "[...] constitutionalism is the protection of an inert temporality, a vassal of history, and the constitutionalist is its inanimate narrator" (Sanín-Restrepo 2012, 18). Without a doubt, liberal constitutionalism is a fundamental element in the process of encrypting the people:

> The most sophisticated encryption machine of coloniality is the constitutional idea. Through it, hierarchies (racial, gender, national) are established, the goods of common use are privatized and democracy is destroyed in the name of itself, whilst capitalism is installed as the only global truth ... Why is the Constitution the perfect machine? Because it binds people and democracy as agency and structure in a formidable and impenetrable clockwork. (Sanín-Restrepo 2020, 7)

As I discussed in another work (Matos 2017), an effectively democratic politics needs to abandon the terrain of liberal constitutionalism, whether it is encrypted based on classical forms (Montesquieu, Sieyès, etc.) or "modern" ones (Habermas, Dworkin, etc.) and deny the traditional legal-dogmatic distinction between original constituent power and derived constituent power, stating that there is only one constituent power, without adjectives and in constant production. Constituent power is not, as constitutionalists teach, a theoretical and distant vanishing point that appears in the political-legal system as a symbol of a supposedly popular origin, which would justify the command derived from it. On the contrary, constituent power reveals itself as a continuous and *an-archic* process, as a constant producer of norms, subjectivities and conflicts that find their always temporary and precarious solutions in the very movement of its affirmation.

Thus, radical democracy—that is, *an-archic*, constituent and nonrepresentative—is the only true democracy as it does not require prior titles for the autonomous and collective exercise of political power (Rancière 2005, 46). Accordingly, we must recognize constituent power as a singular, indivisible and permanent process. In a radical democracy, such power takes the place of sovereignty, typical of the *nomic* and *archic* systems of constituted power, today implemented in capitalist and political-liberal structures considered by constitutionalists as insurmountable. The latter forms a conservative *doxa* that intends to eternalize the present and its institutions, celebrated as alleged insurmountable points of arrival for the political development of human societies (Negri 1996).

According to Antonio Negri, the function of legal-constitutional thought is to tame and control constituent power, using various strategies to do so, ranging from the creation of dualism between original constituent power and derived constituent power to the identification between constituent power and political representation. All of these strategies serve to encrypt constituent power in constituted power. However, these mystifications are not able to mask constitutionalists' true intention, who seek to deny the absolute, indeterminate and potential character of constituent power, seeing it as an always dangerous emblem of the democratic excess that traditional law aims to contain and limit (Negri 1992). According to Negri, constitutionalism is not a democratic doctrine, but rather an ever-renewed attempt to subject multitudinous power to the limits of political liberalism.

In fact, contrary to what constitutional law professors think and teach, liberalism and democracy are not synonymous, but opposite and irreconcilable ideas (Barber 1984). According to Ellen Wood, as the popular masses entered the political scene at the end of the nineteenth century, it was necessary to depotentiate—encrypt—the notion of democracy, transforming it into a kind of worldview that denied its active political role. Rather, democracy was translated in the form of passive enjoyment of constitutional safeguards and rights, thus encrypting the collective contestatory potential of democracy in the form of individual rights and privacy. This is how liberalism came to play a *substitutive* role concerning democracy (Wood 1995, 227). Nonetheless and obviously, liberalism does not acknowledge such substitution, preferring to encrypt the democratic-constituent power under the form of the *republic*, thus making the multiplicity and difference of the hidden people unspeakable and unthinkable, as they are now transformed—linguistically and empirically, as this is how the encryption of power operates—into a dense representative network that has its culmination in North American republicanism, as Sanín-Restrepo and Machado-Araujo (2022) demonstrate.

It is true that several of the liberal principles were transformed throughout the nineteenth and twentieth centuries to guarantee more or less broad scopes of protection for individuals before the State, even evolving certain guarantees of a social nature. Notwithstanding, it is necessary to remember that the central concepts of liberalism—individual liberty and constitutional limits imposed on political power—have premodern origins in the feudal struggle of European property lords in the context of the process of centralization of national States and the consequent strengthening of monarchies (Wood 1995, 229–30). Liberalism is not, therefore, the new name of a deradicalized, reformed and "reasonable" democracy, but the heir of the proprietary *nómos*—in this version, the medieval one—which for at least 2,500 years has determined the hierarchical and unequal modes of human sociability in the Western world.

With this reference to its medieval origin, I do not intend to deny the modern meaning of political liberalism—which, moreover, can only be understood in conjunction with two other modern creations: the national State and capital—but to archaeologically indicate the nondemocratic, counterrevolutionary and aristocratic sources of the ideas of limiting political power. If historically the principle of containment of political power, which later crystallized as liberalism, could function as a decelerator in the centralization of State power, nothing prevented this function from being later directed, already in Modernity, against the democratic-constituent excess of the multitudes who then no longer accepted the tutelage of the "better men."

The clash between liberal and democratic visions is inevitable, given that the constituent power expresses a radical *an-archic* will, opposing representation and the system of checks and balances, both characteristic of liberalism. In this dimension, returning to an idea from Marx, Andreas Kalyvas states that "the constitutional State confronts its objective limit in the constituent power, the totality of people as a conscious and concrete political subject who decides the institution of politics without and independently of the State" (2013, 66). As shocking as it may seem to many, the word "democracy" has a literal and non-negotiable meaning, if one really wants to understand its specificity: it is about the self-organization of the *démos* and nothing more than that. In turn, liberalism is made up of a set of apparatuses whose function is to prevent, moderate or relativize the popular government of the *démos*. Furthermore, there is an ontological distinction that separates these two orders of ideas, since democratic-constituent power turns to the future, never to the past. The opposite is the case with liberal constitutionalism:

> The constitutionalist paradigm is always that of the "mixed constitution," of the mediation of inequality in inequality, therefore a non-democratic paradigm. The paradigm of constituent power, on the contrary, is that of a force that erupts, breaks, interrupts, and undoes all pre-existing balance and all possible continuity. [...] In the concept of constituent power is the idea that the past no longer explains the present, and that only the future can do so. [...] Constitutionalism is a legal doctrine that knows only the past, it is a continuous reference to the time that has passed, to the consolidated powers and their inertia, to the spirit that folds in on itself—while constituent power, on the contrary, is always strong and future time. (Negri 1992, 10)

One of liberalism's strategies to encrypt—that is, limit and disempower—constituent power consists of linking it to the notion of sovereignty, understood as the domain of the One, as thought by Jean Bodin and the conservative tradition following his wake (Hobbes, Schmitt, etc.). This creates a false relationship between constituent power and State sovereignty. However, if we consider the history and the ontological structure of constituent power, we realize that it is connected not to sovereignty, but to democracy. Indeed, democracy is constituent power's radical truth. Constituent power should not be confused with the sovereignty, as endeavored by Bodin, translating the first into the absolute and perpetual power to command entrusted to the ruler, as stated in chapter VIII of the first book of his treatise *Les Six Livres de la République* (1993, 74). Thus, sovereignty evokes the supreme power of *commanding*, while constituent power points to the *collective possibility of building* new political-legal orders, which explicitly hearkens back to the Latin origins of the word "constitute": *co-* (together) *-instituere* (to build, to create, etc.). Insofar as it concerns a continuous and collective process of constitution, the constituent dimension, unlike sovereign power, does not possess an origin, since it does not point to a Being, but rather to a contingent, historical, and potent praxis.

The constituted power of the State is repressive and static, aiming for continuity and permanence; constituent power, on the other hand, is dynamic and productive, pointing to change and renewal. However, to make the revolutionary and contestatory possibilities of constituent power impossible—possibilities that were theorized since the last moments of the Middle Ages by Marsilius of Padua,[1] by the monarchomachs and by English revolutionary authors such as George Lawson and Algernon Sidney—from the end of Modernity onwards, constituent power began to be encrypted and seen as a specific type of sovereignty. If before it was the king who had the power of command at his disposal, now this passes, without fractures, to the side of the people encrypted in the form of "sovereign people," thus embodying the highly mystical and enigmatic idea of "popular sovereignty." In fact, however, popular sovereignty empties constituent power, encrypting democracy and transforming it into a centralized institution of coercive and hierarchical power.

With the victory of Sieyès's centralist ideas in the French Revolution, to the detriment of Condorcet's more democratic ones,[2] constituent power ended up encrypted by the apparatus of political representation, appearing then as a logical paradox and a political risk, whose resolution takes place as a plebiscitary and protopopulist instrument capable of guaranteeing the "recourse to the people" by dictators such as Louis Napoleon (Kalyvas 2013, 61). In this way, constituent power began to be seen as a systemic anomaly and an institutional threat, and should therefore be limited—that is, encrypted—by liberal constitutionalism, as sustained by constitutionalist credo. In this vein, we can name Bruce Ackerman (1998), Andrew Arato (2011, 2007), David Dyzenhaus (2007, 2012), Jürgen Habermas (1992, 1996), Hans Lindahl (2007), and Ulrich Preuss (1995), all of them concerned with negating and limiting constituent power.

There is no doubt that liberal thought wants to domesticate constituent power. Perhaps that is why one of the most radical theories on the subject stems from a self-confessed opponent of political-legal liberalism. In the eighth chapter of his *Verfassungslehre*, dedicated exclusively to the discussion of constituent power, Carl Schmitt (1983) states that constituent power is unconstitutional and permanent, and that it is not possible to limit it through predetermined legal forms and procedures. In effect, limiting constituent power would mean constitutionalizing it. This cannot but lead to an absurdity, since restricting constituent power would require assuming that there are instances of power superior thereto. Such an idea does not make sense in a true democracy, a political formation in which the source of normativity resides in the multitudinous subjects and not in metaphysical dimensions, external to the constitutive and productive agonism of politics. This obvious observation had already been highlighted, with surprising honesty, by James Wilson, one of the "founding fathers" of the United States and one of the six original Supreme Court justices appointed by George Washington:

> There necessarily exists in every government a power from which there is no appeal; and which, for that reason, may be termed supreme, absolute, and uncontrollable. Where does this power reside? [...] Perhaps some politician, who has not considered, with sufficient accuracy, our political systems, would answer, that in our governments, the supreme power was vested in the constitutions. This opinion approaches a step nearer to the truth; but does not reach it. The truth is, that, in our governments, the supreme, absolute, and uncontrollable power *remains* in the people. As our constitutions are superior to our legislatures; so the people are superior to our constitutions. Indeed the superiority, in this last instance, is much greater; for the people possess, over our constitutions, control in *act*, as well as in right. The consequence is, that the people may change the constitutions whenever and however they please. This is a right, of which no positive institution can ever deprive them. (Wilson 1787)

According to Schmitt, constituent power is not only uncontrollable as Wilson explains, but also inexhaustible, as it remains active even after the creation of a given Constitution. This entails the ever-present possibility of questioning the constituted political system. According to Schmitt, the Constitution is not simply a set of norms, but the incarnation of the national will translated into a political decision. For the German jurist, in the case of disregard of this will by the representatives of the people, it is up to the popular political subject to retake its original position, that is, the position of constituent power.

Here it is important to emphasize that I do not uncritically borrow Schmitt's ideas, as they served him in supporting a plebiscitary political-legal proposal of an authoritarian nature. In fact, I accept Andreas Kalyvas's prompting, who states that it is possible to use, in a selective and critical way, some of Schmitt's constructions of constitutional law to think about a "politics of the extraordinary," which can even result in a radical democracy (Kalyvas 2008). Of course, Schmitt would reject such a democracy with disgust. What I take from the German constitutionalist's constructions is his clear understanding of the incommensurability of constituent power, and not the political use of such a conception for conservative purposes. I am aware, however, that my speech risks being the target of misinterpretations, since the simple affirmation of constituent potency does not automatically guarantee any radical-democratic construction, as Schmitt's theory eloquently elicits.

The problem is that constituent power always appears ontologically as potency, not involving any concrete, necessary or determined factual contents. In fact, the mere emergence of constituent power is not equivalent to the emergence of democratic forms of social organization of power, contrary to what Negri believes and preaches throughout his work. As Ernesto Laclau and Chantal Mouffe well noted, the discursive scope of democracy makes it possible to affirm political logics as diverse as those of right-wing populism, totalitarianism and radical democracy, since in this discourse one does not assume beforehand any teleology that might preventively control social articulations (2001, 168).

In this horizon, Claude Lefort describes the great democratic transformation of Western societies as the establishment of a void in the place where solid laws, powers and knowledge previously existed.[3] Since time immemorial, human beings have organized themselves with a view to a theopolitical authority that represented them, a scheme that ceased to exist when democracy emptied the political center of society. From then on, all laws became questionable and precarious, disappearing the notion of a social center, upon which the legitimacy of political representation pivoted. According to Lefort, democracy brought the experience of inapprehensibility and uncontrollability of society, so that the people proclaimed sovereign never integrate or unify themselves, being permanently disputed and latent. Hence the need, constitutionalists might add, to encrypt it. In any case, for the French author, what characterizes the democratic revolution is a double negation: that of a power linked to a body and that of a fixed, transcendent and immutable law (1981, 180–3).

Indeed, democracy is an empty place that involves a paradox: power emanates from the multitude, but it belongs to no one and is not identified with any specific operations of social spheres that, like law, economics and science, have their own rules of functioning. Hence the danger of totalitarianism, this kind of desperate response to the democratic paradox. Faced with the constitutive democratic indetermination of the multitude (the hidden people), totalitarianism intends to fully occupy the void left by the demolition of traditional structures of domination, thus instrumentalizing the concept of a unified people so that it serves as the operator of an integral government in which society and the State are merged. Therefore, totalitarianism can be seen not only as a danger directly derived from democracy, but as a corrupt structure—in the sense that Hardt and Negri give to that word—of political power, which only occurs in previously democratic contexts. Against the collapse of the unified body of the sovereign sponsored by democracy, totalitarianism appears as the opposition to this collapse, as a closed, uniform and angry response, wherethrough the new totalitarian body merges society with the State.

It is worth noting here, however, an idea I develop at greater length in another text (Matos 2025), namely, the absence of guarantees in a radical-democratic theory such as that of *an-archy*. Unlike constitutionalism, the *an-archic* thought cannot begin from any fixed presupposition or value that would "guarantee" democracy (representative democracy, in the case of constitutionalism). Nevertheless, the *an-archic* thought can affirm that, having acknowledged the contingent and potential dimension of reality, the most appropriate political regime is radical democracy, for only it accepts and embraces the flux and indeterminacy of the real, conditions that, as we saw in the very first sentence of this essay, are wholly rejected by thinkers like Schmitt. Although they may be employed to think constituent power and *an-archy*, authors such as Schmitt and Heidegger are not true radical democrats, insofar as they remain tied to an archic universe, at least in their political convictions and praxis. They are merely useful instruments for the theory of *an-archy*, not its masters, and even less its guarantors.

Disinversion

To face the permanent risk of encrypting democracy into totalitarianism, it is necessary to think constituent potency in close relation with the continuous subjectivation of the social subjects of power. This operation is similar to what Walter Benjamin (1991) proposed in the literary milieu: to effect the fusion between narrator and reader in a way that brings out the truth of the text. In an isomorphic perspective, in the field of politics and law, the fusion between ruler and ruled could function as a process of decryption and cast into light constituent power, then understood as an inexhaustible and radically democratic process, something tantamount to revealing the truth of politics as a whole. Instead of being approached as the array of constituted institutions and structures (*la politique*), politics consists of what authors as different as Alain Badiou, Carl Schmitt, Chantal Mouffe, Claude Lefort, Ernesto Laclau, and Jean-Luc Nancy call "the political" (*das Politische, le politique*). In Sanín-Restrepo's words:

> Politics [*la política*] is the institutionalized order where negotiation takes place between those institutionally included, according to precise procedural keys of political language anchored to the rules of law. [...] Politics guarantees the harmony of what is institutionally established and refers to the rules of the game that allow the distribution of benefits, rewards and positions within an already established social agreement; It ranges from written constitutional norms (the formation of deliberative quorums in the legislature) to implicit norms of the balance of power (party quotas within the public administration). According to Politics, what is fundamental is the maintenance of the given order and the controlled defense of speeches that satisfy a standard established by the status quo; It is about regulating the conflict within a zone of legal demarcation that reduces it to institutionally ordered claims. The political [*lo político*] is conflict in its most primal form; It is the excess or residue that institutionally articulated societies cannot contain. [...] The political precedes legal language, since it is in the political where all language is generated. Politics is the adaptation of language to the forms that language itself created. (2012, 36–7)

However, it cannot be forgotten that one of the first and most famous distinctions between "politics" and "the political" is due to Cornelius Castoriadis, who uses the masculine (*le politique*) and feminine (*la politique*) French articles in a way that challenges Sanín-Restrepo's rendition thereof. For Castoriadis (2010)—and also for Jacques Rancière, who follows him in this naming convention—the political constitutes the translation of instituted power, that is, of instituted society, while politics refers to the radical imagination that puts and deposes institutions and laws. As far as I am concerned, in line with Sanín-Restrepo and most of the authors cited in the previous paragraph, I believe it is more appropriate to link the ontological instance to the political and the institutional-procedural instance to politics, as originally proposed by Schmitt, for whom politics refers to a mere technique and the political (*das Politische*) to a specific conflictual existentiality (1991, 2002, 27).[4]

In any case, the distinction goes beyond the simple use of the masculine, feminine or neuter article in French and German. What really matters is the visibility of the perception according to which what is commonly called politics has two complementary and tensioned spheres, which correspond, in short, to constituent power and constituted power. The use of the masculine, feminine or neutral article is up to anyone's choice, as long as the substantial concepts that underlie such vocabulary decision are clear, as they are in both the work of Schmitt and Castoriadis. Finally, Claude Lefort further develops this distinction in a useful way, claiming that the political would be related to the object of political philosophy and politics to the object of political science (1991, 31).

The political, as a permanent and inexhaustible space for the conflicting construction of sociability, corresponds to the truth of politics. Here comes the fundamental difference between truth and knowledge proposed by Alain Badiou. For him, this difference correlates to the distinction between situation and event, and the ones between law and politics, constituted power and constituent power, politics and the political (2014, 47–56). However, it is not a question of assuming an ontological or metaphysical concept of truth, understood as a higher level of cognition of the real that would be opposed to an apparent domain. The truth I refer to with Badiou is presented as *fidelity to oneself* and *novelty*. In fact, it is an untimely surprise, something impossible to be understood by the linguistic networks of existing knowledge, standing beyond both origin and command.

It is not possible to sustain, in a radical democracy, the existence of truths in the sense of knowledge and objective themes that would necessarily integrate the political terrain, as preached by the tradition of Marxism that still insists on its universal subject called "class" and its "scientific" methods of analysis called "materialism" or "dialectics." According to Laclau and Mouffe, democratic discourse is discontinuous because it no longer identifies with the discourse of the universal, constituting itself, on the contrary, in a polyphonic way based on the renunciation of the idea of a privileged epistemic access point from which one might "make the revolution" or "lead the masses" (2001, 191–2). This reading is remarkably close to the idea of truth as novelty proposed by Badiou, since it gives up all essentialism and universalism.

Considering that truth is not defined by knowledge, it can only occur as thought, never as judgment, a form through which it has been insistently presented at least since Plato. Likewise, constituent power can only be experienced in the very act of its production. Both—truth and constituent power—are linked to baseless—that is, *an-archic*—decisions that have no references in the world of constituted power and knowledge. Once this scheme is accepted, several consequences arise in the field of the political. Foremostly, if the political reveals itself as the truth of constituent power, it must be taken as something inexhaustible, always remaining alive in the subjectivities of the multitude that produce the real. The subject of constituent power—always a potency of itself—is never exhausted in the real acts that define a certain institutional political model, unlike what occurs in the process of encrypting the multitude into a sovereign, unified, abstract, rhetorical, depotentiated and, finally, exhausted people. Who develops this idea is not a "postmodern" thinker, but Marx himself.

In the summer of 1843, before surrendering to the economistic dogma according to which the structures of production would condition the superstructural sphere of politics, the young Karl Marx, as he undertook a devastating critique of Hegel's philosophy of law and the State, had already intuited in the unfinished book published posthumously in 1927, *Zur Kritik der Hegelschen Rechtsphilosophie*, the pivotal connection between constituent power and democracy, rejecting with a resolute gesture the bourgeois restrictions imposed by constituted power.

This dense work by Marx, contrary to what one might think, remains absolutely up to date if one stops reading it simply as a libel against the right-wing Hegelians or an attempt to critically reposition the author in relation to the left-wing Hegelians of his time. More than a criticism of Hegel's idealist method of thought, Marx's text constitutes a permanent warning about the intrusion of the transcendent into the domains of immanence, an encrypting operation that can only be carried out successfully when the predicate takes the place of the subject, as fleshed out by Hegel's thinking. In this way, even though the political model directly criticized by Marx—the monarchical-liberal Prussian State—no longer exists, the ideal encryption structures that founded it remain active, and must once again suffer the criticism that, in Marxian style, is not directed at a given empirical phenomenon, but to the mechanisms and apparatuses that allow the functioning thereof.

Marx begins by noting that Hegel inverts the relations between family/civil society and the State, giving logical priority to the latter. Thus, a mere abstract idea begins to determine effective existentiality, configuring a process that repeats itself endlessly throughout Western political philosophy. With this, "[...] the condition becomes the conditioned, the determinant becomes the determined, the producer becomes the product of his product" (Marx 1976, 207). Against this perspective, Marx opposes the fact that the State is produced from the multitude (*die Menge*), that is, from the ways in which it is configured as family and civil society, and not the other way around. Hegel, armed with his typical method of inversion, does not confer to this fact its specific empirical significance, preferring to subordinate it to the abstract idea of State, thus foreseeing the "rationality" that is reflected in the empirical multitude.

The movement of Hegelian thinking—and of conservative thought in general—is always the same: affirming an essentiality or necessity outside of the real that, however, in order to justify itself, ends up making reference to that same real, which appears at the end of the process as its result and not as fact itself (Marx 1976, 207–8). According to Marx, Hegel transforms the idea into a subject and the subject—that is, whoever actually produces and is effective—into a predicate. Nevertheless, this does not prevent development from continuing alongside the predicate (1976, 209), which, after this operation, ends up domesticated and displaced from its ontological centrality. This is the same inversion relationship that exists today between political representation (idea) and people (subject turned predicate), making possible the encryption process described in the previous section.

Furthermore, Hegel mystically transforms real predicates into autonomous subjects, such as "The Idea" or "The State." But, to do so, he needs to renounce the autonomy of the effective subjects—the people, the multitude—who then appear artificially at the end of the process, as if they were its results. In turn, Marx dialectically proposes an inversion of the Hegelian inversion, that is, a disinversion, adding that one must start from the subject and consider its objectifications, which will lead the philosopher to state the obvious: it is the people who make the Constitution, and not the contrary. The results of Hegel's method are catastrophic in terms of political philosophy, since he presupposes sovereignty as an abstract, autonomous and objective idea and then links it to the subjects who produce it, weakening and encrypting them instead of seeing in such forms the effective expression of political power (Marx 1976, 224–5). According to Hegel, power is elsewhere, misty and abstract, only slightly reflected in real subjects and processes, never departing from or depending on them.

Afterwards, Marx deepens the criticism against Hegel by applying his method of disinversion—one of the main strategies for the decryption of power, since the inversion is a form of encryption—to the idea of democracy. To start, Marx notes an insurmountable contradiction in Hegelian thought, which presupposes a double sovereignty: that of the monarch, the most "real," and another, so-called popular, which would have its source in "confused thoughts" wherein the "disorganized representation of the people"[5] lies. Given this structure, Marx draws attention to the fact that the monarch only *represents* the unity of the people, being, therefore, a mere symbol, since sovereignty does not exist thanks to the monarch, but rather the opposite, that is, the monarch only exists through the people. The people is the concrete and the State is the abstract. Hence the truth of sovereignty derives, because, due to an internal necessity of this unifying concept, it cannot be double as Hegel intends (Marx 1976, 290).

After all, does sovereignty reside in the people or in the monarch? At this point Marx presents a bold reading, maintaining that democracy is the truth of monarchy, an idea that will soon be deepened to encompass all types of government. According to Marx, monarchy cannot be justified by itself—it needs a title, Rancière would say—while democracy can. In monarchy, Marx continues, the part determines the character of the whole. In democracy, the entire *démos* is always present, which is why it is the genus—presenting itself as content *and* form—of all other structures of government, mere species and empirical declensions of the original and concrete experience of democracy (1976, 230–1). The memorable words of Marx deserve to be cited *in extenso*:

> In monarchy the whole, the people is subsumed into one of its modes of existence, the political Constitution; in democracy, the *Constitution itself* appears only as *one* determination and, in fact, as self-determination of the people. In monarchy we have the people of the Constitution; in democracy, the Constitution of the people. Democracy is the solved *riddle* of all Constitutions. Here, the Constitution is not only *in itself*, according to the essence, but according to *existence*, according to reality, in its real foundation, *the real man, the real people*, and posited as the latter's *own* work. The Constitution appears as what it is, the free product of man; [...] Hegel starts from the State and makes man the subjectified State; democracy starts from man and makes the State the objectified man. In the same way that religion does not create man, but man creates religion, so it is not the Constitution that creates the people, but the people creates the constitution. [...] Democracy is, therefore, *the essence of all political constitution*, the man socialized as a *particular* constitution; it relates to the other constitutions like the genus with its species, but the genus itself appears, here, as existence and, therefore, as a *particular* species in the face of existences that do not contradict the essence. Democracy relates to all other forms of State as its Old Testament. The man does not exist because of the law, but the law exists because of the man, it is *human existence*, while in other forms of State the man is *legal existence*. This is the fundamental difference of democracy. All other *state forms* are a precise, determined, *particular form* of State. In democracy, the *formal* principle is, at the same time, the *material* principle. That is why it is, firstly, the true unity of the universal and the particular. (1976, 231–2)

For Marx, the power of the Constitution is linked to the power to organize the universal, which even goes beyond the text, translating itself as the legislative power of the people, that is, permanent constituent power: "Legislative power is the power to organize the universal. It is the power of the Constitution. It exceeds the Constitution" (1976, 257). Insisting that it is not the Constitution that creates the people, but the people that create the Constitution, Marx can then shift the focus of the Hegelian analysis previously centered on the State to inquire about the true instance of production of political power. In this way, Marx disinverts the idealistic and reactionary relations typical of Hegel's thought to affirm the free work of the people on itself (self-institution), thus centralizing the thought on the real—and, therefore, on the universal.

Self-Institution

One cannot, however, take the previous Marxian statement in a literal sense, as if the people had an ontological existence prior to the Constitution and therefore, like the creator in relation to the creature, could impose their priorities on the created entity. Following this line of thinking entails falling prey to a type of "archism," that is, in the words of James Martel, "a mode of politics that engages in hierarchy, order and taxonomization and which is, at least in its Western mode, highly concordant with the idea of encryption" (2020, 34). Marx only intends to indicate that it is the living work of the people—the young philosopher had not yet coined the category of the proletariat—that corresponds to the effective instantiation of political power, and the constituent subject is not something prior or external to the act of constituting, as it constitutes itself for itself (Kalyvas 2013, 70), dealing, always on a collective level, with the continuous, problematic and indispensable autonomous institution of society that Cornelius Castoriadis insistently talks about.[6]

This autonomy has nothing to do with the individualist projects of Kant, for example. Democratic autonomy only exists collectively, given that the *nomói* to which it refers only occurs in society. That is why autonomy, self-institution and constituent power form a single reality. Self-institution is radical and non-individualistic autonomy, in the sense that only a human community gives itself its laws, including and especially those that limit it, and this issue cannot in any way be resolved through appeals to political representation (Castoriadis 2005b, 104–6). In the words of the Greek philosopher:

> To participate in power is to participate in *instituting power*. It is to belong in a regime of equality with the others, to a community that explicitly self-institutes itself. Freedom in an autonomous society is expressed through two fundamental laws: no acting without equal participation in decision-making; no law without equal participation in the implementation of the law. An autonomous community has as its motto and self-definition: *we are those whose law is to provide our own laws.* (2005c, 99)

Even though the constituent power is continually productive, there are limits to its potency, according to Castoriadis. However, such limits are only defined by the community itself and not by strange and separate bodies, much less by a deified text called Constitution. No norm or procedure—insofar as both are always expressions of historical conjunctures—can appear in the social scenario as technical means of eliminating the risks of collective *hýbris* inherent to every democratic process (Castoriadis 2005b, 116–17). Only democracy can limit democracy, only democracy can exceed and correct itself.

A beautiful example of the idea that only democracy can control democracy is given by the very same Castoriadis, as he evokes the figure of the *graphé paranómon* ("proceeding against the law"), an institute of Athenian direct democracy through which the citizen who had proposed a law that was later declared unsuitable for the *pólis* would be condemned, and the law annulled. As a result, every law proposal addressed to the Athenian *ekklesía*—and effectively any topic could be the subject of a proposal—had to result from a serious meditation of its proponent, since, due to provocation from another citizen, he could be declared guilty and penalized by a popular jury.[7]

In this way, within the *pólis*, there operated a dynamic in which a law could be proposed by one citizen and later contested by another, with the final decision entrusted to a collective body—generally composed of between 501 and 1,501 citizens—thus eliminating the need for a separate, hierarchical, and elitist authority to control the constitutionality of laws.[8] The current constitutional courts would have seemed to an Athenian citizen something at once absurd, dangerous and ridiculous. Indeed, if laws are made *by* and *for* the people, why entrust to a nonpopular organ the task of judging them? Castoriadis concludes: "Thus, the *démos* appealed to the *démos* against itself. [...] The people dictate the law, the people can make mistakes, the people can correct itself" (2005b, 118–19).

The *graphé paranómon* is part of the general context of Greek direct democracy that, no matter how many defects it may have in contemporary eyes, embodied a type of social organization in which the State was not opposed to the governed, given that the latter, to the extent that they were in fact rulers, became confused with the State itself, making it impossible to highlight different formal political groups in the social body such as "us" and "them," rulers and ruled, judges and those under jurisdiction (Olalla 2015, 20). The unity—problematic and imperfect, certainly, but not encrypted—of the Greek political experience brought with it the impossibility of establishing a separate government, even though such a threat always haunted the *pólis* and was present in the intentions of many aristocrats. For this reason, it was always necessary to affirm, like Thucydides, that the city of Athens was not in its boats, walls or institutions, but in its citizens themselves (*History of the Peloponnesian War*, 7.77), who exercised, in Aristotle's words, *aóristos arkhé*, that is, an indefinite power (*Politics* 1275a, 32).

With the example of the *graphé paranómon*, it is clear that, at the limit, every self-institution of society refers to a self-limitation that needs to permanently deal with the indeterminate, the open and the chaos that substantiate the *an-archic* human existence. In this dimension, indeterminacy can be understood as a result of the assumption not only of a radical and conflictive *public space* potentially open to all proposals for collective life, but mainly of a *public time* through which the political community reflects on its past and its openness toward a future that has always been immeasurable (Castoriadis 2005b, 114).

Marx sees in constituent power a manifestation of the democratic power that exists *before*, *outside*, and *beyond* any Constitution, forming a nonalienated potency made by and for humans. The democratic human being does not exist for the law, he is not an empty shell that only gains existence—spectral, of course—from the encryption promoted by the grammar of abstract bourgeois rights that define him as a "person," as if he were a universal equivalent similar to currency. In radical democracies, this relationship is reversed and the law comes into existence for the humans, assuming *an-archic* characteristics that today can be summarized under the rubric of indetermination, plurality, productivity, and the desire for freedom.

The democratic-constituent subject cannot be eternally encrypted in the networks of language and power established by the constituted power, just as truth is not limited by knowledge. In this way, democratic politics is conceived in terms of the inexhaustibility inherent to constituent democracies, without allowing these to be encrypted, since, by definition, the constituent does not depend on the constituted. When politics begins to define and limit constituent power, we are no longer facing a truly democratic regime, but rather a tyranny, an absolutism or any sort of oligarchy, even if it receives the conventional and pompous name of "representative democracy" or "rule of law" (Sanín-Restrepo 2012, 22).

Maintaining that the characteristic power of *an-archy* is constituent power means that the latter must be approached as something unfinished because it is a collective work in progress that enables the continuous reconstruction of solutions and pacts necessary for social life. If the word "democracy" has any meaning, it must be understood as an effective and liberated self-organization of human groups, determined geographically and historically, and not as a series of procedural and abstract norms bequeathed by tradition. In *an-archic* radical democracies, the avant-garde mythologies of the "people's hero," the reformist ones of the "fight for rights" or those of the "gradual takeover" of the State make no sense. Democracy shall be constantly constituent in act—it is already constituent in potential—as long as it embodies itself in the *an-archy* that self-institutes it. Until this happens, the duty of radical-critical thinking remains to affirm and reaffirm, in a constant manner, not only the misery of this current reality, but the concrete possibility of building many others.[9] The very idea of constituent *an-archy* indicates that its construction is multiple and collective, thus denying the possibility that a single person or a few may claim the right or duty to establish norms for others. Coinstituting is then coestablishing in cooperation.

Conclusion

Doing politics means building worlds and one of the biggest scandals in human history is that we all received *this* world readymade. Even though such prior construction is to some extent inevitable and even useful—just like language and its encrypting dynamics—it cannot determine the unfeasibility of radical transformations in our inherited world. The possibility of broad changes should be a basic assumption of any democratic organization—even "nonradical" ones—as noted by Thomas Jefferson, for whom the earth belongs to the living and not the dead. Considering that the will and power of men—argues Jefferson—extinguish themselves with their deaths, it is not fair to accept that one generation imposes, even though majority rules, a certain constitutional order on the next generation. For him, this would be as intolerable as the intrusion of a foreign nation into the political life of a sovereign people (1904–5, 187).

What Jefferson states through a discourse still embedded in premodernism—he justifies his position by invoking the natural law of life and death—can be read today, in an *an-archic* key, as a (de)foundation for constituent productivity, refusing to assume both the immutability of established institutions and the impossibility of building new mechanisms for organizing and distributing social power. If each generation must be the master of itself, it is up to each one to institute itself indefinitely, assuming tradition as a living and operative memory, never as an impediment or denial of becoming. In this sense, the theory of encryption of power seems extremely useful, insofar as it historicizes, relativizes, criticizes and makes possible the destitution of political mythologemes that guarantee the archic dimension of power, always converting *potentia* into *potestas*.

The philosophical hypothesis developed in this chapter indicates the need to retake an important dimension of being and thought, relating to the absence of a fixed, unitary and transcendent/transcendental foundation, in order to understand constituent power as an *an-archic* creative power and not as a domesticated residue that serves only to create rhetorics that ground the constituted power. It is in this sense, therefore, that I prefer to speak of *constituent an-archy*, a result of the process of decryption of both the people and sovereignty and, even more so, of the constitutionalized and innocuous version of constituent power. Conversely, from the standpoint of *an-archy*, constituent power does not form a system with constituted power, nor divides itself into original and derived.

It is worth adding that the idea of decryption does not seek a more original experience or foundation. In other words, decryption "does not try to filter the true meaning of a proposition controlled by a given context, but to discover how this given context, this 'language game,' was constructed through the primordial exclusion of difference" (Sanín-Restrepo 2018, xx). In this sense, decryption is profoundly *an-archic*, for in its work of stripping away the sclerotic layers of meaning from the ontological onion that is the world, it does not aim to find any hidden central core, but to expose the horror and beauty of nothingness (Schürmann), of the nothing-of-revelation (Scholem) that, paradoxically, continually constitute us as entities of potency. Thus, behind sovereignty and the encrypted constituent/constituted power dyad that grounds it, there is not a kind of a more original power, but only the *an-archic* experience of multiplicity, potency and flow, which opens itself as collective forms-of-life for which being "born from Nothing" is no longer a curse, but a condition for a joyful self-institutive use of themselves.

Notes

1 Based on the work of Alan Gewirth, Kalyvas states that already with Marsilius of Padua, at the end of the Middle Ages, a democratic conception of constituent power emerged, incompatible with the transcendent and unified order that had prevailed until then (see Gewirth 1951, 167–225 and Kalyvas 2013, 43–9). Marsilius would have thought the constituent power as a more genuine alternative to the struggle between Pope John XXII and the holy Roman emperor Louis IV. As the Italian thinker understood, the people were independent of the power that intended to represent it, having an autonomous life in relation to the State form that, in turn, would be dependent on the people. Hence the superiority of the constituent power over the constituted, since the act of creating a community is superior and logically prior to the act of commanding it, just as in Aristotelian philosophy the cause is always superior to the effects it generates. Furthermore, the entire group (the people) is greater in mass, virtue, and wisdom than its isolated part (the ruler) (see Marsilius of Padua 1956, 46–55).

2 On February 15, 1793, Condorcet presented his draft Constitution to the French National Assembly. According to him it was necessary for the people to ratify the constitutional text and any subsequent reform. Condorcet saw an obvious

difference between the drafting and the approval of the Constitution, the first task being the responsibility of the Assembly and the second of the French people (see Condorcet 1804).

3 It would be interesting to oppose Lefort's thesis about democracy as an empty space—which, in fact, is accepted by many constitutionalists—against Agamben's reading about both the state of exception and the apparatus of glory. In the first case, Agamben argues that the empty space, which he calls "kleromatic," is characteristic of the state of exception, and not of the rule of law (Agamben 2003). In the second case, the empty space arises from a process of glorification. Glory is precisely the apparatus through which the people are separated from what belongs to them (power) (Agamben 2007). However, the discussion of these ideas would go far beyond the limits of this text, and is only suggested here for future development.

4 Michel Foucault, without mentioning Lefort's name, appears to criticize him in the course "The Government of Self and Others," by saying that he does not agree with the division between politics and the political:

> [...] the problems of *dunasteia*, of power, are political problems in the strict sense, and nothing seems more dangerous to me than that much vaunted shift from politics (*la politique*) to the political (*le politique*), which in many contemporary analyses seems to me to have the effect of masking the specific problem and set of problems of politics, of *dunasteia*, of the practice of the political game, and of the political game as a field of experience with its rules and normativity, of the political game as experience inasmuch as it is indexed to truthtelling and involves a certain relationship to oneself and to others for its players. (Foucault 2011, 159)

5 Original citation of Hegel as used by Marx:

> Aber Volkssouveränität, als im Gegensatze gegen die im Monarchen existierende Souveränität genommen, ist der gewöhnliche Sinn, in welchem man in neueren Zeiten von Volkssouveränität zu sprechen angefangen hat—in diesem Gegensatze gehört die Volkssouveränität zu den verworrenen Gedanken, denen die wüste Vorstellung des Volkes zugrunde liegt. (Marx 1976, 229)

6 In Castoriadis's vast work, one can profitably read his definitions of radical imagination, instituted society, and instituting society in two central texts: Castoriadis (1987, 2007).

7 It should be added that alongside the *graphé paranómon*—which provided for relatively mild penalties, such as fines and the deprivation of political rights in the case of repeat offenses—there was a much more fearsome figure, the *graphé nómon mé epitédeion theínai* ("proceeding against law not beneficial to the community"), which reserved the death penalty for those who deliberately legislated against the common interests of society. See Olalla (2015, 55).

8 In this sense, in an article specifically dedicated to discussing whether the ancient Athenian *graphé paranómon* can be seen as an antecedent of current judicial procedures for constitutionality control, Melissa Schwartzberg states: "Far from providing the expert guidance and constitutional stability ostensibly offered by contemporary judicial review, the *graphe paranomon* was democratic decision-making at its most sophisticated and robust" (2013, 1062).

9 From this perspective, Castoriadis's words are melancholically inspiring:

> What it is about, then, is something different from calmly managing the existing consensus, from increasing the "spaces of freedom" by millimeters or from demanding "more and more rights." How to do it is another question. A great collective political movement cannot be born from the will of a few. But while this collective hypnosis lasts, there will be, for those of us who have the privilege of being able to speak, a provisional ethics and politics: unmasking, criticizing, denouncing the existing state of affairs. And for everyone: behave and act exemplarily wherever you are. We are responsible for what depends on us. (2005a, 142)

References

Ackerman, Bruce. 1998. *We the People: Transformations*. Cambridge: Harvard University Press.

Agamben, Giorgio. 2003. *Stato di Eccezione*. Torino: Bollati Boringhieri.

Agamben, Giorgio. 2007. *Il Regno e la Gloria: Per Una Genealogia Teologica dell'Economia e del Governo*. Vicenza: Neri Pozza.

Agamben, Giorgio. 2014. *L'Uso dei Corpi*. Vicenza: Neri Pozza.

Arato, Andrew. 2007. "Redeeming the Still Redeemable: Post Sovereign Constitution Making." *International Journal of Culture, Politics, and Society* 22(4): 427–43.

Arato, Andrew. 2011. "Multi-Track Constitutionalism Beyond Carl Schmitt." *Constellations* 18(3): 324–51.

Badiou, Alain. 2014. *Infinite Thought: Truth and the Return of Philosophy*. London: Bloomsbury.

Barber, Benjamin. 1984. *Strong Democracy: Participatory Politics for a New Age*. Berkeley: University of California Press.

Benjamin, Walter. 1991. "Der Erzähler: Betrachtungen zum Werk Nikolai Lesskows." In *Gesammelte Schriften*, Band II, edited by Rolf Tiedemann and Hermann Schweppenhäuser. Frankfurt am Main: Suhrkamp, 438–65.

Bodin, Jean. 1993. *Les Six Livres de la République: Un Abrégé du Texte de l'Édition de Paris de 1583*. Edited by Gérard Mairet. Paris: Librairie Générale Française.

Castoriadis, Cornelius. 1987. *The Imaginary Institution of Society*. Translated by Kathleen Blamey. Cambridge, MA: Polity.

Castoriadis, Cornelius. 2005a. "¿Qué democracia?" In *Escritos Políticos*, edited by Xavier Pedrol, translated by Vicente Gómez. Madrid: Catarata, 129–42.

Castoriadis, Cornelius. 2005b. "La Pólis Griega y la Creación de la Democracia." In *Escritos Políticos*, edited by Xavier Pedrol, translated by Xavier Pedrol. Madrid: Catarata, 103–27.

Castoriadis, Cornelius. 2005c. "Socialismo y Sociedad Autónoma." In *Escritos Políticos*, edited by Xavier Pedrol, translated by Xavier Pedrol. Madrid: Catarata, 89–101.

Castoriadis, Cornelius. 2007. "Radical Imagination and the Social Instituting Imaginary." In *The Castoriadis Reader*, edited by David Ames Curtis. Oxford: Blackwell, 319–37.

Castoriadis, Cornelius. 2010. "Politique et la Politique." In *Démocratie et Relativisme: Débat Avec le MAUSS*. Paris: Mille et Une Nuits, 46–53.

Condorcet, Marquis de [Marie Jean Antoine Nicolas de Caritat]. 1804. "Sur la Nécessité de Faire Ratifier la Constitution par les Citoyens, et sur la Formation des Communautés

de Campagne." *Œuvres Complètes* XV. https://fr.wikisource.org/wiki/Sur_la_n%C3%A9cessit%C3%A9_de_faire_ratifier_la_constitution_par_les_citoyens,_et_sur_la_formation_des_communaut%C3%A9s_de_campagne.
Deleuze, Gilles. 1990. *Pourparlers (1972–1990)*. Paris: Minuit.
Dyzenhaus, David. 2007. "The Politics of the Question of the Constituent Power." In *The Paradox of Constituent Power and Constitutionalism: Constituent Power and Constitutional Form*, edited by Martin Loughlin and Neil Walker. Oxford: Oxford University Press, 129–47.
Dyzenhaus, David. 2012. "Constitutionalism in an Old Key: Legality and Constituent Power." *Global Constitutionalism* 1(2): 229–60.
Esposito, Roberto. 2020. *Pensiero Istituente: Tre Paradigmi di Ontologia Politica*. Torino: Einaudi.
Foucault, Michel. 2011. *The Government of Self and Others: Lectures at the Collège de France, 1982–1983*. Edited by François Ewald and Alessandro Fontana. Translated by Graham Burchell. New York: Palgrave Macmillan.
Gewirth, Alan. 1951. *Marsilius of Padua: The Defender of Peace*. New York: Columbia University Press.
Habermas, Jürgen. 1992. *Faktizität und Geltung: Beiträge zur Diskurstheorie des Rechts und des Demokratischen Rechtsstaats*. Frankfurt am Main: Suhrkamp.
Habermas, Jürgen. 1996. *Die Einbeziehung des Anderen: Studien zur Politischen Theorie*. Frankfurt am Main: Suhrkamp.
Jefferson, Thomas. 1904–5. *The Works of Thomas Jefferson. Vol. XI: Correspondence and Papers (1808–1816)*. Edited by Paul Leicester Ford. New York: G. P. Putnam's Sons. http://files.libertyfund.org/files/807/Jefferson_0054-11_EBk_v6.0.pdf.
Kalyvas, Andreas. 2008. *Democracy and the Politics of the Extraordinary: Max Weber, Carl Schmitt, and Hannah Arendt*. Cambridge: Cambridge University Press.
Kalyvas, Andreas. 2013. " 'Democracia Constituinte.' Translated by Florência Mendes Ferreira da Costa." *Lua Nova: Revista de Cultura e Política* 89: 37–84.
Laclau, Ernesto, and Chantal Mouffe. 2001. *Hegemony and Socialist Strategy: Towards a Radical Democratic Politics*. Second ed. London: Verso.
Lefort, Claude. 1981. *L'Invention Démocratique: Les Limites de la Domination Totalitaire*. Paris: Le Livre de Poche.
Lefort, Claude. 1991. *Pensando o Político: Ensaios Sobre Democracia, Revolução e Liberdade*. Translated by Eliana de Melo Souza. Rio de Janeiro: Paz e Terra.
Lindahl, Hans. 2007. "Constituent Power and Reflexive Identity: Towards an Ontology of Collective Selfhood." In *The Paradox of Constituent Power and Constitutionalism: Constituent Power and Constitutional Form*, edited by Martin Loughlin and Neil Walker. Oxford: Oxford University Press, 9–24.
Marsilius of Padua. 1956. *Defensor Pacis*. Translated and edited by Alan Gewirth. Toronto: University of Toronto Press.
Martel, James. 2020. "The One Who Made the Lock Also Made the Key: Thomas Hobbes on Encryption and Decryption in the Face of Sovereign Power and Authority." *Revista da Faculdade Mineira de Direito* 23(45): 34–48.
Marx, Karl. 1976. "Zur Kritik der Hegelschen Rechtsphilosophie." In *Werke*, Band 1. Berlin: Dietz, 203–333.
Matos, Andityas Soares de Moura Costa. 2015. *Filosofia Radical e Utopias da Inapropriabilidade: Uma Aposta* An-árquica *na Multidão*. Belo Horizonte: Fino Traço.

Matos, Andityas Soares de Moura Costa. 2017. "Desinstituição e Desobediência Civil: Entre o Estado de Exceção e a Democracia Radical." *Revista Filosófica de Coimbra* 26(51): 9–50.
Matos, Andityas Soares de Moura Costa. 2022. *A An-arquia que Vem: Fragmentos de um Dicionário de Política Radical.* São Paulo: sobinfluencia.
Matos, Andityas. 2025. *Decrypting Political Theology: Genealogy, Tendencies, Antagonisms.* London: Bloomsbury.
Negri, Antonio. 1992. *Il Potere Costituente: Saggio Sulle Alternative del Moderno.* Carnago: SugarCo.
Negri, Antonio. 1996. "O Pensamento que Resiste à Ordem." Interview granted to Folha de São Paulo. www1.folha.uol.com.br/fsp/1996/3/24/mais!/37.html.
Olalla, Pedro. 2015. *Grecia en el Aire: Herencias y Desafíos de la Democracia Ateniense Vistos desde la Atenas Actual.* Barcelona: Acantilado.
Preuss, Ulrich Klaus. 1995. *Constitutional Revolution: The Link Between Constitutionalism and Progress.* Translated by Deborah Lucas Schneider. Atlantic Highlands, NJ: Humanities Press.
Rancière, Jacques. 2005. *La Haine de la Démocratie.* Paris: La Fabrique.
Sanín-Restrepo, Ricardo. 2012. "Cinco Tesis Desde el Pueblo Oculto." *Oxímora: Revista Internacional de Ética y Política* 1: 10–39.
Sanín-Restrepo, Ricardo. 2018. "The Meaning of the Encryption of Power as the Razor's Edge of Politics." In *Decrypting Power.* London: Rowman and Littlefield, ix–xxx.
Sanín-Restrepo, Ricardo, and Marinella Machado-Araujo. 2022. "Keys to Decrypt the Republic Against Democracy." *Law and Critique* 33: 41–62.
Schmitt, Carl. 1983. *Verfassungslehre.* Berlin: Duncker & Humblot.
Schmitt, Carl. 1991. *Der Begriff des Politischen: Text von 1932 mit Einem Vorwort und Drei Corollarien.* Berlin: Duncker & Humblot.
Schmitt, Carl. 2002. *Römischer Katholizismus und Politische Form.* Stuttgart: Klett-Cotta.
Schmitt, Carl. 2021. *Politische Theologie: Vier Kapitel zur Lehre von der Souveränität.* Berlin: Duncker & Humblot.
Schürmann, Reiner. 1982. *Le Principe d'Anarchie: Heidegger et la Question de l'Agir.* Paris: Seuil.
Schwartzberg, Melissa. 2013. "Was the *Graphe Paranomon* a Form of Judicial Review?" *Cardozo Law Review* 34: 1049–62. www.cardozolawreview.com/content/34-3/SCHWARTZBERG.34.3.pdf.
Wilson, James. "Speech to the Pennsylvania Convention, November 24, 1787." https://teachingamericanhistory.org/document/speech-to-the-pennsylvania-convention/.
Wood, Ellen Meiksins. 1995. *Democracy Against Capitalism: Renewing Historical Materialism.* Cambridge: Cambridge University Press.

4

Sovereignty, Anarchy, and Encryption of Power

Simón Royo-Hernández

Presently, anarchic ontology is emerging as a significant current of thought, with a community of philosophers collectively contributing to its development. This concept originates from Reiner Schürmann's interpretation of Heidegger's philosophy. Schürmann posits that Western thought has historically been built upon principles of domination, foundational authority, command, and hierarchy—referred to as *arché*. He suggests that, instead, philosophical inquiry should be rooted in its opposite: *an-arché*, which denotes the unfounded, nonhierarchical, and free of government.

Ontological anarchism aims to develop a philosophical framework that aligns with contemporary political anarchism. This framework is grounded in the principles of prominent nineteenth-century anarchists, whose ideas have been revitalized to address modern issues. Among such anarchist authors we share and are in tune with Reiner Schürmann, Andityas Matos, Ricardo-Sanín-Restrepo, Catherine Malabou, Tomás Ibañez, Jordi Carmona, Valerio Di Angelo, and other thinkers, in opposing the foundational thought that, starting from principles, has justified both the rule of the few over the many and of hierarchy in a vertical and pyramidal structure that is deemed as simply the true nature of things:

> Politics, as the primal opening of being and the point of definition of language and its meanings (where power above all is a relation) has been captured in stringent models of unity and permanent qualifications of life where hidden logos (an unseen telos as arché) dictates and justifies any and every kind of hierarchy as natural. (Sanín-Restrepo 2018, xiii)

Our common sense, language and concepts, are encrypted by power, muzzled by millennia of traditional hierarchical thinking, codified in such a way that servitude is experienced as freedom.

For at least two and a half millennia, metaphysical thought, organizing through hierarchies, fulfilled its function of pyramidal ordering. As a result, the notion of equality among beings often clashes with this ancient imposition. Therefore, we must be cautious not to create new forms of oppression under the guise of freedom. Avoiding efforts by those who consider themselves superior to impose happiness on others despite their natural stupidity, as this leads to dictatorship and top-down revolutions. If a free and equal community is achieved, it must remain vigilant against the emergence of new hierarchical and separate powers.

Against the sovereignty understood as "everyone being a king," which is typical of neoliberalism, anarchism understands sovereignty as "no one can be a king," no one governing, not even oneself. In this view, a confederation of selves with their differences—this plurality that we mistakenly call individuals—must regulate themselves democratically, preventing any-one-self from achieving hegemony and becoming a tyrant or dictator

The theory of the encryption of power is defined as "the imposition of institutional simulations that condition, neutralize or prohibit political agency (action), reducing it to static and solid models of identity that are presented as the only form of power" (Sanín-Restrepo and Machado-Araujo 2020, 2).

By establishing a simulacrum of democracy through liberal individual representative democracy, the true hierarchical nature of power—its *arché*, principle, command, and hierarchy—has been encrypted. This power remains in force, hidden beneath a rhetoric of equality that is never truly realized.

From an *an-arché* perspective—without principle, command, or hierarchy—this process of encryption can be revealed, which would suffice to break its spell and dissolve its government. As Etienne de La Boétie said:

> If the country refuses consent to its own enslavement: it is not necessary to deprive him (the tyrant) of anything, but simply to give him nothing; there is no need that the country make an effort to do anything for itself provided it does nothing against itself. ([1548] 1975, 44)

We conceive of sovereign power, the principle, and the foundation that governs and administers terrestrial life, as a false construction of existence and its possibilities. It is easy to reject when this power is presented as dictatorial and fascist. However, when it is presented as constitutional, democratic, and republican, it becomes more difficult to resist. By masking the former as the latter, the fraud operates in such a way that people lend their support to what oppresses them, instead of resisting and refusing the domination that is falsely presented as liberation.

The potentialities of existence of beings are absorbed by the powers and structures of constituted power that dominate the world through their hierarchical arrangements. To counter this, we must begin with an anarchic ontology where all beings are considered equal in value, despite their notable differences in modes of existence. This approach aims to dismantle existing power structures and foster communities where the potentialities of beings can truly unfold without being repressed, subjugated, or dominated. "Hence, any being (a neutrino, a baby, a star, a cell) exercises power as it exists" (Sanín-Restrepo and Machado-Araujo 2020, 4).

As I have expressed it:

> Anarchism is the political movement that has most ardently emphasized that the egalitarian and libertarian community it calls the "commune" provides the

> best conditions for human beings and other beings to realize their full potential with minimal obstacles and impediments. In such a community, mutual aid and cooperation prevail over predation and hierarchization. The process of unfolding possibilities stands in stark contrast to the obedience demanded by hierarchical ontologies. (Royo-Hernández 2024)

We adhere to an *an-archic* thought to advocate for an-archy, which challenges the transcendent metaphysical thinking that has imposed an essentially hierarchical way of knowing and exercising power, dictating a struggle for survival in a world of scarce resources

As Brazilian philosopher Andityas Matos has sharply argued, from an anarchy perspective: "It is necessary to think about life—and consequently death—from a different point of view ... To the conception of life as a scarce commodity for which human beings fight to the death, one can oppose the image of an infinite reserve of life that denies competition and favors hybridization, cooperation, and miscegenation." This way of thinking and practice is encapsulated in the concept of "biopotency" (Matos 2023, 41).

Biopotency overflows the encryption of power, since the totalitarian power that seeks the total administration of existence, hidden under the mask of a false democracy and freedom, will always be incapable of absorbing all existence. Biopolitical power, despite its vastness, remains finite and can never subsume the infinite reserve of life that we term biopotency.

> The people, even when encrypted as the "sovereign people," inherently possess an element of irreducibility with respect to constituent power. This element can never be fully regulated or nullified by the decisive measures of the State and capital. (Matos 2024, 200)

Andityas Matos's concept of biopotency shows us the hidden people Sanín-Restrepo speaks of—those excluded from the simulacrum of totality presented as human rights and national constitutions that supposedly include them. By flattening out differences, these rights become those of the abstract man, aligning with the transcendent model of the European, white, Western individual, typical of globalized capitalism and colonialism.

> We stand before the constitutive paradox of the legitimacy of liberal constitutionalism. On the one hand, we discover the rigid zone of codified law, of codified reality, that manifests itself in archetypal concepts such as the totality of the people as constituent power (We the People), or the totality of the human rights model (everyone) that announces an abrasive universality that holds together the fruit of reality. On the other hand, we have the excess that is compulsory in order to make such totality work as such, the all but one, the all minus one, as the exact mathematical formula of liberalism, the totality minus what it needs to exclude to keep itself immaculate. (Sanín-Restrepo 2016, 35)

To promote radical democracy, we must deactivate the Hobbesian presumption that "man is a wolf to man," which aligns with the notion of scarce resources. Critics argue against radical democracy and the establishment of libertarian communes by claiming that human violence and asocial psychopaths necessitate a repressive and hierarchical system to keep them in check. Curiously, this thanatological argument, while rejecting the Rousseauian counterpoint of the human being's benevolent nature, has generated the greatest violence through its monopoly by legislative, military, and State bodies.

To the vertical and hierarchical biopolitical violence of the market and the State aimed at guaranteeing the property of a few to allow the survival of the majority, equipollent violence is contrasted as a possible conflict between equals and in common that is managed horizontally in a fair way, in the midst of a horizontal coexistence of cooperation and search for harmony.

In the globalized biopolitical order, anarchists are labeled as antisocial or criminal, whereas the anarchanthrope views selfish neoliberals and their gospel of competition as the real antisocial criminals. Thus, we encounter two diametrically opposed positions. This is not because anarchists are naive Rousseauians blind to the existence of violence—a term that is somewhat ambiguous, as even the closing of a door requires some degree of force and energy. Rather, it is because the violence against the community that a member may exercise can be addressed in two distinct ways: either through hierarchical repression and vertical control by power holders over slaves, or as a conflict among equals to be resolved by free individuals—two fundamentally different approaches.

> When we acknowledge that the true people of democracy are the hidden people, that their economy is to support the entire structure of modern law through their exceptionality, and that the distinctive feature of the constituent power lies in its potency to act or refrain from acting irrespective of the constituted act, and we directly oppose these axioms by juxtaposing them with the classical definition of democracy, we create a union of meanings so solid that they expose modern liberalism's artifice, revealing how its concealment of the people in democracy is both helpless and incapable of reconstituting itself as a political unit. (Sanín-Restrepo 2012, 34)

Biopotency defeats encryption by unveiling it, showing that the anarchanthropes—those who think and act an-archically, spring from the hidden people. Dissidents and the excluded are the people of the democracy to come, a radical democracy hidden by the encryption of power that simulates exploitation as freedom:

> The anarchanthrope's attitude involves participating in a revolution without a revolutionary subject and fostering a community of interconnected differences. Its antithesis would be the randroide,[1] an anarcho-capitalist or libertarian, that cynical psychonarcissist aligned perfectly with globalized capitalism. The more it merges with the individualistic mass of those addicted to self-interest and the private sphere, the more identical they become to their consumerist lot, despite believing themselves to be freer and more unique. We must now become cognizant of the

> declassed, the excluded, foreigners, and refugees to engage in the radical action our time demands. This is the historical situation we find ourselves in, requiring us to reject collaboration with the system and consistently demonstrate our profound disagreement with the established order. (Royo-Hernández 2019, 130)

The history of Modernity and the Enlightenment is the history of a deception, of the process of consummation of the encryption of power that has allowed the simulacrum of globalized democracy, the history of a triumphant capitalism that, as it increases its domination over the world, feels comfortable enough of to take some masks off, such as that of the rule of law so it can return to govern despotically. A New Enlightenment would then be nothing more than the new face of a renewed deception, another simulacrum of democracy to govern the masses by making them believe that in their servitude lies their freedom.

The enlightened are cynical elitists who know that their good life cannot be generalized and yet they maintain for the masses the illusion of universality and progress, of the advancement of reason and the welfare State, a position that they hold, ambiguously, both enthusiastically and discreetly.

> At two thousand marks net a month, counterenlightenment quietly begins; it banks on the fact that all those who have something to lose come to terms privately with their unhappy consciousness or cover it over with "*engagements*." (Sloterdijk 1987, 7)

From the moment that one begins to earn around 4,000 euros a month, and all the rulers earn more than that, the enlightened man begins to cynically maintain his principles of emancipation of humanity, just as the hypocritical priest disenchanted with the discovery of the death of God, did before him, with the principles of religion.

That is something that the enlightened occasionally show, because, although their discretion leads them to hide such an open secret, they cannot at all times contain outbursts of sincerity:

> Hegemonic powers, once they have been induced to start talking, cannot stop themselves from letting out all their trade secrets. Once discretion is assured, they can be marvelously honest … For that reason, the awakened knowledge that rulers have places discreet limits on itself. This knowledge foresees social chaos if ideologies, religious fears, and conformities were to disappear overnight from the minds of the multitude. Itself without any illusions, it realizes the functional necessity of illusions for the social status quo. This is the way enlightenment works in the minds of those who have recognized the origin of power. Its caution and its discretion are completely realistic. There is in enlightenment a breathtaking soberness in which it understands that the "golden fruits of sensual pleasure" thrive only in the status quo that puts the chances for individuality, sexuality, and luxury in the laps of the few. It was in part to such secrets of a weary power that Talleyrand referred when he commented that only those who lived before the revolution really got to taste the sweetness of life. (Sloterdijk 1987, 32)

The French Revolution brought the bourgeoisie to power, yet they never ceased to covet the aristocratic power they had overthrown but couldn't acknowledge they were occupying. Secretly, they worked incessantly to create a facade—a "molasses of gerontoplasm"—to appear as the champions of Reason and Freedom, the standard bearers of Light against Darkness, all while climbing to the pinnacle of that pyramidal government enabled by money and power

In *Simulacra and Simulation*, a 1981 work, Jean Baudrillard says that in simulation

> it is no longer a question of imitation, nor duplication, nor even parody. It is a question of substituting the signs of the real for the real, that is to say of an operation of deterring every real process via its operational double, ... that offers all the signs of the real ... To dissimulate is to pretend not to have what one has. To simulate is to feign to have what one doesn't have. One implies a presence, the other an absence. But it is more complicated than that because simulating is not pretending: "Whoever fakes an illness can simply stay in bed and make everyone believe he is ill. Whoever simulates an illness produces in himself some of the symptoms" (Littré). Therefore, pretending, or dissimulating, leaves the principle of reality intact: the difference is always clear, it is simply masked, whereas simulation threatens the difference between the "true" and the "false," the "real" and the "imaginary." (1981, 2–3)

The encryption of power oscillates between pretense and simulation, between masking and *fake news*, progressively moving from the former to the latter. Those in power are not merely hypocrites and cynics; they don't just pretend we're in a consolidated democracy—even if they don't believe it themselves. They also claim to be the most democratic people in the world, creating ambiguity around whether their stance is genuine or fabricated, real or imaginary.

This is the fate of those who propose an *arché* as the origin of politics and philosophy, a foundation, principle, fundamental model, which must rule and govern:

> Liberalism presents us with a contradictory niche of political origins, an original unbound power creating a power that replaces, describes and limits it; in other words, the very negation of the power (krátos) of the demos. The kratos of democracy means unlimited, founding (unfounded) and ever-present power, whose definitive category is a "power" that cannot be reduced to a framework that contains and determines it. (Sanín-Restrepo 2011, 100)

The result is the generalization of corruption, which replaces constituent power with constituted power, which governs from above through a clientelist pyramid of favors that revolve around the top without ever reaching the broad base that sustains it:

> It is not the troops on horseback, it is not the companies afoot, it is not arms that defend the tyrant. This does not seem credible on first thought, but it is nevertheless true. Almost a third of the Roman emperors were killed by their own soldiers. If things are to change, one must realize the extent to which the

> foundation of tyranny lies in the vast networks of corrupted people with an interest in maintaining tyranny. that there are only four or five who maintain the dictator, four or five who keep the country in bondage to him. Five or six have always had access to his ear, and have either gone to him of their own accord, or else have been summoned by him, to be accomplices in his cruelties, companions in his pleasures, panders to his lusts, and sharers in his plunders. These six manage their chief so successfully that he comes to be held accountable not only for his own misdeeds but even for theirs. The six have six hundred who profit under them, and with the six hundred they do what they have accomplished with their tyrant. (La Boétie [1548] 1975, 71–2)

It is not only due to the armies and the police, to the laws and repression, to the prisons and impositions, by which the sovereign governs, the *One* has a network that emanates from its summit to the middle of its empire that actively collaborates in the maintenance of the current power, of which a few hundred subjects loyal to domination are subsidiary:

> The six hundred maintain under them six thousand, whom they promote in rank, upon whom they confer the government of provinces or the direction of finances, in order that they may serve as instruments of avarice and cruelty, executing orders at the proper time and working such havoc all around that they could not last except under the shadow of the six hundred, nor be exempt from law and punishment except through their influence. The consequence of all this is fatal indeed. And whoever is pleased to unwind the skein will observe that not the six thousand but a hundred thousand, and even millions, cling to the tyrant by this cord to which they are tied. (La Boétie [1548] 1975, 72)

A chain of favors creates the sovereign's servants, and every system of domination follows this vertical structure. The encryption of power provides an additional reason for voluntary servitude, complementing those identified by La Boétie. According to him, nature makes us free, but customs, superstitions, and religions can lead us to conform and even favor our chains. This occurs because, beyond traditional means of subjection, power masquerades as the government of reason and freedom, when in reality it governs through greed and slavery.

Anarchy is either excluded and buried or supposedly absorbed by liberalism that dictates that everything must remain under its totalitarian administration. As a result, constitutions, the highest expressions of the law, become mere democratic simulations of dictatorships.

> By merging the nation-state with society as a mere reflection of law, liberalism aims to eradicate any potential for individuals to find personal meaning or foster communal expressions outside the confines of a predefined juridical existence. Modern law endeavors to erase diverse territories, fragmentations, collaborative ties, anonymous political and artistic works, social networks, and any community

> initiatives that do not conform to the fundamental homogeneity of the nation-state and its societal constructs. (Sanín-Restrepo 2016, 120)

Liberalism and neoliberalism eliminate difference to impose a singular identity. They deterritorialize by creating desertic landscapes and reterritorialize by normalizing diverse spaces into homogeneity. This uniformity of the modern, rational, monolithic subject stems from its alienation from the community and the plural characteristics that define and constitute it. The constituted traps and reduces the constituent. Recognition becomes erroneous and simulated, making it impossible to fulfill human rights as the proposed teleological horizon. By eliminating differences and unifying the subject, modernity seeks to legitimize what is given once and for all, so that it can only continue through its conservation and increase characteristics of the will of the sovereign power, which now pretends to be democratic by asserting that its constitution has been approved by the people.

> What is fundamental to democracy is that the construction of the community begins with the principle that no one should be qualified to govern based on natural attributes like strength, wisdom, or wealth. Democracy reverses the logic of the arche as a pre-political category, redefining it as a formula for social organization. (Sanín-Restrepo 2012, 35)

The hidden people, composed of the excluded and marginalized, refugees and displaced people, deserters and dissidents, represent the true democracy—one that threatens the *arché* and embodies the multitude in anarchy. Conversely, those with full citizen rights in the simulacrum of representative democracy are the ones who, whether voluntarily or involuntarily, render servitude to the sovereign.

Democracy embodies anarchy as it fundamentally rejects the concept of sovereignty. It represents the collective power of the commons, which can either be assimilated by existing power structures or be marginalized by it.

> The technical mechanisms through which contemporaneity has submerged law and politics fail to disguise the fact that the idea of hierarchy, on which both depend, derives from a Greek compound that designates the sacred order: *(arché) (hierós), hieroarché*. To live under a hierarchy means to live under a divine order that ensures the continuous passage from the many—the people—to the one who must govern. However, this sacred flow necessitates an intermediary body of functionaries—ranging from the least important to the most powerful—capable of connecting the ideal unity of government to the real foundation on which political power is exercised. (Matos 2023, 70)

A new *oikos-nomos* understood as a biopotency in radical democracy, in commune, emerges and confronts the neoliberal economy and the sovereign paradigm. The multiplicity and difference of the subjects is authentically recognized without admitting simulacra, identities decay replaced by singularities. The hidden and ungovernable people in an anarchic commune are already the here and now, in us and in others, in the excluded and deserters, in the temporarily autonomous zones and the anti-camps.

From a Rousseauian perspective, the transition from the state of nature to culture—marked by the ecological integration of humans into nature, the Golden Age, and the animistic and pantheistic veneration of all existence—can be recounted less enthusiastically than Eurocentrism has done. Animistic prehistoric cults, which valued natural phenomena and animals as equal, superior, or beneficent powers, represented the integration of humans into a harmonious and balanced ecosystem from which human beings would be torn away by the introduction of agriculture and writing during the Neolithic revolution, contemporary with the emergence of the first empires.

The common and the commune are temporarily autonomous spaces, liberated zones, which subsist as long as they are not colonized by a hierarchical power that submits them to its mandates. That spatiality is also a being, then there is an anarchic ontological space that coincides with the nature of things. For this reason, anarchists such as Elisée Reclus prioritized space over time and geography over history. Geography is history in space: ecology, mutual aid, cooperation, joy. That space existed at the beginning of everything, in the past; it reexists in the present and will exist in the future, therefore it is our eternal present.

From an anarchic ontological perspective, the commune emerges as a surplus, a communism of abundance. This stands in stark contrast to the communism of Marxist scarcity, as the anarchist commune will be composed of beings with heightened capacities and diminished needs. Furthermore, the elevation of both common and individual power will be intertwined with a decrease in common and individual need. As we know, a wise individual like Socrates required little in terms of material possessions to live a fulfilling life. Communal rules will continuously evolve from the dynamic interactions and compositions of the individuals who inhabit it. These compositions of individual bodies give rise to the collective body, which is inherently free and equal from its inception.

The order of liberated beings, previously misconstrued as chaos, is in fact synonymous with free order. This constitutes the foundational ontological space within which all entities—things, people, actions, thoughts, the very harmony or symphony of matter and the body—emerge and interact. This anarchic ontological framework provides the basis for a harmonious political order.

The relationship between anarchic ontology and political anarchism is one of inherent harmony. Free beings are naturally inclined toward anarchic political organization, and conversely, an anarchically organized society fosters the freedom of its members.

The ultimate goal is to achieve the autonomy of social space from capitalist domination. This involves cultivating temporarily autonomous zones of shared life, thought, and action within the present moment—an ongoing process of revolt rather than a singular revolutionary event:

> Revolution is the goal set by those who believe only in the things of this world and, therefore, are concerned with the circumstances and the moment of its possible realization in historical time according to the relations of cause and effect.

> Revolt, on the contrary, implies a suspension of historical time, an intransigent commitment to an action whose consequences are not known or foreseeable, but which, for that very reason, does not reach agreements or compromises with the enemy. While those who do not see beyond this world are concerned only with the balance of forces in which they find themselves and are willing to unscrupulously set aside their convictions, the men of revolt are the men of the non-existent, who have suspended historical time once and for all and can, therefore, to act unconditionally in it. (Agamben 2024)

Therefore, the apparent dissociation between the anarchic ontology of many contemporary philosophers and traditional political anarchism does not stem from an internal division within anarchy itself. Rather, it arises from the inability one and the other to bring harmony to both sites of emergence of anarchy.

Note

1 Randroid is a term used, often pejoratively, to describe the followers of Ayn Rand's philosophy of Objectivism.

References

Agamben, Giorgio. 2024. "Sobre las cosas que no son." Ficción de la Razón. https://ficciondelarazon.org/2024/07/04/giorgio-agamben-sobre-las-cosas-que-no-son/. Accessed December 19, 2024.

Baudrillard, Jean. 1981. *Simulacra and Simulation*. Paris: Editions Galilee.

La Boétie, Étienne De. [1548] 1975. *Discourse on Voluntary Servitude*. Auburn, AL: Ludwig von Mises Institute.

Matos, Andityas. 2023. *La An-arquía que Viene*. Madrid: Ned Ediciones.

Matos, Andityas. 2024. "An-arquia contra a soberania: Constituent An-archy Against Sovereignty." *Revista Justiça do Direito* 38(2): 193–224.

Royo-Hernández, Simón. 2019. *El Sujeto Anárquico: Reiner Schürmann y Michel Foucault*. Madrid: Editorial Arena.

Royo-Hernández, Simón. 2024. "Ontología anárquica y anarquismo político." *Ficción de la Razón*, December 16. https://ficciondelarazon.org/2024/12/16/simon-royo-hernandez-ontologia-anarquica-y-anarquismo-politico/. Accessed December 20, 2025.

Sanín Restrepo, Ricardo. 2011. *Teoría Crítica Constitucional: Rescatando la democracia del liberalismo*. First ed. Quito: Corte Constitucional para el Período de Transición.

Sanin-Restrepo, Ricardo. 2012. "Cinco Tesis desde el pueblo oculto." *OXÍMORA Revista Internacional de Ética y Política* 1: 10–39.

Sanín-Restrepo, Ricardo. 2016. *Decolonizing Democracy: Power in a Solid State*. London: Rowman & Littlefield.

Sanín-Restrepo, Ricardo. 2018. "Introduction: The Meaning of the Encryption of Power as the Razor's Edge of Politics." In *Decrypting Power*, edited by Ricardo Sanín-Restrepo. London: Rowman & Littlefield, ix–xxx.

Sanín-Restrepo, Ricardo, and Marinella Machado Araujo. 2020. "A Teoria da Encriptação do Poder: Itinerário de uma ideia." *Revista da Faculdade Mineira de Direito* 23(45): 1–17.

Sloterdijk, Peter. 1987. *Critique of Cynical Reason*. Translated by Michael Eldred, Foreword by Andreas Huyssen. Theory and History of Literature, Vol. 40. Minneapolis: University of Minnesota Press.

5

Nomadic Sovereignty Opposed to the Archist Plantation System

Vincent Pisters Møystad and Anthony Faramelli

Introduction

The starting premise of this essay is that an analysis of power best comes from below. That is, from those excluded from power, relegated to a heterogenic position vis-à-vis the State. We aim to demonstrate an analysis of how power is encrypted and decrypted from the grounded position of lived resistance. Specifically, we will look at two key texts, a Zapatista 1995 communique attributed to Subcomandante Marcos titled "Power as a Mirror and an Image" (2004, 153–60) and *The Dragon and the Hydra: A Historical Study of Organizational Methods* (2006) by the late Russell Maroon Shoatz, Black Panther and Black Liberation Army member and political prisoner (Shoatz et al. 2013, 101–31). We will demonstrate how each of these texts contains an analysis of how State power is encrypted and, more significantly, an analysis of what exceeds and remains existential to the State.

To develop this analysis, we will first propose a theory of the plantation as the *0-degree point* from which the State emerges. We will situate the plantation as an extractive social-technological (metabolic) assemblage that is foundational to contemporary expressions of archism. We will use this to demonstrate how the plantation is the metamodel that structures power in contemporary liberal democracies. We will then look at how power functions as a mirror, creating a simulacra of power for the State, demonstrating how extractive operations of power enacted by the plantation are in turn subject to encryption and mystification through speculative epistemologies imposed by State structures. Finally, we will look to develop a concept of nomadic sovereignty that exceeds and is existential to the State, while also operating within State structures. We will be utilizing a theoretical framework that draws from Rancière, Glissant, Wynter, Deleuze, and Guattari. While this conceptual framework provides us with both the tools and vocabulary to build our argument, this is not an attempt to "understand" Marronage and Zapatismo through Western philosophy, to make these movements "speak" to Western academia. Nor do we suggest that these philosophies directly inform or underpin these movements. Here we follow Deleuze and Guattari's assertion that a concept is only a tool to aid analysis. Like any other tool, it can be used, misused, and set aside once it is no longer useful. In other words, we are using these concepts to illuminate an analysis of power that is already operative in both Marronage and Zapatismo.

Importantly, we are not suggesting that there is a direct link between Marronage and Zapatismo. Nor do we claim that there are any active lines of affiliation, let alone communication, between them. While both Marronage and Zapatismo emerge from the extractive violence of colonialism, the plantation system, and the persistent problems of coloniality, they are situated within very different historical, cultural, and social contexts. They also employ different forms of organization and resistance. However, they do rhyme in multiple important ways. It is our hope that by staying with the tension and looking for this "rhyming scheme" between Marronage and Zapatismo, we can develop a critical analysis of power from the lived experience of resistance. An analysis that, to paraphrase the Zapatistas, comes from below and to the left. In keeping with this ethos of resonant heterogeneity, the text itself is polyphonic, shifting registers between historical analysis and conceptual experimentation as well the voices and perspectives of its authors. Rather than seeking to smoothen the ensuing frictions, we have elected to keep these as generative gaps in which echoes and resonances can unfold and find force.

The Plantation as Archism

On November 4, 2021, a group of Zapatistas gave a talk at a meeting with activists in East London. They told the history of the Mexican State as originating with the colonial plantations. The plantation is a social-technological (metabolic) assemblage that, due to its extractivist relationship to land, always presupposed the existence of a State. That is to say that the plantation institutes a recursive logic that encrypts power, manifesting the State as a technical object that, thanks to the recursive logic of the plantation, appears to us as inevitable. The State becomes a totalizing simulacrum that is immanent to the power that it presupposes. In other words, the State exists because the plantation logic insists that it must exist. As such, following the thought of Sylvia Wynter, C. L. R. James, and others, the extractivist model of the plantation is foundational to contemporary expressions of archism. The extractive operations of power enacted by the plantation are in turn subject to encryption and mystification through speculative epistemologies imposed by State structures.

For Wynter, the plantation is taken as paradigmatic, premonitory, and foundational to the development of modern iterations of archism, whether understood as specific protocapitalist (or indeed capitalist) "economic" arrangements (Williams 2022) the biopolitical convergence of State power and speculative finance (see Baucom 2005), or indeed the infrastructures of repression and surveillance necessary to maintain the (relative) stability of such arrangements (Browne 2015). Katherine McKittrick, in her piece *Plantation Futures* (2013), coined the oft-cited image of the "ugly blueprint" to describe the early modern plantation economy's relation to our present conjuncture. While all earlier human societies had been characterized by an oscillatory and mutually constitutive (or at least "oscillatory") relationship to nonhuman being, Sylvia Wynter writes, "With the discovery of the New World, and its vast exploitable lands, that process which has been termed 'the reduction of Man to Labour and Nature to Land' had its large scale beginning" (2022, 295). In Wynter's account, which may be taken here as broadly representative of a far wider range of study and theorization of the plantation as paradigmatic or premonitory, plantation arrangements are structured first and foremost around crop monoculture, grown for export. The ecological impact of this approach to the cultivation of land continues to be felt today: indeed, the ecological devastation of the plantation logic has led some anthropologists and ecologists to deploy the term "plantationocene" (Barua et al. 2023). The clearing of human beings, as well as a wide range of other animal and plant species, some companion and some wild, has been a necessary predicate of the cultivation of monoculture, as has the transportation of cultivars around different parts of the world. The ecological footprint of the plantation model is a *migratory* one in McKittrick's terminology (2013), but not thereby nomadic, a point to which we shall return in greater depth later. It carries the migratory potentials of the fungible, the mobility that turns the cultivar into a commodity, land into fixed capital, and human beings into units of labor power (Gomez 2021); a highly mobile machine, but one geared toward the production of exchange value rather than errantry (Glissant 2010). Against the ethograms of plant intelligence (Fuller and Goriunova 2019, 101), the plantation imposes the archism of taxonomy.

The plantation is also characterized by the drive to render fungible, and thus control, human being and praxis. The process known as the Plantation of Ireland, more or less contemporaneous with the beginnings and early consolidation of plantation logics in the Americas, was less focused on the production of agricultural monoculture and more with the replacement of potentially rebellious populations with more pliant ones, a process understood by its advocates and organizers as roughly analogous, even a necessary predicate, for the unfolding of plantation of the Americas (Taylor 2003). Russell Maroon Shoatz's study of the organizational forms assumed by the resistance of enslaved peoples, discussed at greater length below, also highlights the slavers' preference for the widest possible range of sociocultural backgrounds among the enslaved, as well as the high mortality rates on plantations, as techniques for the prevention of the constitution of cultural formations that could sustain organized resistance. On one level then, plantation consists of the destruction of human societies with connections to the land, or forms of countersovereignty that generate friction for the plantation's command-and-extract logics. At the same time, the plantation logic seeks to constitute a human labor force that is fundamentally fungible and predictable.

This process of displacement and reshaping of human lives would take intensive, as well as expansive form as plantation logics consolidated throughout the early modern period. Meredith Whittaker has persuasively demonstrated the widespread circulation of tracts that sought to advise planters and factory owners alike on the correct management of laboring bodies, suggesting methods of discipline, punishment, and accounting that prefigure both the time-and-motion studies of high-modern industrialism and the development of computational logics. Charles Babbage, famed as one of the originators of the computer through his contributions to the theorization of the *analytical engine*, was also the author of tracts on labor discipline in the factory. Such tracts were part of a circulation of management practices between plantation and factory, to which Babbage's contribution was the "Babbage Principle"; the breaking down of tasks into ever smaller constitutive parts requiring less "skill," striving for the displacement of any form of embodied knowledge (and by extension, social power or capacity for organization) on the part of the laboring body (Whittaker 2023).

In the accounts of Yusoff (2018) and Fiori (2020) these processes are thought together as mechanisms for energy extraction, different moments in a social-ecologic metabolic process in which humans and environments are reordered for a concentrated and accelerated thermodynamic process. Donna Haraway has given this ordering perhaps its most succinct characterization as "enclosure and extraction" (quoted in Barua et al. 2023). To enclose and extract are both archist gestures, a spatial and thermodynamic reordering predicated on clear relations of command and obedience.

For Wynter, the techniques of control and command pioneered enclosing-extractive activities of the plantation form the diagrammatic precedent for the exercise of modern State power "under Hitler and Stalin," as captured in her dyad of "emporium-imperium" (2022, 294). The plantation thus appears as the form of the State particular to modernity. However, as Wynter is keen to underline, this process of enclosure and extraction that results in the emporium-imperium necessarily produces an excess, an outside.

In *Plot and Plantation*, Sylvia Wynter contrasts the plantation, the site of capital accumulation, with the plot, the patch of land allocated by planters for small-scale subsistence agriculture to the people they enslaved. In Wynter's account, the plot comes to represent a zone of comparative autonomy for enslaved people through its function as a site of self-organized production of use values, albeit within the rigid constraints of the wider plantation economy (2022, 295). In Wynter's account, this space of communal food production remains also a site for the propagation of a folk culture. In generating forms of production, sociality and commensality in direct opposition to the plantation economy, the plot "recreates traditional values-use values. This folk culture becomes the source of guerrilla cultural guerrilla resistance to the plantation system" (Wynter 2022, 295). The plot and plantation thus come to exist in direct opposition to one another, a relationship that continues after the formal abolition of slavery and across the continued struggles over land, subsistence, and culture that persist into the present:

> The plantation was the superstructure of civilisation: and the plot was the root of culture. But there was a rupture between them, the superstructure was not related to the base, it did not respond to the needs of the base, but rather the demands of external shareholders and metropolitan market. The plantation was run by the manager class, the colon class. This class and the laboring indigenous class faced each other across barricades that are in-built in the very system which created them. That is why the clash in 1865 and the clash in 1938 and the future clashes are unavoidable unless the system is transformed. (Wynter 2022, 295)

Wynter's account succinctly traces out the contours of Black liberation struggle as operating in conditions of constraint imposed by a spatialized organization of violence, and surveillance, while emphasizing the centrality of autonomous activity, self-valorization, and (agri)cultural politics. Wynter is careful to define this position against what she calls the "heroic folkish mythology of a Hitler" (2022, 295), that is, a sentimentalized racial past deployed as an element in State building, and instead proposes the plot and its attendant "guerrilla cultural resistance" as a generative of alternative value practices from which to formulate a critique of the present.

The (Neo)Liberal State and the Encryption of Power

Ultimately, reading the plantation as the 0-degree point of the contemporary archic State necessitates a theory of how archic power is encrypted or, to use the terminology of Deleuze and Guattari, captured. Following the work of Ricardo Sanín-Restrepo, encryption of power refers to the "imposition of institutional simulations of difference that condition, neutralize or prohibit political agency, reducing difference to static and solid models of identity that pose as the only form of power" (2020, 19). In "Treatise on Nomadology: The War Machine" and again in "Apparatus of Capture," both from *A Thousand Plateaus*, Deleuze and Guattari build on the work of Georges Dumezil to argue that the State historically emerged from two contradictory apparatuses that nevertheless work together, a double articulation of two processes, an apparatus of capture that bonds (the "magician-emperor") and an apparatus that creates contracts and treaties (the "jurist-priest") (2002, 351, 424). Throughout the first section of this chapter, Deleuze and Guattari (2002, 351–6) chart how the act of bonding takes actions and practices (such as agricultural practices) and turns them into work. By doing this the action becomes artificially separated from the person performing the action, in other words the work is separated from the worker. This in turn creates identities that are contingent on the State and alienated from their practices. The second apparatus, the jurist-priest, hierarchizes the State, distributing identities into class positions, through the creation of contracts. The opposition between these two apparatuses "is only relative; they function as a pair, in alternation, as though they expressed a division of the One or constituted in themselves a sovereign unity" (Deleuze and Guattari 2002, 351).

War is not contained within either apparatus (Deleuze and Guattari 2002, 353). While repressive apparatuses like the police are incorporated into the State (355), war is a "pure form of exteriority, whereas the State apparatus constitutes the form of interiority we habitually take as a model, or according to which we are in the habit of thinking" (354). War cuts into and distributes the organization of the State (352). As such, it is fundamentally at odds with the historic State form.

This analysis, however, lacks the same consistency when looking at the neoliberal State. Neoliberalism is a destructive force that works by creating markets by destroying old ones. It "operates a reorganization of the [State] that is superimposed by the market"

(Faramelli 2018a, 23), reorganizing the State alongside its own destructive conditions (23). In other words, neoliberalism is a War Machine that disorganizes and destroys the State in order to make it anew. It creates its own crisis and then offers its destructive drive to reorganization as the only solution to the crisis. This is a fundamentally more complex form of encryption of power than the historic State analyzed by Deleuze and Guattari in "Treatise on Nomadology: The War Machine."

The Zapatistas offer such an analysis in the essay "Power as a Mirror and an Image" (Marcos 2004, 153–60). While this essay is far from the only time Marcos employs mirrors in an analysis of State power and resistance, it is by far the most crucial in demonstrating the encryption of power by the neoliberal State. The essay is broken down into four chapters where each chapter represents a mirror. As the narration passes through each mirror, we can see how archic power becomes encrypted, creating a simulacrum of power that is more real than reality.

In writing that is characteristically poetic and performative, the first section, or "The First Mirror," of this essay (Marcos 2004, 153–6) is a critical analysis of how "Mexico" moved from a "mirror," a heterotopic space of mediation, to an "image," a simulacrum of neoliberal governmentality. This chapter is divided into two sections, each section dubbed a deceit; however, a close reading shows that this chapter engages with four distinct spatial levels of analysis. The first space is a heterotopia of mediation where power creates a simulacrum of itself:

> In the [neoliberal] Power the mirror reflects a double image: what is said and what is done. The mirror hides nothing. The resources are gone, it is not the same as before. Its surface is mildewed and stained. It can no longer "reverse" reality. On the contrary, it shows the contradiction. But in making this evident, it controls it and puts it at its service. Now it simply attempts to make the contradictory image seem "natural," as "evidence," and "unquestionable." (Marcos 2004, 153)

The neoliberal State frames the contradiction of power, the double apparatuses utilized by Deleuze and Guattari, in such a way as to solidify its power. It does this by positioning economic, political, and social instability as existing outside the frame of governmentality, rather than as integral aspects of neoliberalism. In other words, power creates a crisis that is seen to be exterior to the State while positioning itself as the only possible solution to the crisis. This allows power to present the false choice that it is "I or fascism," "I or anarchy," and "I or chaos" (Marcos 2004, 154).

This is a space that is fundamentally tautological (Marcos 2004, 155). However, Marcos argues that mediation alone is not sufficient to freeze the image. The movement to an image needs codification of the statements of Power; it needs legality to structure its territory (2004, 154–5). The most dramatic event of legality used to structure the space of Mexico happened in 1994 when the North American Free Trade Agreement (NAFTA) came into effect. Writing on the structuring effect of legality, the second apparatus of the State, Subcomandante Marcos noted that legality is a tautological mirror.

> In its image, in the reflection it obtains itself, Power says:
>
> *"I exist because I am necessary,*
> *I am necessary because I exist,*
> *therefore:*
> *I exist and I am necessary."*
> As the image it receives of itself is enough to satisfy itself, the Power believes it is enough, and once again the mirror in front of the mirror, eternal. (2004, 155, emphasis in original)

Throughout the essay Marcos notes how the reality of the encryption of power is evident in the events of 1994 and 1995 in Mexico. As noted above, 1994 was the year that Mexico entered into the NAFTA with the United States and Canada. The move was intended to fully integrate Mexico into the neoliberal world order (Faramelli 2018b, 137). This process involved ending the *ejido* system of communal subsistence farming that was guaranteed in the Mexican Constitution. "This was literally intended to make Mexico, the dark land of rural farmers, become (North) America, the land of light, law, and economic progress" (Faramelli 2018b, 138). The radical reorganization of Mexico so that the State conformed to neoliberal conditions resulted in economic, social, and political polycrisis throughout 1994 and 1995. Here we can see how power is encrypted precisely by folding in the exteriority of the War Machine. Crisis is no longer the exception, but has become the rule.

Nomadic Sovereignty

Marcos finishes his essay with the Fourth Mirror. This section, uncharacteristically brief and poetic in comparison to the rest of the essay, creates a space that is exterior to the simulacra of power created by the previous mirrors. The section reads:

> Send, through the ocean of the east, a greeting to the men and women who, in Europe, discovered that they share with us, the same ailment: the illness of hope.
>
> Instructions to see the fourth mirror:
>
> Find a mirror, place it in front of you and assume a comfortable position,
>
> Breath deeply. Close your eyes and say to yourself three times:
>
> "I am what I am, a little bit, of what I could be. The mirror shows me what I am, the crystal what I could be."
>
> Once this is done, open your eyes and look at the mirror. No, don't look at your reflection. Direct your look downward, to the left. Ready? Good, now pay attention and in a few moments another image will appear. Yes, it is a march: men, women, children and old people who come from the southeast. Yes, it is one of the

> highways which go to Mexico City. Can you see what is crawling on the left flank of the caravan? Here? There, on the ground! Yes, that tiny, black thing! What is it? A beetle! Now pay attention because that beetle is . . . . (Marcos 2004, 160)

The essay concludes with the Zapatista march to Mexico City that happened in 1995, specifically focusing on the conceptual persona of Don Durito. Marcos created the character of Don Durito as a children's story. Durito is a knight-errant beetle modeled loosely on Don Quixote. It's significant that this essay ends with hope—which Marcos positions as an illness not because it causes dis-ease, but because it is infectious—contained within a movement that exists to trouble the State and a conceptual figure who is defined by errancy. In other words, hope is contained within nomadic movement.

Movement holds a privileged position in the thought of both the Zapatistas and Deleuze and Guattari (and, as we will see later in this text, Glissant). Returning to nomadology, the nomad is understood to be heterogenic to the State. It is "distributed by turbulence across a smooth space, in producing movement that holds space and simultaneously affects all of its points, instead of being held in space in a local movement from one specified point to another" (Deleuze and Guattari 2002, 363). In this way the nomad is able to avoid capture by the State, to avoid being subsumed by State systems, enabling the nomad to be able to corrupt other institutional arrangements within the State system (366). What defines the nomad is intensive movement, their inner psychic life (381). In other words, the nomad is in motion even when staying still.

This is not to say that the nomad exists fully outside the reach of the State either. As Leonie Ansems de Vries argues in her essay "Politics on the Line" (2013), everything in Deleuze and Guattari happens in the middle, meaning that resistant flows emerge from within lines of power (126–47). Because the nomad is defined by intensive movement, they emerge from within the territory of the State, but because they exist both inside and exterior to the State, they trouble the State apparatuses of power. They decrypt power. To decrypt power is to fundamentally reject, "politics as the imposition of any conditions, qualifications or purpose (*Entelecheia*)" (Sanín-Restrepo and Machado-Araujo 2020, 26). This resonates with Deleuze and Guattari's argument that also works against and undoes the consolidation of encrypted State power (2002, 358). Later in the text they go on to write:

> It is the secret power (*puissance*), or strength of solidarity, and the corresponding genealogical mobility that determine [the War Machine's] eminence in a war body. This has to do neither with the monopoly of an organic power (*pouvoir*) nor with local representation, but is related to the potential (*puissance*) of a vortical body in a nomad space. (366)

The existence of the nomad within the State always asserts new nomadic political claims that trouble and destabilize the State (Deleuze and Guattari 2002, 368). By doing so, we argue that the nomad enacts a sovereign position. Not sovereign within the States' understanding of the term, but rather, following Bataille, the sovereignty that refuses or escapes being "put to work." A pure excess and expenditure, rather than a Heideggerian standing reserve.

The Dragon and the Hydra

Indeed, there are strong resonances between Deleuze and Guattari's argument and Russell Maroon Shoatz's intervention in *The Dragon and the Hydra: A Historical Study of Organisational Methods* (2013). In this text, Shoatz presents a historical overview of Maroon revolts across the Americas, distinguishing between movements that sought, or were compelled, to construct organizational forms that mirrored the hierarchical military machinery of the plantation system and those who succeeded in maintaining more distributed and participatory modes of organization.

The Dragon and the Hydra forms part of Maroon's prison writings, gathered in the anthology *Maroon the Implacable* (Shoatz et al. 2013). A member of the Black Panther Party and later the Black Liberation Army, Shoatz was incarcerated in 1973 and would spend over twenty years in solitary confinement before his eventual release in 2021. His repeated escape attempts in the 1970s and 1980s earned him the nickname Maroon, a name that would precipitate a long-standing commitment to theorizing the practice of Marronage as a revolutionary strategy. As part of various study collectives and correspondence groups while imprisoned, Shoatz developed a political outlook that both built on and criticized the legacies of Marronage, both as a historical practice and a political orientation in the present toward Exodus and flight as vectors of revolutionary change (2013, 8).

Like other theorists of the Black Radical Tradition, the analysis of historical modes of resistance in the African diaspora and the attempt to theorize these as part of modern movements toward universal emancipation became a means to broach questions of political organization in the present. Shoatz's discussion of the politics opens with a repudiation of democratic centralism and the role of the vanguard party as conceived by contemporaneous Marxist Leninist groups (2013, 105). Shoatz diligently deparochializes the debates around organizational form in the European and European diasporic labor movements:

> What you'll read here is going to look a lot like anarchism [but] what follows cannot properly be termed anarchism, because the practitioners themselves never knew that word, nor were they in contact with people of that view … Still, [anarchism is] welcomed as a sister set of ideas, beliefs, and concepts, so long as the anarchists understand that they stand on equal footing, in a spirit of intercommunal self-determination. (2013, 107)

Shoatz discusses groups such as the Boni Maroons of present-day Suriname, who have been able to maintain their autonomy from the British, Dutch, and Surinamese States over the course of several centuries. Dutch colonial accounts emphasize the capacity of the Boni and related groups to dissolve, reconstitute themselves, flee or attack at short notice, as well as their capacity to cultivate the territories across which they moved. Indeed, Dutch soldiers would often set out in search of Maroon food caches to supplement their own meager rations, predicated on the far more archist plantation economy (Shoatz 2013, 113).

The Boni are the paradigmatic example of a range of practices of nomadic sovereignty across the Americas, the Plot armed and on the move, such as the Windward Maroons of Jamaica and the Seminole of Florida. The titular *Hydra* was the colonial nomenclature for such decentralized, polycephalous formations: Shoatz points out that the Hydra is also one of the largest constellations in the night sky, and one that has no identifiably brighter star than others. The image of the Hydra is one that has been picked up by a number of historians, notably Peter Linebaugh and Marcus Rediker (2000) to denote the nexus of rebelling peasants, religious dissenters, witches, Indigenous *résistants*, and Africans' refusal of enslavement that opposed the twin project of colonization and enclosure. To slay the Hydra is, of course, one of the tasks of Hercules, and this myth formed part of the self-understanding of the emergent Atlantic bourgeoisie:

> From the beginning of English colonial expansion in the early seventeenth century through the metropolitan industrialization of the early nineteenth, rulers referred to the Hercules-hydra myth to describe the difficulty of imposing order on increasingly global systems of labor.
>
> The many-headed hydra variously designated dispossessed commoners, transported felons, indentured servants, religious radicals, pirates, urban laborers, soldiers, sailors, and African slaves as the numerous, ever-changing heads of the monster.
>
> But the heads, though originally brought into productive combination by their Herculean rulers, soon developed among themselves new forms of cooperation against those rulers, from mutinies and strikes to riots and insurrections and revolution. Like the commodities they produced, their experience circulated with the planetary currents around the Atlantic, often eastward, from American plantations, Irish commons, and deep-sea vessels back to the metropoles of Europe. (Linebaugh and Rediker 2000, 5)

Shoatz argues that where Maroons compromised the participatory and decentralized approach in favor of centralized, State-like forms of organization, the struggle took place on a terrain favorable to the colonial State, allowing the movements to be repressed or co-opted through their leadership structures. Shoatz points to the destruction of Jamaica's Leeward Maroons, who operated with a centralized authority structure (2013, 115).

The paradigmatic example of a counterarchism in the context of plantation uprisings is, of course, the Haitian experience. Shoatz devotes some time to recounting C. L. R. James's account of the Haitian Revolution; in the process of overthrowing French and planter rule, the leading cadres of the revolution reinscribed the archist principle and plantation logics into revolutionary Haiti (2013, 120–1). For Cedric Robinson, C. L. R. James's account is a parable for the world communist movement of the 1930s, with Toussaint, Dessalines, and other leading cadre standing in for the vanguard party and Enlightenment, republican ideals standing in for a Marxism that increasingly came to dominate and commandeer the vernacular radicalisms from which it had emerged (2021, 276).

For Shoatz, the lesson is clear and unequivocal: "I contend that such centralization will only make it easier for our oppressors to identify and level repression against us" (2013, 126). Shoatz proposes instead a process of coordinated autonomous struggles from a multitude of positions, which he terms "the Mosaic" (Robinson 2021, 128).

In *Poetics of Relation* (2010) Edouard Glissant points out that nomadism, while it may rupture existing social arrangements, is not movement without constraint or pattern. Glissant distinguishes two forms; arrow-like nomadism, the nomadism of conquest, which is always a frustrated desire for rootedness, and circular nomadism, which is patterned on and maintained through external constraints. Arrow-like nomadism conquers, settles, and reinstitutes an order determined by filial legitimation to a root (Glissant 2010, 17). Circular nomadism is driven by some environmental compulsion to move: "Populations that move from one part of the forest to another, ... hired laborers in their pilgrimage from farm to farm, circus people in their peregrinations from village to village" (Glissant 2010, 12).

Thus, while the association of nomadism and anarchism may be a seductive one, it cannot be taken for granted. A resonant problematic emerges in the attempts to theorize Marronage as political concept that overcomes the problem of power. In *Freedom as Marronage* (2015), Neil Roberts attempts precisely such a maneuver, thinking the Maroon not only as a historic personage but as a modality of the political: "Freedom materializes in the liminal and interstitial spaces between our imaginings of absolute unfreedom and the zone of its opposite ... Marronage philosophy runs counter to the idea of fixed, determinate endings" (2015, 174).

In Roberts's schema, marronage can be understood as a concrete practice of freedom, and indeed a conceptualization of freedom as a vector in the political, but it is not a State. Roberts is less critical of the formation of Haiti as a State, casting this as a form of maroon sovereignty, though by comparison to the more critical account of C. L. R. James, Roberts's is a little lighter on historical detail. In Roberts's account, Dessalines overcomes the limitations of a sovereign marronage toward a sociogenic marronage, marronage as the foundational act of a new political order, which, while not breaking fully with plantation logics, encodes a capacity for popular revolt into the social fabric (2015, 135). In other words, the Haitian State is not so much the conclusion to a historical process of emancipation, but an ongoing attempt at Marronage.

Given the shifting conceptual-historic registers of Roberts's text, this remains a difficult claim to evaluate. In his review of Roberts's work, Gary Wilder instead characterizes Marronage as a predicament, an "independence within a framework of inescapable global economic and geopolitical inequality in relation to which there was no stable outside" (Wilder 2017, 4). For Wilder, this reading of Marronage as a predicament and possibility, expressed in Roberts's text as the Haitian proverb "beyond the mountains are other mountains," becomes a potent heuristic for understanding the paradoxes and contradictions of nomadic sovereignty Wilder adds "more hopefully, we might reconsider recent experiments in autonomous democracy without State sovereignty in places such as Mondragon, Chiapas, Buenos Aires, and Rojava, as examples of late-modern marronage" (Wilder 2017).

Conclusion

In *Hatred of Democracy* (2006) Jacques Rancière succinctly outlined the tension that underlines modern democratic States, arguing that, while the State can be more or less democratic, every State is, in essence, an oligarchy (138) insofar as every State is a government by wealth (88). For Rancière "democracy" is the enactment of an emancipatory politics that resists oligarchic power and the privatization of life. In other words, democracy is the resistance to reducing life to the sphere of "public life," the area that is codified, legislated and controlled by a system of representation where those in power secured their place by exploiting the nondemocratic schisms within a given society, and "private life," the sphere governed by the capitalist accumulation and ownership (107–9). In this sense democracy means

> [the] impurity of politics, the challenging of governments' claims to embody the sole principle of public life and in so doing be able to circumscribe the understanding and extension of public life. If there is a "limitlessness" specific to democracy, then that's exactly where it lies: not in the exponential multiplication of needs or of desires emanating from individuals, but in the movement that ceaselessly displaces the limits of the public and the private, of the political and the social. (Rancière 2006, 121)

Far from simply reproducing the binary division between direct democracy and representational democracy, Rancière disentangled democracy from the juridical-political State (2006, 104–6) and locates it solely within non-State actors' resistance to State domination (106–7). This leads Rancière to situate democracy at the "micropolitical" level, the level in which particular subjectivities, rather than larger institutional bodies, relate to power. In doing so Rancière proposes that the democratic process is the process of micropolitical emancipation.

Hatred of Democracy's introduction notes how a hatred and critique of democracy have existed as long as the concept itself (Rancière 2006, 9–13). The novelty of Rancière's intervention is that it realigns the analytic focus from representation and State forms of governance, what is termed "macropolitics," to the subjectivization of individuals by their democratic resistance, or "micropolitics." Subjectivization, the micro process in which subjects are formed by a heterogenic set of relational and contingent factors that exist at the intersections between different subjects (60–1), is opposed to the notion of identity, the macro process in which subjects are formed through a system of representation that is fundamentally based on the fearful exclusion of others (59, 63–4).

Rancière argues that "the current dead end of political reflection and action is due to the identification of politics with the *self* of a community" (2006, 59). The "self of a community" is the place where the community is governed, either by formal laws and structures or informal norms, that is to say that it is how the community forms an identity. The self of community therefore is not politics, but rather policy, and if we are to maintain a distinction between policy and politics, then the notion of "identity politics" becomes a misnomer (59). Politics in this sense means the force of action that relates to an individual, contingent on specific sociohistorical circumstances. Emancipatory politics then is the politics of the self as an other. It is the bringing together of different subjectivities to work in concert with one another, while still retaining their own particular traits, an anarchic heterology (59–62).

This characterization of emancipatory politics as micropolitical anarchic heterology resonates with Wynter's discussion of the practices of the Plot as the "principle of organization of decentralized groups with total participation in the context of an overall framework of belief" (1970, 183). Wynter traces this principle across a range of folk practices, case as African cultural continuities that have been repurposed and recoded into practices of collective an-archic becoming. Jonkunnu, Myal, and Revival, Rastafarian communes and slum communities, the heirs of the plot, were all constituted through a process of self-organization in the absence of and direct opposition to encrypted modes of power.

Across these different cultural forms, Wynter argues that participants will take on a specific function within a wider organizational process, one that offers both affordances for individual self-expression and a role in the collective "laboring of spirit," as in the offices of Pocomania: "Leader, Governess, Mother, Shepherd, Water Maid, Cooing Dove, Train Driver, Conductor; all functionaries who have a role and a function in the organization of the group and in the order of the spiritual journey" (1970, 184).

The performance of such a function within a collective and counterhegemonic organizational framework is thus both individuating and constitutive of collective experience, and crucially, it is wholly at odds with the archic Babbage Principle and the principles of enclosure and extraction that structure the plantation and slum. In the immediate context of the performance, participants undo their own enclosure and resubjectivize themselves as part of other forms of organization. In *Black Metamorphosis*, Wynter tracks this basic schema across Jamaican peasant/folk culture, rooted in the Plot, right through to urban slum practices of Rastafari encampments, Garveyite mobilizations, and the emergent dancehall cultures of the 1960s and 1970s, as contemporaneous instantiations of the Plot (1970, 135).

Wynter thus conceives of the plot not as a mythical arcadia to be regained, but rather as a mode of resistance to be transversally deployed. What remains implicit in *Plot* (but is better developed in the *Metamorphosis*) is the proposal that the superstructure of the plantation may be unresponsive to the needs of the base but is nevertheless predicated on it; the plantation requires the generative ungovernability of the plot and its attendant social formations, even as the plot constitutes a continuing challenge to the plantation. Jacques Rancière makes a similar point: "Inegalitarian society can only function thanks to a multitude of egalitarian relations. It is this intrication of equality in inequality that the democratic scandal makes manifest in order to make it the basis of public power" (2006, 48).

What Wynter proposes across these texts is thus a mode of resistance that works to undo the encryption of the plantation system through counterposing a mutually constitutive practice of autonomy and the construction of alternative modes of sociality rooted in self-valorizing production. Beyond the concrete example of the plot, (or, elsewhere, provision ground) as a site of mutual aid and commensality, it is in performance as a site of intersubjectivization that Wynter casts as paradigmatic for the practice of nomadic sovereignty. Indeed, in the lengthier passage cited above, Wynter characterizes the *culture* of the plot as the "base" upon which the "superstructure" of the plantation feeds. The Plot, understood here as an emblem of the wider "cultures of participation" discussed in *Black Metamorphosis*, is engaged in a struggle for its autonomy from the plantation, not a greater share in its proceeds.

In Wynter's account, the plot becomes an instantiation of what is sometimes known as Petit Marronage; the smaller (whether considered spatially or temporally) acts of resistance that are predicated on clandestine or minor forms rather than open insurrection. For Saidiya Hartman, the key emancipatory charge of this minor marronage is specifically its incommensurability and inscrutability to power, in contrast to projects of Marronage that have aimed to create opposing State forces:

> When you look at the histories of Maroon communities who are able to create those complicated state forms, they're in a domain of politics where they are involved in these treaty forms with slaveholding powers. For me the petit marronage is actually more consonant with my own thinking about a history of anarchist projects which describe the way we have always lived, these decentered headless societies. It seems that there's a potentiality there, as opposed to making an alternative that has to be legible in terms of the given. We also see this in the Zapatista territories in resistance in Mexican Chiapas, the adoption of a form of anti-State democracy that is an anarchic micro-political process of emancipation. This entails a complete refusal of the possibility of any State being able to be a "government of the people" since all States are, "always exercised by the minority over the majority" (Rancière 2006, 83). It is a heterology of democracy that requires a form of political organization that focuses on micro-politics and the process of subjectivization without falling into the static monomania of identity where a group is defined solely by what it opposes. (Rancière 2006, 59; Deleuze and Guattari 2002, 215)

Ultimately, our analysis here is not intended to offer a neat and tidy theory of revolutionary change. Nor do we propose that the nomadic position is in and of itself emancipatory. Rather, we are proposing that by working through the polyvocality of multiple resistant theories and politics we can find a methodology to decrypt power. It is our hope that by staying with the dissonance of these multiple voices we can find a rhythmic pattern to follow. An errant path from below and to the left.

References

Ansems de Vries, Leonie. 2013. "Politics on the Line." In *Deleuze and Fascism: Security, War and Aesthetics*. London: Routledge, 126–47.

Barua, Maan, Rebeca Ibáñez Martín, and Marthe Achtnich. 2023. "Introduction: Plantationocene." Society for Cultural Anthropology. https://culanth.org/fieldsights/introduction-plantationocene.

Baucom, Ian. 2005. *Specters of the Atlantic: Finance Capital, Slavery, and the Philosophy of History*. Durham, NC: Duke University Press. https://doi.org/10.1215/9780822387022.
The Black Outdoors. 2016. "Fred Moten & Saidiya Hartman at Duke University." www.youtube.com/watch?v=t_tUZ6dybrc.
Browne, Simone. 2015. *Dark Matters: On the Surveillance of Blackness*. Durham, NC: Duke University Press. https://doi.org/10.1215/9780822375302.
Deleuze, Gilles, and Felix Guattari. 2002. *A Thousand Plateaus*. Boston: MIT Press.
Faramelli, Anthony. 2018a. *Resistance, Revolution and Fascism: Zapatismo and Assemblage Politics*. London: Bloomsbury Philosophy.
Faramelli, Anthony. 2018b. "Mirrors and Masks: The Political Space of Zapatismo." In *Spaces of Crisis and Critique: Heterotopias Beyond Foucault*. London: Bloomsbury Philosophy, 131–52.
Fiori, Nicholas. 2020. "Plantation Energy: From Slave Labor to Machine Discipline." *American Quarterly* 72(3): 559–79.
Fuller, Matthew, and Olga Goriunova. 2019. *Bleak Joys: Aesthetics of Ecology and Impossibility*. Minneapolis: University of Minnesota Press.
Glissant, Édouard. 2010. *Poetics of Relation*. Ann Arbor: University of Michigan Press.
Gomez, Pablo F. 2021. *Pieza de Indias*. London: University of London Press. https://read.uolpress.co.uk/read/new-world-objects-of-knowledge/section/2b8931c8-1f7d-4eb3-b673-0b4ae64721ae#:~:text=The%20concept%20of%20the%20pieza,yet%20been%20purchased%20or%20evaluated. Accessed October 11, 2025.
Linebaugh, Peter, and Marcus Rediker. 2000. *The Many-Headed Hydra: Sailors, Slaves, Commoners, and the Hidden History of the Revolutionary Atlantic*. London: Verso.
Marcos. 2004. "Power as a Mirror and an Image." In *¡Ya Basta! Ten Years of the Zapatista Uprising*. New York: AK Press, 153–9.
McKittrick, Katherine. 2013. "Plantation Futures." *Small Axe: A Caribbean Journal of Criticism* 17(3): 1–15. https://doi.org/10.1215/07990537-2378892.
Murray-Román, Jeannine. 2022. "Care Webs and the Creole Garden in Manthia Diawara's *Édouard Glissant: One World in Relation*." *French Screen Studies* 22(1): 77–90. https://doi.org/10.1080/26438941.2021.2003555.
Rancière, Jacques. 2006. *Hatred of Democracy*. London: Verso.
Roberts, Neil. 2015. *Freedom as Marronage*. Chicago: University of Chicago Press.
Robinson, Cedric J. 2021. *Black Marxism: The Making of the Black Radical Tradition*. London: Penguin.
Sanín-Restrepo, Ricardo, and Marinella Machado-Araujo. 2020. "The Theory of Encryption of Power: Itinerary of an idea." *Revista da Faculdade Mineira de Direito* 23(45): 18–33.
Shoatz, Russell Maroon. 2013. *Maroon the Implacable: The Collected Writings of Russell Maroon Shoatz*. Oakland, CA: PM Press.
Taylor, Alan. 2003. *American Colonies: The Settlement of North America to 1800*. Revised ed. East Rutherford: Penguin.
Whittaker, Meredith. 2023. "Origin Stories: Plantations, Computers, and Industrial Control." *Logic(s) Magazine*. https://logicmag.io/supa-dupa-skies/origin-stories-plantations-computers-and-industrial-control/. Accessed March 30, 2025.
Wilder, Gary. 2017. "The Promise of Freedom and the Predicament of Marronage: On Neil Roberts's Freedom as Marronage." Small Axe Salon. https://smallaxe.net/sxsalon/reviews/promise-freedom-and-predicament-marronage-neil-robertss-freedom-marronage. Accessed March 30, 2025.

Williams, Eric Eustace. 2022. *Capitalism and Slavery*. Penguin
Wynter, Sylvia. 1970. *Black Metamorphosis*. Unpublished manuscript.
Wynter, Sylvia. 2022. *We Must Learn to Sit Down Together and Talk About a Little Culture: Decolonising Essays, 1967–1984*. Edited by Demetrius L. Eudell. Leeds: Peepal Tree.
Yusoff, Kathryn. 2018. *A Billion Black Anthropocenes or None*. Forerunners Ideas First from the University of Minnesota Press. Minneapolis: University of Minnesota Press.

6

Iñuggusiqput (Our Way of Life): Iñupiat (Re)vitalization as Decryption

Zackary Taktuk Smith

When the earth was young, the Arctic was a warm and bountiful place. Without grating winters nor scarcity, the first peoples of the Arctic resultingly "did not work in their minds because they did not have to worry or think about how to survive." (Oquilluk 1973, 7). Despite the limitations in the uses of their faculties, people got along and were peaceful among themselves. "Even though these people did not use their minds very much, they knew how to govern themselves. There were not fights among them; and they did not know what war was" (Oquilluk 1973, 17).

This is the setting of one of the origin stories of the Iñupiat as recounted by William Oquilluk in *People of Kauwerak: Legends of the Northern Eskimo.*[1] Iñupiaq storying generally comes in two forms—unipkaaq and uqaaqtuaq (Topkok 2015). The former, unipkaaq, refers to legend stories, whereas uqaaqtuaq are personal stories. Many unipkaat (the plural for unipkaaq in the Iñupiaq language), including the one cited above, began long ago and have been transmitted from our elders and ancestors, from generation to generation. Oquilluk's accounting of the origin and history of the Iñupiat from the place-based perspective of Qawiaraġmiut (people of Qawiaraq/Kauwerak) exemplifies that of an unipkaaq. Both forms of storying for Iñupiat contain real truths, accounts, and histories, alongside metaphorical and allegorical revelation that "describe our own cultural values and show us to continue on with our own journey" (Topkok 2015, 9).

Whereas the Arctic was once without both winter and scarcity, the First Disaster marked the introduction of the unforgiving winters that we are familiar with today. Prior to the First Disaster, there was a prophet named Aungayoukuksuk who foresaw the coming extreme shift in climate and sought out a young man who was noticeably curious and inquisitive—traits uncommon for that time. Not only was this young man of an active mind, but Aungayoukuksuk too noticed his penchant toward being respectful and helpful toward others. These attributes led Aungayoukuksuk to conclude that the young man was a quality prospect to be taken under his wing to prepare for the coming disaster. Upon Aungayoukuksuk establishing a relationship with the young man, he went on to name him Ekeuhnick, which means "burns like that which was burning and went out—a glowing coal"—a foreshadowing of the coming disaster (Oquilluk 1973, 17).

Aungayoukuksuk goes on to teach Ekeuhnick many things in preparation for the First Disaster. Most notably, Aungayoukuksuk emphasizes the importance and necessity to harness the power of imagination:

> I will give you Wisdom and the Power of Imagination because your Eskimo people have none of these. You have to make every effort to teach them many things they have to learn to do to live in the changes to come. You must organize yourselves and struggle to live when this time comes. Now, the people live without problems. You will have to encourage them into a process so they will learn a new way of life. When this climate changes they will never know how to survive from destruction. (Oquilluk 1973, 19)

The power of imagination encapsulates both observation and creativity. In the context of the First Disaster, Ekeuhnick harnesses the power of imagination to navigate life when overnight the Arctic transformed from a place of warmth and leisure to frigid, unforgiving temperatures. To survive the changing landscape, Ekeuhnick not only had to harness this power to observe the now-frozen tundra but also had to teach others to deploy this power. Upon the arrival of the First Disaster, Ekeuhnick, along with the people, immediately endeavored toward observation and creative experimentation, learning how to use furs as clothing, start and maintain fires, set net for fish, build homes and boats, how to survive in the now frigid Arctic.

The deployment of the power of imagination indicates that Iñupiaq prophecy does not promise nor limit any sort of a future. For Aungayoukuksuk, he had no access to know what would come of the changing weather, no knowledge of what life would entail or what would be required to survive—this was not available to him. Rather, the emphasis on the power of imagination illuminates that Iñupiaq knowledge, worldview, and belief embody creative experimentation and adaptation across a series of changing circumstances where the future is open. Additionally, not only does the power of imagination operate as an ongoing articulation of the present into the future, but it also does not merely retreat into the past. In this way, Iñupiaq prophetic knowledge is not fixed nor omnipotent, but democratically experimental and fluid.

Whereas the First Disaster marked the transition from a warm Arctic to a frigid one when the earth was young, the Fourth and Fifth Disasters are marked by the 1918 influenza pandemic, which Oquilluk refers to as "The Terrible Sickness" alongside the cultural and language loss resultant from the Terrible Sickness and the loss of Iñupiaq lands (Oquilluk 1973, 157; Native American Rights Fund 1975). During the Terrible Sickness, missionaries and boarding schools were already present and mobilized throughout Alaska, including the Arctic North. Between boarding schools, missionaries, and the near wiping-out of entire villages because of the 1918 pandemic, there arose a crisis of belief across Iñupiaq communities. As Harold Napoleon (1996) notes, the inability for shamans to combat the pandemic resulted in the transition away from shamanism to that of Christianity. For Napoleon, that transition marked a so-called victory for Christian missionary work, whereby cultural knowledge, language, festivals, songs and dances would be banned. "The survivors embraced Christianity, abandoned Yuuyaraq (way of the human being in Yugtun, the language of the Yupik), discarded their spirit world and their ceremonies, and buried their old culture in the silence of denial" (Napoleon 1996, 13).

The Fifth Disaster, demarcated by the loss of lands that correspond to Alaska transitioning into the forty-ninth State, ultimately culminates in the Alaska Native Claims Settlement Act of 1971 (ANCSA). Just as how the Fourth Disaster corresponds to the end of shamanism and the completion of Christianity in Iñupiaq communities, the Fifth Disaster culminates in the envelopment of Iñupiat into neoliberal capitalism through the creation of land claims being held by designated Alaska Native regional corporations whereby Alaska Native peoples are classified as shareholders.

The response to both disasters operates under the global movement of decolonization, which many refer to as Indigenous (re)vitalization. Indigenous (re) vitalization consists of the movement toward returning to Indigenous language, cultural, knowledge systems, and the assertion of sovereignty and self-determination. I contend that Iñupiaq (re)vitalization is not merely a return to ways of knowing and being but too functions as active articulation within Indigenous temporality that profanes the settler State as being naught but a small chapter over the course of a history that stretches back to time immemorial. The tool of this modernity-making within the "time immemorial" of Iñupiaq temporality is the power of imagination found in the Iñupiaq prophetic tradition—whereby prophets democratically open space-time for the community to endeavor in active creation and adaptation in the face of change and disaster. The radical assertion of Iñupiaq articulation in the ruins of the profaned settler State, therefore, is not returning to an imagined past that never was, nor is it stepping outside of the contaminated space of coloniality. Rather, it is the active and modern articulation of the power of imagination that generates affirmative anti-archist lifeways that decrypt the perceived totality of the settler State.

The decryptive and anti-archist generative deployment of the power of imagination operates in three main spheres: sovereignty, religion, and law. Regarding sovereignty, I contend that the counter-articulation of an Indigenous sovereignty politicizes Indigenous culturation. Indigenous sovereignty is not a replication of colonial sovereignty, nor is it a colonial self-fetishization to return to an imagined past. Instead, Indigenous sovereignty as counter-articulation functions to decrypt the eliminatory and exceptional violence of the settler State as a citation of colonial anxiety and weakness, as opposed to strength. Moreover, although the ANCSA could easily be framed as a colonial envelopment of Alaska Native peoples in neoliberal capitalism, the collective response of the ANCSA, *Iñupiat Ilitqusiat* (Iñupiat spirit), signifies a sharp and significant return to language, culture and cultural values that operate within an Iñupiaq temporality whereby time is marked by the sequencing disasters that go as far back to when the earth was young—thereby both decrypting the neoliberal colonial entrapment of the ANCSA and profaning the settler State as only a small temporal "blip" on the Iñupiaq timescale.

Secondly, whereas Napoleon (1996) cites the shift to Christianity as a defeat of the shamanic tradition of the "old ways," I contend the move is the same as listed above. Instead of Iñupiaq defeat into Christianity through missionaries and boarding schools, finalized in the aftermath of the pandemic of 1918, I contend that the Iñupiaq prophetic traditions deploys the power of imagination into the shift into Christianity through the prophet Maniilaq. Maniilaq was a real person who was a shaman before Western contact. In his shamanic contemplations, he foresaw a singular omnipotent figure in the sky that would be brought by outsiders. Although this brought great distress to Maniilaq because he surmised the probability of unfriendly relations, he nonetheless served to spread the word for the coming change of belief. Embodied in Maniilaq, then, there are two core elements. Firstly, rather than shifting from shamanism to Christianity, the figure Maniilaq represents the convergence of the two, since it is the vehicle of shamanic knowledge that brings Christianity. Secondly, this prophetic insight occurs before colonial contact, thereby decrypting the colonial narrative of Christianity being a site of submission and consolidation of archist colonial reign. Instead, Christianity becomes a piece of the assemblage of the power of imagination of Iñupiaq articulation into modernity in an Iñupiaq temporality.

Moreover, the articulations of and relationships to Sedna, the woman of the sea exemplify Christianity as within Iñupiaq temporal framing and agency. Before Christianity, shamans would appease Sedna if animals retreated to her due to humans not acting in relationship and respect. As Christianity became more and more prevalent, Sedna would be cast as either a Christly figure or as a demonic one. Nonetheless, even as the formal practices of shamanism would fade, the animate and relational world and cosmology that informed the relationship between shamans and Sedna (alongside other iñua, spirits/owners of certain realms) remains even within the Christian worldview. Resultingly, Iñupiaq articulations vis-à-vis the power of imagination decrypt narratives of Christianity and open the animate world that requires nonanthropocentric governing frameworks that correspond to Iñupiaq values that are incommensurate with the sovereignty of the settler State and capital.

If Christianity is an expression of Iñupiaq articulation via the power of imagination within an Iñupiaq temporal framing since time immemorial that contains within it an animate and relational cosmology, then what sort of governing framework, or law, could arise in the power of imagination? I contend that the maxim often stated among Iñupiat is that of "the only real law is God's law." Being that Iñupiaq worldview and belief prior to Christianity both resulted in the survival of Iñupiat across time, and itself forecasting Christianity, Iñupiaq worldview in all its articulations are consigned by God as good. This sentiment resonates in another popular Iñupiaq maxim, "thank you God for making me Iñupiaq." The logics of Iñupiaq law operate within the cosmology of cultural values with the land, animals, and all things (since all things are animate), where thought and action are rewarded or punished by animals, land, and other animate beings, of which are consigned by God. Therefore, the only real law is that of the second commandment—all instantiations of law that operate above, or violate, the cosmological relationship in the animate world informed by respect and reciprocity are idolatrous. In result, the vehicle of the power of imagination both operates to decrypt the sovereignty, religious narrative, and legitimacy of law of the settler State, and presents the possibility of anti-archist, nonanthropocentric lifeways, otherwise known as *Iñuggusiqput* (our way of life).

On Sovereignty

The development of US federal Indian policy situates Native peoples within a liminal state of "peculiarity" (Rifkin 2009). The presentation of Indigenous peoples as peculiar illuminates the fundamental lack that they are situated in pertaining to US law. Stemming from the Marshall trilogy, Indigenous nations are rendered "domestic dependent nations" under the "wardship" of the settler State (*Cherokee Nation v. Georgia* 1828). Existing as both separate nations within the geography of the settler State, alongside being subsumed by its sovereignty relegates Indigenous nations and peoples as being neither wholly sovereign nor wholly citizen. In other words, Native tribes, being recognized as "domestic dependent nations," operate in a classification that places them outside of being fully sovereign while also denying them full incorporation into the US legal framework. Being in a position of "peculiarity" renders Indigenous nations as being incompatible with legal protection and political recognition, whereby sovereign power reduces them to an indefinite "subject to change" status. This ambiguous position of "peculiarity" of an ever-changing goalpost in the relationship between law, sovereignty, Native nations and the settler State opens Native peoples to what Agamben (2005) refers to as the "state of exception."

The settler State not only regulates Native peoples through exceptional violence from the negative cleavage of the status of "peculiarity" in US policy but also deploys the ideological apparatus of interpellation. Whereas the former seeks to eliminate Indigeneity through extra/nonjudicial violence, the latter reinforces colonial power structures whereby all Indigenous claims of land rights, self-government, and cultural expression are conditional upon State-defined norms, and inculcates a relationship of dependency to the settler State. This reification whereby the settler State accommodates Indigenous identity claims in ways that ultimately reinforce settler power while obscuring Indigenous dispossession is what Coulthard (2014) refers to as the "politics of recognition." Not only does the "politics of recognition" circumscribe Indigenous claims into the prerogatives of settler State hegemony, but it too is a creative force. As Foucault reminds us, "one never governs a state, a territory, or a political structure. Those whom one governs are people, individuals, or groups" (2004, 122). The "politics of recognition" then is the biopolitical act of reconstituting the subjecthood of Indigenous peoples into the bowels of the settler State. Channeling Fanon, Coulthard continues:

> Where colonial rule is not reproduced through force alone, the maintenance of settler-state hegemony requires the production of what he [Fanon] calls "colonized subjects": namely, the production of the specific modes of colonial thought, desire, and behavior that implicitly or explicitly commit the colonized to the types of

> practices and subject positions that are required for their continued domination. (2014, 16)

Both the biopolitical subject-making of "the politics of recognition" and the procedural obfuscation of the status of "peculiarity" in Indian law is what Sanín-Restrepo refers to as "encryption." Encryption explains how power structures and juridical systems obscure their actual operations, embedding them behind layers of ideology, procedure, and language. To encrypt is to determine "what and who makes up the world, or how can the world be … [Encryption] devour[s] all reality and permanently reflect[s] the image of an unchangeable and insurmountable state of things" (Sanín-Restrepo 2018, x). In other words, encryption deploys an invisible hegemonic violence that not only imposes an ordering of fate—demarcating what is even possible—but also constitutes who is even possible. Encryption thus necessitates a "solidification" of power that eliminates alternative modes of being (Sanín-Restrepo 2016, 2018).

Moreover, the transition from genocidal violence to the politics of recognition is not a ceasing of eliminatory violence, but rather encrypts the active, current, and changing dynamics of eliminatory violence into a narrative of past-tense encounters and histories that have been addressed and ameliorated within the parameters of settler governance and apology performance. For Wolfe (2006), settler colonialism is inseparable from eliminatory violence; it is a structure (that is always restructuring). Whereas the settler State seeks to encrypt via the narration of colonialism as a past-tense, singular event, the logic of elimination discursively ebbs and flows discretely in both the politics of recognition as assimilation and the hidden matrix of the state of exception as displacement, legal erasure, and genocide.

If encryption serves as the settler-colonial frame that determines who and what are possible within a hidden hegemonic violence that is continually (re)structured, then archism is the maintenance of this violence as sovereignty. For Martel, archism is "a system of violence and hierarchy that is so ubiquitous in the world that it does not—normally—even have a name" (2023, 1). He continues, "Archism is a form of projection of authority, the assertion of a deep, ontological basis for power that is in fact based on nothing at all" (2). Archism, embedded within hegemonic normalcy through encryption, perpetuates settler State sovereignty, which relies on violence because it is ultimately rooted in nothing. This is evident in US Indian law and policy, where the Marshall trilogy is built upon the foundational fiction of the "Doctrine of Discovery," whereby Pope Alexander VI granted European nations the right to "discovered" lands in the name of Christendom (Agtuca et al. 2023). Because archism lacks a genuine foundation, it must perpetuate violence via the peculiar status of Native peoples to maintain and sustain itself.

For Martel, the assimilative recognition of Indigenous peoples into the apparatus of the settler-colonial State functions as absorption into settler temporality. Through performative participation in the entrenchment of settler sovereignty, Indigenous peoples are presented with a guarantee of teleological progress and improvement. Martel argues that archism holds that "The future is a kind of (false) promise that no matter how terrible things may seem in the present, there is a plan, a grand scheme that ensures that everything will work out just fine. The future is a guarantee and a stopgap to prevent any sense that archism is itself unjust and that it must be upended" (2023, 1). Pacification into settler temporality thus articulates the structural eliminatory violence of US federal Indian law and policy as a necessary element of the supposed arc of progress framed by encryption. Archism, then, is the justificatory trap of encryption that assists in the maintenance of remaining hidden the supraviolence of the state of exception via the distribution of false promises, in contradistinction to Iñupiaq prophecy where there is no promise or guarantee in post-disaster future. Rather, the unpromised future is continually negotiated and expressed in the means of the power of imagination.

If encryption frames what is possible, archism articulates it. Archism, in its liberal variant, even acknowledges its own role and complicity in colonial violence, gender violence, institutional racism, and economic exploitation, but simultaneously asserts that "there is no alternative." It legitimizes itself through the logic of "T.I.N.A." (There Is No Alternative), seizing temporality by positioning itself as the only viable framework while offering empty promises of future resolution. Archism thus justifies and perpetuates present inequities as the "best possible outcome" while ensuring that alternatives remain unthinkable. In this way, archism articulates sovereignty as both an inevitability and an empty construct; it is the hierarchization and colonization of time.

In the face of the fated parameters of encryption inscribed by archist sovereignty, what does it mean to invoke Indigenous sovereignty? Jodi Byrd proclaims that "If there is one unifying principle that the field of Indigenous studies asserts as foundational, inviolable, and central, it is the concept of sovereignty" (2020, 501). Despite the Western, colonial, and religious attributes of (Westphalian) sovereignty (Agamben 2011; Foucault 2007; Martel 2012; Byrd 2020), the assertion of Indigenous sovereignty, rather than replicating or mirroring Westphalian sovereignty, is both a refusal against settler governance predicated upon elimination, inferiority, and racialization, and an act of affirmation of Indigenous political traditions that are inexplicably connected to land and place. This connective affirmation is what Glen Coulthard refers to as *grounded normativity*, which means "the modalities of Indigenous land-connected practices and longstanding experiential knowledge that inform and structure our ethical engagements with the world and our relationships with human and nonhuman over time" (2014, 13). To invoke Indigenous sovereignty then is to assert, defend, and embody "as we have always done" (Simpson 2017, 31). The land-based custom and practices within Indigenous worldview encapsulates a nonanthropocentric, animate, relational world where all things are given agency (Kovach 2021). Just as Wolfe (2006) begins his essay as stating that "land is life," "mni Wiconi" translates to "water is life" in Lakota (Dietrich and Knopf 2023, 19). Moreover, it signifies that life is alive. Not only does this serve to illuminate the animate interconnectedness that informs Indigenous worldview, but than being in "grounded normativity" necessarily means recognizing that Indigenous lifeways are both incommensurate with, and rivals against, the settler State.

The invocation of Indigenous sovereignty is not an either–or, a battle of totality between a singular existence of Indigenous sovereignty, or settler sovereignty. As Audra

Simpson (2014) describes, Indigenous sovereignty coexists with settler sovereignty. Simpson ultimately describes the possibility of a nested Indigenous sovereignty existed within settler sovereignty not as a "cartography of refusal" against colonial recognition informed by "the prior experience of sovereignty" that continues into the present (2014, 33). Indigenous sovereignty therefore functions as a point of refusal, creating pockets of resistance against the settler State that contains the sovereign expression of time immemorial.

Indigenous sovereignty, rather than simply exuding a nostalgia that seeks to return to a time prior to colonial contact, is instead a wrestling-away of the hegemony and monopoly of time and history. That is, Indigenous sovereignty (re)situates grounded normativity that reconstitutes history from the Indigenous temporal position. It is a decentering of colonial encryption whereby the settler State organizes and periodizes events and accounts that reify sovereignty as archism. This is what Rifkin (2017) refers to as "temporal sovereignty." In other words, temporal sovereignty refers to the ability of Indigenous peoples to assert and maintain their own temporal frameworks, challenging the dominance of settler-colonial impositions of a linear, progressive time that Martel (2023) outlines as a false promise of archism.

But, why sovereignty? For Audra Simpson (2014), the assertion of sovereignty from the position of Indigeneity is to combat sovereign power's attempt to depoliticize Indigenous peoples through techniques of disciplinary control. Jodi Byrd attests to this, "the technologies of biopolitics that have defined the twentieth and twenty-first centuries subject those peoples to settler-colonial rule by depoliticizing them into a population subjected to control" (2014, 134). In other words, to specifically invoke sovereignty is to assert the politization of Indigenous struggles for land and self-determination. The assertion of Indigenous sovereignty contains a paradox other than merely reconstituting sovereignty as a word game. Whereas Simpson (2014) asserts Indigenous sovereignty as a politics of refusal, refusal still denotes the necessity of recognition, such as the example of the use of Haudenosaunee passports rather than Canadian ones.

In contrast, for Turner (2006), rather than refusal, the work toward Indigenous sovereignty requires recognition. Fully realizing the power of encryption of the State, he seeks to blast through encryptive constraints through the savvy cadre of "Word Warriors," specially trained Indigenous peoples who can adeptly translate Indigenous modalities into the settler State for positive policy outcomes that assist in the practical improvement of Native communities. For Turner, there is still hope in the assimilative allure of liberal pluralism in the domain of recognition.

Nonetheless, the tension that this presents is that, as both Martel (2012, 2014) and Sanín-Restrepo (2016, 2018) illuminate is that there is no being outside of power, and it is no different for the pursuits of Indigenous sovereignty. To constrain the pursuits of Indigenous self-determination purely through the bowels of settler-colonial institutions, only serves to reify the hidden power of encryption, thereby functioning within the container of possibility set forth by the settler State within the temporal formation of coloniality; to operate purely into refusal without engaging in recognition risks being rendered obsolete and reifying coloniality through nonparticipation. Rather than augmenting these positions against each other as an either–or, Rifkin claims that they are supplemental to each other.

> A politics of refusal opens room for acknowledging the existence of collective forms of being and becoming that give everyday shape and substance to Indigenous peoplehood but that do not mirror state frames and aims. However, such a politics supplements rather than substitutes for the overdetermined role of official Native political institutions in mediating colonial imperatives, in serving as a site of contestation over what will count as governance, and in translating alternative Native norms as policy. (2017, 184)

Indigenous sovereignty is simultaneously the site of the politization of cultural resurgence as grounded normativity that oscillates as a politics of refusal in which to engage in the politics of recognition of the settler State without subsummation. If Indigenous sovereignty is the site of a politicized resurgence that (re)connects with Indigenous pathways that decenters settler temporality and historical narrative, then Indigenous sovereignty is the agent of decryption that reveals the State as archist.

Archism, for Martel, "is a system of control that is eternally insecure about its right to exist whereby it resorts to violence in order to reassert its power over and over again" (2023, 2). Being founded on nothing other than violence, archist sovereignty is profaned as a sign of weakness, rather than strength. Moreover, in *Means Without End*, Agamben states, "Sovereignty, therefore, is the guardian who prevents the undecidable threshold between violence and right, nature and language, from coming to light" (2000, 113). However, upon the decryption of settler coloniality the "mythic violence" of archism illuminates that sovereignty is empty (Agamben 1995). In the case of Indigenous peoples in the United States, the "peculiar" position within US policy is reflective of the archist mythic violence of the sovereign State; rather than being a site of strength, the settler State is confounded with anxiety pertaining to nations existing within its geographic boundary (Rifkin 2009).

Indigenous sovereignty, having the power to decrypt the archism of the sovereign State, opens space-time to other possibilities, of which Martel (2023) refers to as "anarchism." Rather than invoking the Western tradition of anarchism, Martel invokes anarchism as "every other practice in the world, every other way for human beings to arrange themselves politically, socially, and economically[2]" (2023, 2).

Finding inspiration in Graeber and Wengrow's seminal book *The Dawn of Everything* (2021), the declaration of anarchism as other possibilities that aren't archism is not utopian nor a fetish. Just as how Rifkin, in expounding upon an Indigenous temporal sovereignty, states that "Native frames of reference are neither inherently liberatory nor transcendent." Martel doesn't denote the declaration of anarchism as the end of time or the human struggle. Simply, in decrypting the archism of the settler State, in a centered Indigenous temporality, we always have a *chance* to constitute something other-than. Anarchism, then, is the recognition that we always have the chance to change our circumstances, contradictory to the maxim of neoliberal coloniality, "there is no alternative."

The ANCSA exemplifies the complexities of Indigenous sovereignty whereby archist settler-colonial expansion forces Indigenous nations to jump into "encryptive" negotiation to assert the right to exist in the face of elimination. With the Alaska Statehood Act of 1958, and the subsequent passage of Alaska becoming the forty-ninth State in 1959, Indigenous communities were not included in the process of land selection after statehood (Grinage 2024). Unlike the lower-48, Alaska Native communities did not have established treaties with the United States. With the explicit exclusion of being rendered as "bare life," Indigenous communities of Alaska rapidly organized, establishing a variety of local and regional organizations to force the State and federal government to allow Indigenous peoples to maintain their land such as the Arctic Slope Native Association, alongside a statewide organization, The Alaska Federation of Natives (Grinage 2024). Ultimately, the discovery of oil in Prudhoe Bay in 1968 prompted the State and federal government to resolve the question of land claims.

The ANCSA was enacted to facilitate oil development at Prudhoe Bay, which is situated on Iñupiaq lands. The act extinguished all future Native land claims in exchange for approximately 40 million acres—about 11 percent of Alaska's total land—alongside $1 billion in compensation (McClanahan 2006; Grinage 2024). Additionally, Indigenous land claims and compensation were funneled into twelve Alaska Native regional corporations, further embedding Indigenous governance within settler-colonial legal and economic structures. Through colonial recognition, ANCSA's neoliberal framework further encrypted Indigenous existence within corporate structures, reducing landholdings and entrenching capitalist dependencies. For Iñupiat, transitioning to neoliberal capitalism via incorporation signified a stark shift in the relationship to land—that of being of-the-land, to that of for-the-land (Coulthard 2014). In this transition, the assertion of Iñupiaq sovereignty became entangled with incorporation and the pursuit of profit through the sale of oil extraction rights, ultimately becoming absorbed into the framework of archist sovereignty.

Being thrust into neoliberal capitalism via the ANCSA, after having already survived the ravages of the pandemic of 1918 that nearly eliminated entire communities, alongside the experience of BIA boarding schools, the Iñupiat have navigated and survived exceptional eliminatory violence after exceptional eliminatory violence. Despite the issues, challenges, and complexities that go with such a rapid transition in Western corporate neoliberal capitalism, Indigenous organizing and advocacy that led up to the ANCSA is an historical achievement.

Nonetheless, the ramifications of the ANCSA on Iñupiaq communities was not insignificant. As Klausner and Foulks (1982) account, the large singular influx of money and capital, alongside being thrust into capitalistic labor led to a significant transition of lifestyle that departed from the Iñupiaq worldview and cultural values to the Western. Resultantly, increased rates of alcohol and suicide ravaged communities.

To confront and address these ills that emanated from the stark transition into neoliberal capitalism, John Schaeffer (president of the NANA regional corporation at the time) and others created Iñupiat Iḷitqusiat (Iñupiat Spirit, otherwise known as the Spirit Movement). The Iñupiat Iḷitqusiat movement emerged as a response to the sociocultural crises wrought by the ANCSA and corporatization. Community leaders traveled from village to village, warning of the spiritual devastation caused by disconnection from Iñupiat values leading to increased suicide, substance abuse, and fears of intergenerational cultural loss (Schaeffer and Christensen 2010). In response, the movement called for a return to Iñupiaq language, values, and worldview. Coulthard (2014) describes this process as desubjectification—rejecting the colonial State's subject-making apparatus and reconstituting identity through Indigenous frameworks. Whereas the goal of the ANCSA was the elimination of Indigeneity through assimilation as incorporation, the response became its opposite, instead proclaiming the necessity to reconstituting what it means to be Iñupiaq through cultural values and language.

Despite the very real struggles that are negotiated in the post-ANCSA matrix of power, sovereignty, and subjecthood, the neoliberal inclusion of Iñupiat as corporate bodies functions as a failure of encryption evidenced by the movement of (re) vitalizing Iñupiaq language, culture, and worldview catalyzed the spirit movement Iñupiat Iḷitqusiat (Schaeffer and Christensen 2010). To be reconstituted in Iñupiaq culture, values, and language is to be in the Iñupiaq temporal frame that accounts for these phenomena. In Iñupiaq (re)vitalization, the return to story functions as the acknowledgment of the "Indigenous longue duree, the precolonial that tends to be lost in postcolonial projections" (Clifford 2013, 64). Resultingly, the settler State is profaned as naught but a small arc in Indigenous time that stretches time immemorial. Clifford continues, "Thus Indigenous claims always transcend colonial disruptions ... we were here before all that; we are still here; we will make a future here" (2013, 64).

Although the ANCSA sought to incorporate Alaska Native peoples into the assimilative allure of the settler State and neoliberal capital, the Iñupiat Iḷitqusiat movement evidences Indigenous (re)vitalization as a direct allegorical signpost from the attempt of assimilation toward the possibility of anti-archist pathways via utilizing the power of imagination as Iñupiaq articulation of cultural values, language, and custom in current conditions. Moreover, even as the ANCSA has at least perceptibly and partially succeeded in its encryptive endeavor, it simultaneously creates an unintended space of articulations of anti-archist attributes of Indigenous sovereignty from within the corporate setting, resulting in anti-archist articulations hiding in plain sight, avoiding the eliminatory violence of the settler State that misreads the articulations as assimilative.

Religion

Iñupiaq temporality, in (re)claiming storying, it opens the Iñupiaq prophetic tradition that functions as an Iñupiaq articulation of Iñupiaq modernity. It refuses being absorbed as passive participants of a Western modernity whereby Indigenous identity is relegated as something past tense that needs to be "updated" into Western modernity. Iñupiaq prophecy as temporal articulation centers *power of imagination* as a functionary of Martel's concept of anarchism. The power of imagination, stemming from the origin story *The People of Kauwerak* (Oquilluk 1973), is a mapping of critical thinking and adaptation skills that the prophet Aungayoukuksuk bestowed unto Ekeuhnick. The power of imagination is the temporal tool of articulation that centers change and adaptation over time from the positionality of being Iñupiaq. The power of imagination is not a hierarchized tool for a select few, but rather open to anyone. Even though Aungayoukuksuk sought out Ekeuhnick, he (Ekeuhnick) was still nonetheless responsible for introducing the power of imagination to his community. Secondly, the power of imagination is a creative force, rather than the tool of prefigured fated. Iñupiaq prophesizing signals changes to come but does not consign how the power of imagination must be delivered. Iñupiaq prophets therefore gesture what is to come, but without the knowledge of answers to navigate and address. Prophecy then functions as the forecasting of change where everyone is empowered with the power of imagination to creatively (re)constitute Iñupiaqness in each circumstance. Iñupiaq prophecy and the power of imagination then are a means-oriented creative force that is the modality to operate in an open and nonfated future.

Maniilaq was an Iñupiaq prophet and visionary from northwest Alaska who was believed to have lived in the early nineteenth century (Haile 2003). He is known for his spiritual teachings, predictions, and advocacy for changes in traditional ways of life. Not only did Maniilaq predict the arrival of new technologies, such as ships and airplanes, well before Western contact, but he too proclaimed that shamanism was on the decline, predicting the coming of Christianity. Of the latter Maniilaq was accounted as replying to a question as to whether he himself was a shaman since he (Maniilaq) contacted a spirit. "No, I am not a shaman … My grandfather, who dresses in white and lives in the sky with his followers, joins his mind with my mind to reveal the truths about the present and the future" (Haile 2003, 121). Regardless of his self-affiliation, he nonetheless embodies both for he deploys shamanic knowledge for his Christianly insights.

Despite the destruction, pain, and trauma that the missionaries and boarding schools wrought to Iñupiat, the storying of the prophet Maniilaq centers an Iñupiaq temporality to where it is from within the articulation of and centering of Iñupiaq storying and worldview that brings Iñupiat to a modernity on their terms, as opposed to being merely participants in settler modernity whereby "savages" are "saved" by the West. Of the importance of Maniilaq as a figure in the articulation of Iñupiaq temporal sovereignty Paul Ongtooguk (2016) states:

> Maniilaq prepared people for the arrival of the missionaries. The missionaries wrote in their journals of their surprise that some of the Native people not only expected them but knew that they came from a new religion. No matter the explanation for Maniilaq's vision and power—he was an extraordinary person with an extraordinary impact. In the typical textbook history of this time in Alaska the Europeans and the Americans are usually the actors, or the doers. The Russians save Native lives with the vaccine and recruit more Natives into the Orthodox church. The Americans sail up the coast, develop trade and introduce new technology. In contrast, Alaska Natives are described as passive societies. Their role

> as victims of terrible disease is the most powerful image of them. Maniilaq's life demonstrate that at least some Alaska Native societies during this period were not passive. People were aware that change was coming no matter what and they were actively preparing for change. Some traditions were questioned and sometimes overthrown. The all-important traditional values of harmony, balance, and sharing continued though people prepared for contact with "outsiders."

The figure of Maniilaq does not serve to substitute one for the other. That is, Iñupiaq worldview that comprises of relational animacy and place-based spirituality, knowledge, and values, does not get cast aside. Rather, the Iñupiaq worldview is maintained in the paradigm of Iñupiaq Christianity for it is perceived as being given by God for Iñupiat to survive and thrive in the Arctic. This sentiment is found is the popular phrase "thank you god for making me Iñupiaq."

In *Inuit Shamanism and Christianity*, Laugrand and Oosten examine the complex interactions between Inuit[3] spiritual beliefs and Christianity. They explore how Inuit shamanism adapted and transformed under the influence of Christian missionaries. This convergence illuminates that Inuit/Iñupiat did not simply replace one with the other but ebbed and flowed through adaptation and negotiation.

One significant encounter with Inuit Cosmology and Christianity can be found in meaning-making around the image of Sedna, the sea woman. Firstly, Sedna had many names, and in different communities took on different permutations, so the specificity of Sedna is not necessarily important as much as the affiliation and general meaning-making around her character. There are varying accounts of who she was and what she represented, but she was an image often framed within Christianity during the time of transition:

> Later, Sedna was identified with Satanasi, the devil, by missionaries as well as by Inuit. Aksaajuq from Panniqtuuq related: "From what I know, when religion came, missionaries would say that she is the devil, Satanasi. Even the shaman would say that afterwards." The sea woman was always considered dangerous and ambiguous, but she has also been identified with Jesus(i), as on a tape by Donald Suluk from Arviat. (Laugrand and Oosten 2022, 149)

So, the image of Sedna is ambiguous, but nonetheless is framed in extremity within Christian context—either as Christly, or as satanic.

This ambiguity could be reframed as holding a duality, both Christly and satanic. "But while [Sedna] gives mankind all these good things, created out of her own finger joints, it is she also who sends nearly all the misfortunes that are regarded by the dwellers of the earth as the worst or direst" (Laugrand and Oosten 2022, 149). Sedna here is thusly both a creator that helps sustain life and simultaneously associated with the worst of most dire things. Accounts detail further, "She was a person who was deceiving people. We didn't really believe in Nuliajuk ... But when you understand the techniques of survival, Nuliajuk [Sedna] was the one who could assist us" (Laugrand and Oosten 2022, 149). Sedna is resultingly a complex figure. But, nonetheless, she is an image affiliated with both the heavenly and the hellish, both of deception and that of practical assistance of subsistence. But to access the practical help of Sedna, it required shamanistic intervention.

If the people were "unhappy or abusive toward wildlife, the wildlife [would] move away from the camp. The animals would flee to Sedna's shed where they were so numerous, they seemed like maggots" (Laugrand and Oosten 2022, 157). To retrieve the animals, the shaman would have to go get them. The shaman situates themselves at the house was the ritual is to occur alongside establishing connection with the domain of Sedna.

In plunging to Sedna's domain required many things and complete a variety of obstacles. The main task, and main difficulty, however, was appeasing Sedna herself after completing the varying tasks to even arrive:

> When the shaman enters the house, he at once sees Takanakapsaluk, who, as a sign of anger, is sitting with her back to the lamp and with her back to all the animals in the pool. Her hair hangs down loose all over one side of her face, a tangled, untidy mass hiding her eyes, so that she cannot see. It is the misdeeds and offenses committed by men which gather in dirt and impurity over her body. All the foul emanations from the sins of mankind nearly suffocate her. As the shaman moves towards her, Isarrataitsoq, her father, tries to grasp hold of him. He thinks it is a dead person come to expiate offenses before passing on to the Land of the Dead, but the shaman must then at once cry out: "I am flesh and blood" and then he will not be hurt, and he must now grasp Takanakapsaluk by one should and turn her face towards the lamp and towards the animals, and stroke her hair, the hair she has been unable to comb out herself, because she has no fingers; and he must smooth it and comb it, and as soon as she is calmer, he must say: ... "those up above can no longer help the seals up by grasping their forefinger." (Laugrand and Oosten 2022, 158–9)

The image of Sedna, then, can be viewed as fundamentally human, but imbued with the power of an iñua (spirit/entities of certain realms). She is consumed with images and feelings of great pain and harm. With such pain, it is also accounted that shamans need to remove the cause of her pain or else she will continue to withhold sea mammals. Her pain too is bound up with the effect of human action. "The sea woman could not see when the hair covered her eyes. But even though she had only one eye, she would be aware of all of the transgressions human beings made ... Any sins committed by the people give pain to her blind eye, and the angakok has to remove the cause of the pain" (Laugrand and Oosten 2022, 162).

Sedna was not merely appeased however; she was also contended with. Sedna would be accounted as interfering in a variety of ways, whether it be catching her by hook, or harpooning her. So, relationship with iñua were active, revolved around moral phenomena, and often had to be wrestled with.

Both the prophet Maniilaq and Sedna exemplify that the shift into Christianity isn't a break from the past, but a molding of the past into the present contextualized in

Christianity. Even though shamanism isn't practiced anymore, both Inuit and Iñupiat maintain dynamic, active, relational engagements with place that is filled with animacy and agency. Even amidst the archism of settler State sovereignty and the proliferation of Christianity, Iñupiaq worldview, which is grounded in nonanthropocentric cosmology, is continually sustained and rearticulated with agency that gestures toward a non-archist conception of governance that includes active animate agents as co-constitutive parts of authority.

Law

How might Iñupiaq articulation deploy the *power of imagination* to augment a nonarchist governance framework under the banner of Iñupiaq sovereignty? The answer might be contained in a popular maxim among Iñupiat, "*the only real law is God's law*."

If the State is a colonial imposition that Iñupiat were forced to contend with for the purposes of survival, and the (re)vitalization of language, culture, and history fortifies the sentiments of an Iñupiaq sovereignty that functions to profane the settler-colonial State, then the State is revealed as a false idol, a mythic instantiation—a violation of the second commandment. This is what Walter Benjamin refers to as mythic violence—the violence that establishes and maintains law in and through violence—or archism. As the theory of encryption informs us, mythic violence functions as an imposition of fate that operates as a container for what and who are even possible.

If mythic violence is law-making, then divine violence is law-destroying. Benjamin, being a Jewish theorist, God does not necessarily return as Redeemer, but rather God is involved in the world as a conduit to where *things are removed*. That is, divine violence is the removal, or the reveal, of the falsity of power:

> Dissolution of legal violence stems from the guilt of more natural life, which consigns the living, innocent and unhappy, to a retribution that "expiates" the guilt of mere life—and doubtless also purifies the guilty, not of guilt, however, but of law. For with mere life, the rule of law over the living ceases. (Benjamin 1996, 250)

Mythic violence is then of its own end, for its own sake, tautologically violent; whereas divine violence expiates humanity form law, that form of mythic violence. "Mythic violence is bloody power over mere life for its own sake; divine violence is pure power over all life for the sake of the living. The first demands sacrifice; the second accepts it" (Benjamin 1996, 250).

This account of divine violence is inherently anarchist. A simple retort of such anarchy would be the notion of "all kill all," the stereotype of anarchy. A response can be found in the commandment *Thou Shalt Not Kill* because there is no known judgment within the commandment. Benjamin details this:

> This commandment precedes the deed, just as God was "preventing" the deed. But just as it may not be fear of punishment that enforces obedience, the injunction

> becomes inapplicable, incommensurable, once the deed is accomplished. No judgement of the deed can be derived from the commandment. And so neither the divine judgement nor the grounds for this judgment can be known in advance. Those who base a condemnation of all violent killing of one person by another on the commandment are therefore mistaken. It exists not as a criterion of judgment, but as a guideline for the actions of persons or communities who have to wrestle with it in solitude and, in exceptional cases, to take on themselves the responsibility of ignoring it. (1996, 250)

The notion of divine violence and wrestling in solitude when to obey and betray the commandments fits within the nexus of Shamanism and Christianity. Within conceptions of iñua, the relationships were not crowned by fate. That is, they were not sanctioned to any particular law. This notion is confirmed by an Iñupiaq elder, "In those days people did not know anything about going to jail. There were no written laws" (Lee, Sampson, and Mendenhall 1990, 147). Peter Aaquuraq Atoruk continues this notion:

> We are talking here about Eskimo laws. They were like the laws enforced by game wardens today. Long ago people abided by these laws. The difference was that when a person broke a law he was not punished or held up as an example as is done now. If a person did not follow the laws about animals in those days, he brought bad luck upon himself. If he killed an animal just for fun of it, he just brought trouble upon himself. Sometimes, the hunter himself even became disabled because the law then was embedded in everyone's mind. Just as we were taught long ago not to take hunting lightly, we too should teach the young men today. (Lee, Sampson, and Mendenhall 1990, 147)

This conception of law is bound within moral truisms within an animate and relational cosmos. If one acts outside of the moral code of the cosmos, iñua would respond accordingly, but it is not circumscribed with fate or punishment like with mythic violence. There is consequence, but one has the agency to *wrestle in solitude* where to betray or honor the moral valuations ascribed to the sky, earth, and sea, as was described in the harpooning of Sedna. Inuit cosmological law, if we were to call it as such, is not tautologically violent like that of mythic law.

Similarly, despite the neocolonial dynamics of Pentecostalism and Evangelism in Inuit communities, there is still a strand of opportunity, being that Inuit take these conceptions and comport them within their history, culture, and values. A strand that exists within Benjamin's conception of divine violence, Inuit cosmological law, and Christianity is the wrestling with the following or betrayal of moral valuation in solitude. In the Pentecostal and Evangelical rendition, it exists as the notion of the transcendental personal experience. And, in those experiences, being wholly subjective must be wrestled with double to determine whether it is a holy or satanic intervention, of which is not always clear.

The power of imagination is thus a functionary of pure means, which functions as the opposite of law as mythic violence. Pure means is, well, means oriented, of no end. It is the practice of embodiment of Martel's notion of anarchism. The power of imagination functions as pure means for that it does not dictate how to act in the future but rather is an open and democratic process for the opportunity to participate in Iñupiaq articulation. In the profaned ruins of the settler-colonial State whereby Indigenous sovereignty decrypts the hidden archism of sovereignty through its anxious performance of mythic violence, the act of Iñupiaq articulation that disrupts settler-colonial space-time enters the scene as the always possibility of creating alternative forms of governance that are nonanthropocentric, relational, and affirm all animate life—Iñuggusiqput.

Notes

1 The word "Eskimo" will only be used as it is referenced in the literature. Rather than using the words of archism and colonization, the Indigenous people of the North Slope and North West Arctic refer to themselves as Iñupiat (plural), Iñupiak (dual), or Iñupiaq (singular). Iñupiat are also Inuit, which include Indigenous peoples of the Canadian Arctic, Greenland, and the Yupik peoples of the Chukchi Peninsula in Russia and western and southwestern Alaska.

2 Although Martel references "anarchism" in the cited essay, he has since preferred using "anti-archist."

3 This study focuses on Canadian Inuit. Despite differences, there are large commonalities in beliefs with Iñupiaq. For the purposes of this inquiry, I will be weaving Canadian Inuit and Iñupiaq beliefs together.

References

Agamben, Giorgio. 1995. *Homo Sacer: Sovereign Power and Bare Life.* Translated by Daniel Heller-Roazen. Stanford, CA: Stanford University Press.

Agamben, Giorgio. 2000. *Means Without Ends.* Translated by Vincenzo Binetti and Cesare Casarino. Theory Out of Bounds. Minneapolis: University of Minnesota Press.

Agamben, Giorgio. 2005. *State of Exception.* Translated by Kevin Attell. Chicago: University of Chicago Press.

Agamben, Giorgio. 2011. *The Kingdom and the Glory: For a Theological Genealogy of Economy and Government.* Translated by Lorenzo Chiesa. Stanford, CA: Stanford University Press.

Agtuca, Jacqueline, Michelle Demmert, Tami Truett Jerue, and Debra O'Gara. 2023. *Alaska Native Women: Ending the Violence, Reclaiming a Sacred Status.* Fairbanks: Alaska Native Women's Resource Center.

Barker, Joanne, ed. 2017. *Critically Sovereign: Indigenous Gender, Sexuality, and Feminist Studies.* Durham, NC: Duke University Press.

Benjamin, Walter. 1996. *Selected Writings: Volume 1, 1913–1926.* Edited by Marcus Bullock and Michael W. Jennings. Cambridge: Belknap Press of Harvard University.

Byrd, Jodi A. 2020. "Indigenous Futures Beyond the Sovereignty Debate." In *The Cambridge History of Native American Literature.* Cambridge: Cambridge University Press, 501–18.

Clifford, James. 2013. *Returns: Becoming Indigenous in the Twenty-First Century.* Cambridge: Harvard University Press.
Coulthard, Glen. 2014. *Red Skin, White Mask: Rejecting the Colonial Politics of Recognition.* Minneapolis: University of Minnesota Press.
Dietrich, Rene, and Kerstin Knopf, eds. 2023. *Biopolitics, Geopolitics, Life: Settler States and Indigenous Presence.* Durham, NC: Duke University Press.
Foucault, Michel. 2007. *Security, Territory, Population: Lectures at the College de France 1977–1978.* Edited by Michel Senellart, Francois Ewald, Alessandro Fontana, and Arnold I. Davidson. London: Picador.
Haile, Sarah. 2003. *Maniilaq: Eskimo Prophet.* Springville, UT: Bonneville.
Klausner, Samuel Z., and Edward F. Foulks. 1982. *Eskimo Capitalists: Oil, Politics, and Alcohol.* Totowa, NJ: Allanheld, Osmun.
Kovach, Margaret. 2021. *Indigenous Methodologies: Characteristics, Conversations, and Contexts.* Toronto: University of Toronto Press.
Laugrand, Frederic, and Jarich Oosten. 2022. *Inuit Shamanism and Christianity: Transitions and Transformations in the Twentieth Century.* Montreal: McGill-Queen's University Press.
Lee, Linda, Ruthie Sampson, and Hannah Mendenhall, eds. 1990. *Lore of the Iñupiat: The Elders Speak.* Vol. 2. Fairbanks: Alaska Native Language Center, University of Alaska.
Martel, James. 2012. *Divine Violence: Walter Benjamin and the Eschatology of Sovereignty.* Oxfordshire: Routledge.
Martel, James. 2014. *The One and Only Law: Walter Benjamin and the Second Commandment.* Ann Arbor: University of Michigan Press.
Martel, James. 2023. "Anarchism Is the Only Future." *Philosophies* 8(113): 1–10.
McClanahan, A. J. 2006. Alaska Native Corporations: Sakuuktugut, "We Are Working Incredibly Hard." Anchorage: CIRI Foundation.
Napoleon, Harold. 1996. *Yuuyaraq: The Way of the Human Being.* Edited by Eric Madsen. Fairbanks: Alaska Native Knowledge Network.
Native American Rights Fund. 1975. "'The Fifth Disaster': The Colonization of the North Slope." https://narf.org/nill/documents/nlr/nlr3-1.pdf.
Ongtooguk, Paul. 2016. "Maniilaq: Preparing for Change." Alaska's Cultures. https://akhistory.lpsd.com/articles/article.php?artID=279.
Oquilluk, William A. 1973. *The People of Kauwerak: Legends of the Northern Eskimo.* Edited by Laurel L. Bland. Anchorage: AMU Press.
Patkotak Grinage, Beverly. 2024. *Inupiat Nunanat: The Epic Story of Inupiat Self-Determination.* Self-published.
Rifkin, Mark. 2009. "Indigenizing Agamben: Rethinking Sovereignty in Light of the 'Peculiar' Status of Native Peoples." Cultural Critique 73(1): 88–124.
Rifkin, Mark. 2017. *Beyond Settler Time: Temporal Sovereignty and Indigenous Self-Determination.* Durham, NC: Duke University Press.
Sanín-Restrepo, Ricardo. 2016. *Decolonizing Democracy: Power in a Solid State.* London: Rowman and Littlefield.
Sanín-Restrepo, Ricardo, ed. 2018. *Decrypting Power.* London: Rowman and Littlefield.
Schaeffer, John, and John Christensen. 2010. "Iñupiat Ilitqusiat: To Save Our Land and Our People." *Journal of Indigenous Studies* 35(2): 123–45.
Simpson, Audra. 2014. *Mohawk Interruptus: Political Life across the Borders of Settler States.* Durham, NC: Duke University Press.

Simpson, Leanne Betasamosake. 2017. *As We Have Always Done: Indigenous Freedom Through Radical Resistance*. Minneapolis: University of Minnesota Press.
Topkok, Charles Asiqłuq. 2015. "Iñupiat Ilitqusiat: Inner Views of Our Iñupiaq Values." PhD diss., University of Alaska Fairbanks.
Turner, Dale. 2006. *This Is Not a Peace Pipe: Towards a Critical Indigenous Philosophy*. Toronto: University of Toronto Press.
Wolfe, Patrick. 2006. "Settler Colonialism and the Elimination of the Native." *Journal of Genocide Research* 8(4): 387–409.

7

Empire, Archipelago, and Abyss: Spaces of Power and Resistance in James Bond's Caribbean Imaginary

Jonnie Eriksson and Kalle Jonasson

James Bond is dead. At least twice over. After having been blown to bits on an island in the Russo-Japanese archipelago in the finale of *No Time to Die* (2021), Jeff Bezos's Amazon acquired creative control of the Bond franchise from EON Productions in February 2025. At that point, the fate of the secret agent, in the service of the British Empire and its legacy, could be looked upon as having been sealed (White 2025). There is of course an afterlife to Bond, but firmly in the grip of the US marketplace behemoth, thus confirming neoimperialism by means of capitalism.

So, what kind of resting place and legacy can we expect for Bond? What kind of tomb is fitting for an infamous misogynist and chauvinist, serving sovereignty to safeguard the vestiges of empire, in light of the emergent strand of studies called the *theory of encryption of power* (henceforth TEP)? A crypt perhaps ("the crypt conceals a dead body while being a site of reverence to it"; Sanín-Restrepo 2021, 11), or a mausoleum, a cenotaph, a sepulchre, all different variants of displaying or hiding the body (cf. McDonald 2020)? Where will we hide him—if anything remains to be hidden? Or how could he return from hiding—if anything at all remains? (One should remember that Bond himself declares that his hobby is resurrection (Mendes 2012, 01:16:55)).

Encryption and Decryption: The Vicissitudes of Archism

Coined by Ricardo Sanín-Restrepo (2018, 2021), the TEP has appeared in the cross-section between the studies of law, culture, and Indigeneity, and in view of its concern with postcolonialism, Caribbean thinking acts as a whirlpool nexus of the theory. Encryption "is the imposition of institutional simulations of difference that condition, neutralize or prohibit political agency, reducing difference to static and solid models of identity that pose as the only form of power" (Sanín-Restrepo and Machado-Araujo 2020, 19). It all amounts to the act of labeling that reinforces power to centers (be it liberal ideologies, republics, democracies, or sovereignties), which in turn immobilize and make their peripheries invisible. Inspired by a roster of continental thinkers, including Gilles Deleuze, the TEP has mustered a broad range of scholars to understand "structures of power (the state, for example), [but] not their corporality, but their expressions" (Sanín-Restrepo and Machado-Araujo 2020, 21). The TEP thus offers a stark defense for difference, democracy, and the world:

> Everything that can exist and communicate its difference, we call the world. There is only world when it is made up of all the differences that can produce and communicate difference ... Henceforth, power is either the exercise of immanent difference or its privation. When power is nested in the privation of difference it is domination; a primordial denial of power, a false construct of existence and its potentialities that we name potestas. (Sanín-Restrepo and Machado-Araujo 2020, 20)

However, nowadays archistic regimes decrypt no less than they encrypt. Musiol (2018, 157–78) ponders the metaphorical promise of encryption's antithesis, *decryption*, but informs us that Amazon actually chose to remove encryption from its Fire Tablets. This might seem like corporations are acting in line with the TEP, but perhaps it signifies the opposite, especially if we take into account the recent political affiliations of Jeff Bezos and others of his ilk. When, as in the tech-brocracy of present-day United States, decryption is appropriated by the instances that obstructs a democracy of differentiation (*à la* Sanín-Restrepo), this poses a problem for the TEP:

> Encryption and decryption are partial stages of the communication process, and to see encryption and decryption as polar ends, disempowering and liberatory in all contexts, privatizing versus democratizing, is to ignore the complexity of how and where both processes operate, how interdependent they are, and how, in fact, in the technical sense, they are both needed to preserve information and control its flow. (Musiol 2018, 162)

Power changes when the serpent of the "societies of control" slithers out of the molehill burrows of disciplinary society into the openness of information flows (cf. Deleuze 1990, 240–7). Encryption, once the name of exclusionary coding practices, now gives room to explicit showcasing of games of power and domination (such as in the blatant, if unintentional, display of the US government plan to attack Houthi targets witnessed by a reporter from *The Atlantic* (Goldberg 2025)). What would Bond, the secret agent, do in times like these? What secrets are there to police when politics displays itself like a reality show and live imperialist geopolitics is stated to be "great television" (McCreesh 2025)? It might seem as though there is a current mania for decryption, as with the obsession with "free speech" and telling "truth" in face of presumed fake news and cancellation culture, even while installing presidential sovereignty in a post-truth society. Indeed, encryption itself is about hiding in plain sight (Sanín-Restrepo 2016, 4, 2021, 11). Encrypted power may hide in the very systems that we consider democratic or liberal; the principle of such power is termed "archism": "Archism is the opposite of anarchism although it is not often called by that term (usually it doesn't have a name because part of its conceit is that it is natural and just 'the way things are'). Archism is a principle of rule and domination characterized by two key principles, hierarchy and representation" (Martel 2019, 127).

What we will do here is to shift perspectives a bit, by installing one of the most Western, white, and masculine representatives of sovereignty of them all as an asset to the TEP: namely the fictional spy James Bond. Of course, behind the glitz and glamour of his suave persona, Bond could be regarded as a wielder of *potestas* and a motor for imperial momentum. Certainly, "colonialism, … racism and misogyny and other archist practices" (Martel 2020, 46) are amply represented in both novels and films, as evidenced by their academic reception (cf. Black 2005; Comentale, Watt, and Willman 2005; Funnell 2015; Funnell and Dodds 2017). But Bond is a man of many turns. For one, we will turn to his origin in the Caribbean—a region imbued with much hope, knowledge, and resistance in the spyglass of the TEP. Along with the poetics and philosophies of the Caribbean archipelago, we intend to explore the ways in which space can be opened up for an-archic form of thought, however precarious and uncertain such a space might be: "The sole purpose of decryption is to open politics as the place where meaning is yet to be decided" (Sanín-Restrepo 2016, 13). Bond's Caribbean genesis allows for a discussion on how archism, decryption, encryption, and sovereignty permutate when the imperial abode shifts geographically, geologically, and geopolitically: from the archipelagic empire of the UK to the continental empire of the United States ("America" for short), with the an-archi-pelagic realm of the Caribbean as an imaginary sanctuary. Could the Caribbean (philosophy and geography) be seen as a warding off of the hauntological resurrections of sovereignty and empire, as well as the archistic appropriation of decryption?

The thesis of the present text is that James Bond reveals new aspects of empire and sovereignty, in history and the future, in ways that work in favor of the TEP, precisely by tracing his Caribbean origin and travels. The question is which tracks we might find, what spaces they cross, and what they lead back to. What we will attempt in the present text is to review Bond's canonical contribution to postwar popular culture by examining different expressions of imperialism and anti-imperial resistance, charting Bond's Caribbean genesis and nostos, and revealing his paradoxical nonsecrecy (given his profession) as an agent of decryption (for good and bad). One should remember that Ian Fleming subscribed to Jack Buchan's dictum: "If you want to hide something, put it directly under the light" (Shakespeare 2023, xxii).

For this purpose, we pose the following questions: How could encryption and decryption of power be understood following a figure like James Bond, reluctantly running the errands of an all-out sovereignty? How is this reluctance connected to space and territoriality: the relations between Britain and the Caribbean, more specifically, and to the difference between continental and archipelagic empire, more generally? How are the movements of Bond connected to this reluctance and to the Caribbean, and what concepts of power, thought, life, and death do they reveal?

Political issues in Bond have long been investigated. For decades, book-length studies have been devoted to the "political career of a popular hero" (Bennett and

Woollacott 1987), the "politics of James Bond" (Black 2005), the "cultural politics of James Bond" (Comentale, Watt, and Willman 2005), the "geopolitics" of Bond (Funnell and Dodds 2017), and Fleming's "politics of ambivalence" (Kinane 2022). Matters of imperialism, the Cold War impasse and its aftermath weigh heavy, alongside questions of nationalism, racism, and sexism; however, the image of Bond in this regard has begun to change and become more nuanced as the state of art develops, Kinane's "ambivalence" being one explicit indicator.

Geography, and especially motifs of islands and the Caribbean, play a significant role in several such political analyses. While Crane and Fletcher (2017) generally peruse the frequency of insular themes in Fleming's novels and their degrees of fantasy and realism, they remark that the Caribbean islands tend to be portrayed as "either feminised spaces to be enjoyed by Bond" or "malevolently male spaces to be conquered by the hero" (64): "Islands are the epitome of Bondspace, the setting in which James Bond's hyperbolic heroic masculinity is forged" (68). In comparison, Vivian Halloran (in Comentale, Watt, and Willman 2005, 158–77) focuses on the representation of the Caribbean as a reenactment of "the plantation machine or the mythification of piracy," but also as "the one physical and ideological space in which displaced, racially hybrid characters—both villains and heroes—feel at home"; even Bond, so obviously British and white, it seems, is nationally and ethnically deconstructed by Fleming to the point that the Caribbean becomes a hybrid "ethnospace" to work out his crisis of identity. Ian Kinane (2022) provides the most extensive study on the representation of Jamaica in the James Bond novels and films, and he demonstrates that Fleming's conflicted opinions on Britain's colonial heritage and its position in the modern world carries over into fiction. While Fleming is considered a "casual racist" prone to "pseudo-imperial fantasies," Kinane argues that the Bond stories represent a possibility of resisting "imperial rhetoric."

Cinematic Bond originates in Jamaica in *Dr. No* (1962), but then evades the island for decades, instead replacing it with other islands, in the Caribbean or in Asia. In a similar manner, other colonial and postcolonial spaces can also be "encrypted," as is the case with Hong Kong in *Skyfall* (2012): "Bond's pursuit of Silva takes him around the geographical fringes of Hong Kong, to three different cities in East Asia: Shanghai, Macau, and an unnamed island … Each of these places appears almost as encryptions of Hong Kong, referring to the city through rebuses or inside jokes" (Hoa 2012, 6). Encryptions of Jamaica across the Caribbean need to be traced with a sense of such irony.

Geopolitics: The Dialectics of Powers and Territoriality

Geopolitics obsesses over geography and geology as natural domains of power exerting itself spatially. This plays out in ways that may very well lead to associations with the trope of the "Bond villain," just all too real ones. Let's take two topical examples. One: Eight months into his invasion of Ukraine, Vladimir Putin used tectonic plates as a geological metaphor to promote his deterministic view of political changes in the world order, as if global shifts in the dominance of great powers were a natural process outside of the influence of the actions of individual nations:

> All these changes have been happening for many years; some pay attention to them, others do not, but these are tectonic changes in the entire world order. You know, these tectonic plates, they are in constant movement somewhere down there in the Earth's crust. Experts say that they are moving now, and are always in motion yet everything seems quiet, but changes are still happening. And then, they collide. Energy accumulates and when the plates shift, this causes an earthquake. The accumulation of this energy and its outburst have led to these current events. But they have always happened. What is the essence of these events? New centres of power are emerging. (Putin 2022)

Two: A little over two years later, rumblings came from the American continent that things needed to change. On the very day that he assumed the office of president, Donald J. Trump signed an executive order to rename the Gulf of Mexico "The Gulf of America," reasoning that the Gulf has been "an indelible part of America" (as in the United States) and "will continue to play a pivotal role in shaping America's future and the global economy" (Trump 2025). Having laid claim to this body of water, there quickly followed claims to the Panama Canal, to Canada, to Greenland and even to the Gaza Strip; incidentally, Trump would also wheel and deal to gain mineral resources from the territory of Ukraine, thus rubbing his tectonic plate against Russia's, as it were. So, as Putin sees new powers emerging to decenter the West and break supposed American hegemony, Trump sees power restored to his nation by decentering it *from* the West and supposedly manifesting the destiny of a dollarized sovereign.

Usually, imperialism follows ideas of continuity and consolidation. Such nostalgia can lead to a revanchist return of imperialism and geopolitics, as in China, Russia, and Turkey (Tertrais 2023), or for that matter in the phantasmagoria of MAGA-USA, mining for their golden ages in ever-dirtier soil. On the theoretical side, the legacy of Alfred Thayer Mahan and Halford Mackinder, carried by Nicholas Spykman and Zbigniew Brzezinski, slides into Robert Steuckers and Aleksandr Dugin, right into an unearthing of Carl Schmitt's geopolitics of sovereignty and Francis Yockey's Imperium. But there is also an alternative to the model of controlling land masses. History has for millennia seen the alternatives of continental empires (Akkad, Persia, Rome, the Ottoman Empire, China, Mongolia, Russia, Austria-Hungary, the United States) and what one might term archipelagic empires (Greece, Japan, Spain, Portugal, the Netherlands, Great Britain). These alternatives could also be seen, at least at one point in time, as a chronological shift from a classical-continental phase to a modern-maritime phase of empire (cf. Barker 1944), much as one might today imagine an emergent neoimperialism that transforms from geographical territories to technological topologies (cyberimperialism). Still, the geographical fantasy of empire holds a significant sway. For the British Empire, the insular or archipelagic nature of its global territoriality is a particularly romantic idea. Speaking of "Romance as Bond of Empire" (Stokes 1930, 293–304), the very dispersal across the globe of British colonies at the height of imperialism, provides food for fantasy to the nourishing of imperial ideals, in an archipelagic fashion: "To enter on the romance of the British Empire is to embark upon an illimitable sea, for almost every one of its innumerable centers and aspects is a center or an aspect of romance. Islands of the Empire, … is there any limit to the romance of these?" (Stokes 1930, 295–6). The image of Britain as being an island nation or island empire is still prevalent in the historiographic view (Wilson 2002; Riley 2023), even as an "imperial nostalgia" permeates contemporary Britain in various aspects (Mitchell 2021).

Geopoetics and Geophilosophy: Archipelagic Thinking as Theory and Methodology

If our point of departure is in the notion of geopolitics, it is only to seek out alternative ways of thinking territoriality, ones which can resist strategies of domination and the hierarchies of power blocks, instead opening up a space for a thinking and creating with the earth in its immanent difference and dynamics. We thus depart from geopolitics only to explore geopoetics and geophilosophy.

Geopoetics—a multifaceted attention to the relation of man to language and the earth—was invented by the Scottish French poet-philosopher Kenneth White: for him, geopoetics is the quest for "a new expressivity, a *poetics of the world*," which "explores the archaic way and the anarchic voice" (White 2018b, 43). White (2007, 35–54) compares his project to Deleuze's geophilosophy and discerns three geophilosophical approaches: the national, the archaic, and the utopian. They seek, respectively, to characterize different ways of thinking in relation to the territoriality of nations for different people, to find the origins of philosophy itself in the maritime culture of ancient Greece, and finally to create a space for a new world and a new people to come (the thought of a new Earth).

Geophilosophy is introduced as a concept in *Qu'est-ce que la philosophie?* (Deleuze and Guattari 1991, 82–108), with a Nietzschean inspiration to understand different ways of thinking as influenced by environmental conditions (for instance, differences between landlocked and seabound peoples). However, themes concerning territoriality and deterritorialization, nomadic distribution and nomadology, smooth and striated spaces, the geology of morals, the Earth as a Body without Organs, faces as landscapes, methodologies of rhizomatics and cartography, and so on pervade the works of Deleuze, solitarily and in collaboration with Guattari (cf. Deleuze 1968, 1986; Deleuze and Guattari 1975, 1980; cf. Antonioli 2003; Carbone, Broggi, and Turarbek 2012). It is an engagement with geology and geography that could perhaps be traced back to a short essay from the early 1950s on "The cause and reason of desert islands" (Deleuze 2002, 11–17), which hinges on the distinction between islands of continental and oceanic origin, demonstrating a "living combat between the land and the sea." The essay chiefly addresses the island imaginary, as a geographical movement away from continents are complemented by a mythological, human movement away from the world or a creation of a world on the ocean: "Consciousness of the earth and the ocean, such is the deserted island, ready to begin the world anew" (13). The ultimate lesson of the mythology of islands is that they are the site of a second origin or second creation—not divine creation or the issue of pairs (as in the biblical creation myth of a Lord-God separating land from the sea, instituting both sovereignty and continentality), but a rebirth from a usually feminine space (Circe, Calypso), which plunges the idea of origin even deeper into time immemorial: "In the ideal of recommencement there is something which precedes the beginning itself" (17). (Regarding Calypso we may note that the meaning of her name is one who "hides" or "conceals"; and she, on whose island Odysseus is hidden away for seven years, is the "daughter of malignant Atlas, who has discovered / all the depths of the sea, and himself sustains the towering / columns which bracket earth and sky and hold them together"; Homer 2007, I:52–4. We are already pulled toward the depths of the Atlantic.)

The very term "archipelago" encrypts a Greek legacy (by way of a Venetian invention), as the term originally refers to the Aegean Sea, the "main sea" (*archi-pelagos*), and later to its islands; the word thereby also inscribes a literal hierarchy to this territory of Greek civilization. (The Antilles of the Caribbean archipelago only stresses this: Antillia, the "first" island, was originally an imaginary island floating in the Atlantic; White 2018a, 8.) The import of this legacy, shot through with British colonialism, is negotiated by the St. Lucia poet Derek Walcott, in whose works, such as *Omeros* (1990) and *The Odyssey* (1993), Homer's world is transposed to the West Indies. Of the Caribbean people and its poets, Walcott can speak of "the 'New Aegean' race" (1998, 15) and "poets of the 'New Aegean'" (42): "Antillean art is this restoration of our shattered histories, our shards of vocabulary, our archipelago becoming a synonym for pieces broken off from the original continent" (69). Is it a coincidence that Kenneth White, in his travels to the Antilles, in Guadeloupe finds a cemetery with headstones inscribed "Ici repose Madame Homère" and "Ici repose Capitaine Suédois Omer" (White 2018a, 120)?

A more problematic connection between these cultural landscapes is evinced by Édouard Glissant, who would rather see the Mediterranean and the Caribbean as symbolizing different types of seas and archipelagos. Collin and Zerba (in Aurélia, Leupin, and Sainton 2020, 237–60) treat Glissant's critique in terms of a "dialectic between the Mediterranean and the Caribbean" as different archipelagic images of thought: the former enclosing, centering on unity (the philosophy of the One, of the first principle (*archê* in Greek)), the latter instead opening up to difference and diversity (the philosophy of Relation, without hierarchy).

However, Homer constitutes a paradox, since the epics in his name, which provide a specifically Mediterranean origin to Western civilization, are almost Caribbean in character: they (particularly the *Odyssey*) are epics of wanderings (*errance*) and of Relation, demonstrating the difficulty, if not impossibility of a return to the native land. The shared etymological root of the words *nostos* (homecoming) and *nomós* (place of roaming, from the verb *neomai*, to roam) (Aurélia, Leupin, and Sainton 2020, 250) signals the intricate relation between nostalgia and nomadism, which is key in the Odyssean epic. And while there is no etymological link between the words, Odysseus's attribute *polymêtis* (of many ruses) is playfully linked to *métissage* (of mixed races) (248). This association of Greek *mêtis* with Caribbean *métissage* is also extensively explored by Rosello (1992, 143–91) as a way of thinking, typical for the Caribbean identity: ruse as an activity of resistance to power in conditions of powerlessness. White, for his part, addresses *mêtis* in the context of his conception of a "pelagic thinking," in reference to the mythology of its personification, the primordial goddess Mêtis, an "aquatic and polymorph" divinity, paradoxically both female and male, white and black, luminous and obscure (2018b, 48–9). In the "territory of philosophy" ("the kingdom of Ideas"), it is *epistêmê* that reigns supreme, while outside of its domain there is *mêtis*, a dangerous, malign way of thinking, used by fishermen and seafarers to navigate in changing circumstances, associated with Odysseus and the octopus (51–2).

As a note on method, inspired by such poet-philosophies of the mythology of islands and seafarers, we will approach James Bond in a similar way. The following analysis will not be of the representation of places and people in the novels and films, but rather the signification or dramatization of space and movement, where Bond is treated as a mythopoetic figure, similar to Odysseus. James Bond, *anêr polytropos* and *polymêtis*, too, is here viewed as a figuration of moving and thinking in ways that escape the polemical dialectics of geopolitics to poetico-philosophical archipelagic landscapes, and as belonging to an epic expression of power and resistance to dominion.

Édouard Glissant is of special importance in this enterprise, since it is in his poetics and philosophy that notions of archipelagic thinking (and its critical correlate, abyssal thought) is developed in the most sustained way, in a sort of dialogue with Deleuzian geophilosophy (Glissant and Deleuze shared a biographical connection as young students at the Sorbonne; for his remarks on Deleuze's philosophy, see Glissant 2005, 135–40). Studies on Glissant have dwelled on the postcolonial, political import of his poetics (Dash 1995; Britton 1999; Nesbitt 2013; Coombes 2018; Aurélia, Leupin, and Sainton 2020; Khalfa 2023) or highlighted his philosophy of becoming and "the living" (Leupin 2016), while some have recently focused on themes of archipelagic, oceanic and abyssal thinking (Wald Lasowski 2015; Wiedorn 2018; Drabinski 2019; Pugh and Chandler 2023). All these aspects are relevant for our purposes, but the latter is of special significance.

Essentially, archipelagic thinking is opposed to continental thinking, in that it deals with intuitive testing rather than the forming of systems, an "imposing synthesis" in terms of blocks: continental thought surveys from above the "configuration of landscapes" in a general overview, while archipelagic thought seeks out the minor features of the terrain, the rocks and rivers and such (Glissant 2009, 45). The archipelago is a fractal and fragile space, both "passing and remaining," washed by waves and rising seas, or sinking into the abysses of the ocean (47). It resists the thought of conquest and domination, instead seeking to think "all sorts of relations" (46). Developing a poetics and a philosophy of what Glissant terms Relation—nonsystematic connections of differences without hierarchies—is perhaps the core of his project (Glissant 1990, 2009), and the context in which the archipelago becomes more than mere geography.

According to continental thinking, even the oceans are conceived of as a sort of continent, as Glissant says of the Atlantic (2009, 50); continental thinkers see continents everywhere, even when the Caribbean islands were first discovered (48). Archipelagos across the world have historically preceded continental empires: the Ionian islands of Greece, the Pacific archipelagos such as the Easter Islands, the archipelagos of the Indian

Ocean and of Indonesia, or the Scandinavian archipelago in the north, even land-archipelagos such as the Balkans or African villages (48–9). And even after continental thinking leads to conquest and colonization, the systems imposed (such as plantations) disintegrate into a sort of cultural archipelagization (creolization, *métissage*) (52).

Glissant (2005, 146) distinguishes between two types of empires, with two types of movements: one an expansive nomadism, empires of conquest and invasion that know no limits (Romans, Arabs, Mongols); the other a circular motion, enclosing itself from the outside and resisting internal dispersion of the community due to external influence (China, Japan). The age-old ambition of a universal empire, such as Glissant sees in the present-day United States (after the aborted attempt of the Soviet Union), will need to perform both movements: reaching across the whole world and enclosing everyone within it (a totality-world, which neglects or effaces differences). Glissant (155–6) notes that the imperial movements are prefigured in the Homeric epics: the outward movement of conquest in the *Iliad* and the erring around the Mediterranean in returning home in the *Odyssey*. In one sense they are therefore archetypical epics of empire. But they also stage a conflict between the people and the sea, with an anti-imperial and anti-rational force in Poseidon, contra Zeus, which is the nemesis of most empires (with the significant exception of Great Britain).

In opposition to fixed hierarchies that consolidate power structures, the archipelagic is a fluid system of motions: one type of motion being that of magma escaping the hadal trenches and underwater volcanoes to form new islands, and another type being that of the winds and tides that recurrently reshape them. The archipelagic therefore, on one hand, has an origin in the abyssal depths, an unground that rises to the potentials of the imagination, as if founding reality on a "secret" fantasy: "*From the outpourings of the abysses the Ocean created a stretch of archipelagos, not yet inhabited and secretly offering themselves to our imaginations. The reality of these archipelagos took hold in the surrounding*" (Glissant and Chamoiseau 2022, 35, italics in original). On the other hand, there is a motion to-and-fro on the surface of things, a repeated coming-and-going and returning of forces that erode, wash away and silt up material reality, as a constant reminder of change in the world that is.

For Daniel Maximin (2006, 108), the Caribbean archipelago represents a geopoetics that opposes geopolitics ("La Caraïbe oppose aux politiques de l'espace une poétique de l'espace."). This opposition is inscribed in its history: its narrow and fragmented geography has made it impossible to establish an empire there; rather, it has been the place of contestation between imperial powers (109). But Maximin is also attentive to the oceanography and meteorology of the archipelago: it is not just a matter of pieces of land but a space of natural forces connecting the islands across the sea—a geopoetics of cyclones. Similarly, the Caribbean poet-historian Kamau Brathwaite (1994) focuses on the oceanic movements that wash over the archipelago, specifically the tides. Tides move in other ways than the irreversible arrow of time; more roundabout, while still installing difference. Here, we shift from dialectics to *tidalectics*:

> A neologism … on the word "dialectic," where "dia" is replaced with "tid(e)" indicating the idea of a natural and dynamic fluctuation in history, identity,

> and landscape, similar to the motion of the tide of the sea ... [T]he tidalectic as an alternative historiography is modelled on the geophysical attribute of the Caribbean archipelago, in which the movement of the sea shapes the shores of the Caribbean islands: encroaching and then receding, altering the landscape for a moment, only to return it as it was. (Bogetoft Mogensen 2023, 31)

In view of waves, storms, and currents, all is laid bare, not contiguously, but in repeated seasonal sequences. Thus, the weather refreshens and replenishes the Caribbean, hydrologically and meteorologically decrypting and devastating the colonialist and encryptions of its islands and their ecologies. To work tidalectically is to approach politics from a poetic and philosophical point of view (Brathwaite 1994a, 1994b; DeLoughrey 1998, 2009). But is it only cyclical, returning things to what they were? Bogetoft Mogensen (2023, 38) thinks not: "Tidalectic time functions more like a spiral than a circle. It does not return to the exact same moment or spot, rather it spirals, mimicking the sea's movements: tides that expand and retract in relation to the shore, waves that come in, again and again." (In the case of James Bond, as we will see below, he turns back to the Caribbean, but he is always someone else, a new face, in a new time, with new enemies and lovers, jumping in and out of Her Majesty's service, sometimes to quit it.) Riffing off Wayde Compton's (2001) take on tidalectics, Bogetoft Mogenssen (2003, 31–2) directs our attention toward another vision of time by using the *palimpsest* as metaphor. Evading, not only the "missilic" (Brathwaite 1994b) and forwards-thwarting time of the West, Enlightenment, colonialism, and dialectics, but also the neat symmetry of cyclicity, a tidalectic analysis opens up for a viewpoint "where generations wash over generations" (Bogetoft Mogenssen 2023, 37), which "reveals a different understanding of the connection between history and identity, viewing both as palimpsests that can never be wiped completely clean, but only re-written repeatedly, as tides that wash over a beach" (32).

Here an opportunity to reinforce the TEP emerges. For if the powers that be currently appropriate decryption—as when tech bro moguls suggest the opening up of its encrypted devices (see Musiol 2018, 162)—what will become of TEP's deliberating and democratizing agenda? Being focused on overwritings and laying bare of the codes secluding the practices of power, the TEP could be fortified by the palimpsest. Initially a term denoting a proper paper, the typings of which were erased and replaced with new letters, the palimpsest is a medium whose past could be discerned. The new writings aren't encryptions, but overcodings that still let the erased and hidden content be shown (to different degrees). Tidalectics, as a Caribbean methodology of resistance, thus counterappropriates the archistic practice of encrypting, but in a manner that lets the medium be, not only its present, but also its past messages. In a bottle.

However, in the Caribbean the abyss is always nigh. Next to dialectics and tidalectics, we might perhaps suggest a third term, *hadalectics*, in reference to the deepest recesses of the pelagic abyss, the hadal zone (named for Hades, the underworld of the dead in Greek mythology). It is worth noting that the deep-most part of the Atlantic Ocean, the Milwaukee Deep of the Puerto Rico Trench, is located just north of Puerto Rico, and that the Caribbean Sea itself is cut through by the

Cayman Trough, reaching from Cuba to Mexico, at the separation of the American and Caribbean plates. While winds and waves sweep across the surface of the waters that both connect and separate the islands, the beaches give way to the most abyssal zones of the whole Atlantic, hiding in the darkest depths the churning work of swallowing up and spit out molten earth.

These movements are distinct from those centrifugal and centripetal movements that Glissant ascribed continental thought and may symbolize (archi)pelagic thought instead. They are both opposites of the continental paradigm for thought: the thinking of fixed landmasses upon which territories can be delimited. They are instead the epistemological alternatives of archipelagic and abyssal thinking, respectively. Tidalectics accounts for the movements to-and-fro on the surface of the forces of nature, the repetitive coming-and-going of the waves and tides (and the winds), which sweep across the dispersed lands of the archipelago; it is a thought of repetition and return as a rhythm of life. Hadalectics, by contrast, would affirm the fissures hidden in the darkest depths that split the continental plates apart; it accounts for the sinking and rising motions of magma that liquefies earth and the volcanic eruptions that may create new land, and stands for a thought of demise and resurrection.

The geopoetics of islands, winds, currents, waves, and tides, of magma and lava (or for that matter of glaciers) opens up thought from the rigidity of the continental norm for geopolitics, affirming the dynamics of forces rather than establishing domains of powers. In this respect, they are metaphorically an-archic principles, typical for pelagic and archipelagic thought. It would be the object of geophilosophy to explore the ontology and epistemology of all such Earth–Thought relations: to examine and assess the differences between these ways of thinking, how they relate to nature, and how they may concern aesthetics, ethics, and politics.

In the following, we turn to the figure of James Bond, to see how novels and films featuring this illustrious British secret agent (for Bond as an agent of secrets, cf. Wald Lasowski 2020) can be seen to develop geopolitical and geophilosophical themes that challenge the dialectics of power in geopolitics. In particular, archipelagic, tidalectic, and abyssal styles of thought are sought in the tracing of Bond's repeated travels to the Caribbean, where the colonial and imperial past forms the background of a problematic of nostalgia and exotic adventure, while generating a cartography or oceanography of surface appearances and opaque depths.

The Many (Re)turns of a Secret Agent: Caribbean Origins and Adventures

The original name of Fleming's fictional spy was James *Secretan*, as if catching himself, in the very name, in declaring his status as a *secret agent* (indeed, the title of the first chapter in the first novel); the name Secrétan was presumably borrowed from a codename Fleming may have had early in his intelligence career (in turn inspired by a Swiss philosopher, Charles Secrétan). By settling instead upon James Bond, Fleming named him for an American ornithologist specialized in the birdlife of the West Indies, thereby anchoring the agent's identity in the Caribbean archipelago rather than the nostalgia for the naval service of his own youth.

From the very first, Fleming seems to have Bond under the spell of the Caribbean. In the first chapter of *Casino Royale* (1953), "the secret agent" passes under the cover of a wealthy Jamaican, drawing from Bond's experience from that island, and in the assignment to the fictional French seaside resort Royale-les-Eaux he is in fact "being controlled through Jamaica" (Fleming 2012, 5). This fake identity is later expanded upon: "Bond knew Jamaica well, so he asked to be controlled from there and to pass as a Jamaican plantocrat whose father had made his pile in tobacco and sugar and whose son chose to play it away on the stock markets and in casinos" (27). As he checks in at his hotel, he signs the register "James Bond, Port Maria, Jamaica." Fleming seems to insist upon establishing not only a cover, which has little significance for the plot, but an imaginary biography for his newly created character, as if he really stepped out of the world of the *Birds of the West Indies*. Before we know much at all of Bond, now that he is introduced—and long before Fleming refashions him as a Scotsman, fusing his own heritage with that of Sean Connery—he is provided with a faux-but-all-too-true background as a degenerate colonialist. On the face of it, Bond's chosen cover is a fantasy of colonial, patriarchal privilege and capitalist, wasteful hedonism. And still he is emphatically *James Bond* (no alter ego required)—he is just located in the village neighboring Fleming's property at Oracabessa, Jamaica, as if he were inhabiting Fleming's own haunt. From the very first, Bond is indeed controlled through Jamaica; and for all his existence, the Caribbean will haunt him. In the subsequent novel, *Live and Let Die*, Fleming makes a point of contrasting the lush island of Jamaica with the capitalistically dense American continent: "Bond was glad to be on his way to the soft green flanks of Jamaica and to be leaving behind the great hard continent of Eldollarado" (Fleming 2019, 207).

Bond was in many ways a creature of the Caribbean. It was the place of his creation; Fleming came up with the idea for Bond while taking a swim in the bay by his Jamaican property, on the north shore of the island. In his annual, hibernal retreat from his professional duties in England, from 1952 until his death in 1965, Fleming wrote all the Bond novels and novellas in his Jamaican bungalow, Goldeneye (on a typewriter of the "Imperial" brand, no less), and several of his novels featured adventures set on the island, from the second one, *Live and Let Die* (1954), to the very last, *The Man with the Golden Gun* (1965); and if we count the collections of short stories, the posthumous "Octopussy" (1966) would fill the same function.

However, Jamaica did not provide sufficient escape from the realities of politics. If Bond was originally conceived to compensate for the diminishment of the British Empire after the Second World War, his literary career would in reality bear witness to its final dismantling, most symbolically in terms of the Suez Crisis of 1956. With supreme historical irony, Fleming's Goldeneye estate became the place where the sun finally set on the British Empire: Sir Anthony Eden, the physically ailing prime minister, sought refuge to Fleming's home on Jamaica just as the Suez crisis rocked the world, but insisted that he would continue dealing with the affair from there. Thus, it was from Goldeneye that the order came to withdraw from the Suez Canal Zone, sealing the fate of a last imperialist gasp. With yet more irony, the scandal in the press surrounding Eden's Caribbean excursion (and subsequent resignation from office) put Fleming's name in public view and revitalized interest in his novels (Parker 2015, 210–18; Shakespeare 2023, 524–33, 558). So, it might be said that the end of the British Empire literally came to ensure the future of Bond.

Part of this future was that the character entered the world of cinema, cementing his iconic status. During 1962, the first Bond film, *Dr. No*, was shot and released. The irony continues: fittingly, the bulk of the first cinematic Bond adventure takes place in Jamaica (as if it had to repeat his origination there); furthermore, it was shot during the spring, when Jamaica was still a British colony, but released in the autumn, when it had reached independence (as if the film documented the birth of the Jamaican nation). It was also the last film to be set in Jamaica, until the time of *No Time to Die*, released in 2021. All the other Bond stories in which Fleming had made Bond revisit his chosen home, the filmmakers displaced to other territories, and when setting off on their own after having gone through Fleming's œuvre, they continued to have him avoid Jamaica (though Bahamas and Cuba are repeating islands), up until it was time for Daniel Craig to make his final performance in the role. There is a weighted significance to this choice. In the words of producers Barbara Broccoli and Michael G. Wilson: "We believe that Jamaica is Bond's spiritual home, which is why we as filmmakers decided to choose it as the place for Bond to retire from the world in *No Time to Die*" (quoted in Lovatt-Smith and McDonald-Whyte 2023, 133). This bears repeating: Jamaica is Bond's "spiritual home," so it is the place for him to "retire from the world." What is really the significance of this—more specifically, what is this dichotomy between *home* and *world*?

One might be forgiven to assume that Bond's home is Britain. Time and time again, with a mixture of panache and cheekiness, we are reminded of his status as an agent in Her Majesty's service, soaring with a Union Jack parachute and cockily "keeping the British end up" (Gilbert 1977, 02:03:43). Being "British," Bond's nationality is already archipelagic, though. The casting of Bond has historically affirmed his belonging to all the countries of the British Isles: not just England (Roger Moore, Daniel Craig) but also Scotland (Sean Connery), Wales (Timothy Dalton), Ireland (Pierce Brosnan)—indeed, even Australia of the Commonwealth (George Lazenby). As 007 returns, he returns to different homes within the remnants of the empire.

As to "world," the world that surrounds Bond constitutes the axial geopolitics of East–West and North–South. Bond is most often associated with the Cold War and the conflict between East and West, with Russia and Britain battling it out via the deadly intelligence organizations SMERSH (from "death to spies") and MI6 (with a license to kill), the latter in an uneasy alliance with the United States (specifically the CIA). In this respect, Bond fits squarely into the geopolitical contest of power blocks, representing an Atlantic island nation squeezed between two continental Behemoths, tearing Europe apart at critical junctures. But Bond never quite embroils himself in the pivotal centers of power in global geopolitics, such as Washington, Moscow or Beijing; rather, he works in the periphery of power plays, launching himself from London to all manner of zones of interest, whether political or personal, across the globe.

Among his many travels, quite a few take him to the so called Global South—the site of contestation of postcoloniality and neoimperialism: in the Sean Connery films, Bond visits Jamaica, Turkey, and the Bahamas; Roger Moore's Bond travels to the fictional Caribbean island of "San Monique" (standing in for Jamaica and Haiti) but also Lebanon, Thailand, Egypt, Brazil, Cuba, and India; Timothy Dalton brings Bond to Morocco, Afghanistan, Bahamas, and Panama; with Pierce Brosnan, southern destinations include Vietnam, Turkey, Azerbaijan, North Korea, and Cuba; and lastly, thus far, Daniel Craig visits Pakistan, Madagascar, Bahamas, Haiti, Bolivia, Turkey, China, Mexico, Morocco, Jamaica, and Cuba.

If any pattern might be detected in this list of destinations, aside from their increasing frequency, it is perhaps their place in the geopolitical shifts during the decades they cover. First, with Connery in the 1960s, the southern destinations are relevant as bordering on the greater continental conflicts of the Cold War; they are, as it were, US-adjacent (the Caribbean) and Soviet-adjacent (Turkey). The same is true for Moore's first outing in *Live and Let Die* (1973), where the Caribbean island is the nexus in a drug smuggling ring intimately connected to the United States. But Moore's further adventures in the Middle East, in Asia, and in Latin America are rather exotic romances of imperialist mythology (or perhaps ironical sendups, including tongue-in-cheek references to Lawrence of Arabia and Tarzan). Then, with Dalton and Brosnan, as the Cold War comes to an end, there seems to be a thematic need to renegotiate the position of southern sites in relation to shifting balances of power: the Middle East becomes more politicized, China rises, North Korea looms, and so on. Lastly, with Craig and a post-9/11 world (dis)order of global terrorism and digital panopticism, we see a kind of networked globalization, a decidedly postcolonial globetrotting in the worldwide network society.

While some journeys seek out hot spots of Cold War conflict, most, however, trace the machinations of a more nebulous, post-ideological empire, the dark mirror image of which is SPECTRE. (The octopus in the emblem of this shadowy organization is the tentacled analogue to the scaly Leviathan of classical sovereignty: the power that effuses and diffuses rather than collects and consolidates.) Among these many destinations, a significant number are islands, as if emphasizing the fragmented structure of postmodern politics, in the age after classical imperialism. Aside from more Homeric haunts in the Mediterranean (Corfu in *For Your Eyes Only*, Sardinia in *The Spy Who Loved Me*, the Gibraltar peninsula in *The Living Daylights*), the cinematic Bond travels to eight isles of the Global South: Jamaica in *Dr. No*, *Live and Let Die*, and *No Time to Die*; Crab Key (a fictional island off Jamaica) in *Dr. No*; New Providence (Bahamas) in *Thunderball*, *Licence to Kill*, and *Casino Royale*; San Monique (a fictionalized Jamaica/Haiti) in *Live and Let Die*; Khao Phing Kan (Thailand) in *The Man with the Golden Gun*; Jag Mandir (Udaipur, India) in *Octopussy*; Cuba in *Octopussy*, *GoldenEye*, *Die Another Day*, and *No Time to Die*; Hispaniola (Dominican Republic/Haiti) in *Quantum of Solace*. Even a cursory glance makes it evident that, aside from Thailand and India, all these islands are situated in the Caribbean archipelago. The West Indies seem to keep having a consistent pull.

It happens that only one incarnation of Bond does *not* travel to any part of the Global South, nor to any island, but remains steadfastly in continental Europe: George

Lazenby, whose single outing was the most subserviently titled story of them all: *On Her Majesty's Secret Service* (1969). No other novel or film makes Bond so explicitly an agent of classical sovereignty. No other title states so clearly that his power comes from representing the authority of the head of State. No other title hints at the presumed "encryption" of this power—the "secrecy" of his service to the majesty. Nevertheless, the plot makes a mock of this, and doubly so: "her Majesty's secret service" is precisely what Bond states that he *quits* (in a thwarted attempt to resign his position, half way through the story); and in the end he effectively does, driving away from the wedding where Majesty and M have been replaced by Marriage; and so the Caribbean romance is supplanted by a more connubial one, though ending in tragedy.

The greater significance of this for the cinematic Bond mythos is the role played by *On Her Majesty's Secret Service*, Lazenby's singular effort, in the themes of *No Time to Die* (2021), Craig's final outing. At the start of the latter film, Bond has indeed left his service; he is no longer a 00, having quit his job to be with his new love, Madeleine Swann, as if repeating the choice at the end of *On Her Majesty's Secret Service*. But by a ruse of the arch-nemesis Blofeld, Bond suspects that Madeleine has betrayed him for SPECTRE and casts her aside, doubting her "secrets" that they haven't got to yet … Five years later, we find Bond having retreated to a rustic lifestyle in Jamaica, living a relaxed life in a somewhat stylish shack by a cove, not very dissimilar from Fleming's Oracabessa fancy. This is Bond divested of all "bonds" to imperial power (just James, as it were). It is the ultimate elimination of State sovereignty from the figure of Bond—an an-archic recluse in his archipelagic excursion, a full investment in the Caribbean romance, once the conjugal option failed (again).

Motifs of power, dominion, empire, and sovereignty recur throughout much of Bond fiction, novels as well as films. It is the very fact that they are so insistently encoded into the fabric of Bond's character and his universe that might make us wonder if the message is being forcefully repeated to us as a vital characteristic, rather than obfuscated in the ideological veils of the plots.

We learn very well from the title of one novel and film that he is *On Her Majesty's Secret Service* (an agent of the sovereign); we know him from his military title as "Commander" Bond (the one who nominally commands, in a hierarchic chain of command); we know iconically that his codename 007 signifies that he has two kills to merit his position, and we know that he thereby has a license to kill (a sovereign decision on life or death); we know, too, that the cover for the British secret service agency MI6 is the company "Universal Exports" (a euphemism, one might say, for colonialism or imperialism, in capitalist terminology); and, as said, we come to know that the motto of the Bond family, inscribed in their aristocratic heraldry, is "The world is not enough" (in Latin, *Orbis non sufficit*; a hyperbolic statement of transcendent archism).

This phrase returns to prominence in the eponymous Pierce Brosnan film *The World Is Not Enough*, not just in its title but also in its dialogue (Apted 1999, 01:43:19–01:43:28). When Bond is tortured by the female villain Elektra King (what's in a name? a vengeful, female claimant to patriarchal sovereignty), she states: "I could have given you the world," to which Bond responds: "The world is not enough." Elektra curtly retorts: "Foolish sentiment"; Bond chuckles softly: "Family motto." So, as Bond is physically restrained and faces a medieval torture device, he is symbolically fettered to the legacy of his feudal genealogy, outlined in *On Her Majesty's Secret Service*, and to the hubris of its ambition, which foreshadows the colonialism and imperialism of his nation. Ultimately, it is a question in the scene whether he affirms the sentiment of his heraldic motto, stoically refusing Elektra's temptation (because a woman's offer of the world is not enough, or because he already has enough of it), or if he, with fatalistic irony, surrenders to its foolishness (instead affirming her judgment: it is foolish to be bonded to such ambitions).

No doubt, the explicitness of Bond's association with power and sovereignty serves as a ruse. In the case of M's dismissive summation of Bond's character in *GoldenEye*, we can see it as a kind of contract with the audience: once the matter of Bond's outdated sexism and his ties to Cold War politics has been addressed, the narrative can continue to operate with good conscience, so to speak; we can enjoy the spectacle in reassured awareness that the filmmakers are themselves aware of its ideological import, which undercuts the need for critique. The business is sorted, so the pleasure can proceed. In some sense, Bond is a trickster figure in his own mythos, on one hand appearing as exactly what he is, and explicitly so, and on the other hand thereby getting away with whatever subterfuge action imaginable. We are all playing a mythological game to scramble the ideological code. As a result, the overarching ideology of the Bond stories becomes unimportant, since it dissipates and scatters across the surface, getting lost in a mythological and quite symbolic archipelago of places, bodies, images, and phrases.

What is important, though, is this very archipelago, however mythic. There is a utopian strand to the Bond franchise, taken as a whole (the literally *overarching* theme that seeks to go beyond archism), displaced in the fragmentary essays in creolization. There is indeed a fantasy of imperial nostalgia, of masculine prowess, of erotic stylishness—yes, all of the clichés are true; but there is also a phantasmagoria of place and escape: of departing, of retreating, of returning. This is the reason why James Bond is so readily associated with the primary myth of journeying—of departing and returning—in Western mythology: the *Odyssey*.

It is no coincidence that the shadow of Odysseus looms over *Skyfall* (2012), the outing whose title and climax bring Bond back to his ancestral home in the Scottish Highlands. The intertext is made explicit through M's reading of the final lines in Lord Tennyson's poem "Ulysses" during the hearing scene (Mendes 2012, 01:40:20–01:40:48):

> We are not now that strength which in old days
> Moved earth and heaven; that which we are, we are;
> One equal temper of heroic hearts,
> Made weak by time and fate, but strong in will
> To strive, to seek, to find, and not to yield. (Tennyson 1842)

In the context of the story, the intention seems to be to reflect upon the possibly remaining strength of a weakening power (Britain, M, and Bond), and thus a nostalgic lament over a waning empire. Contrarily, Tennyson's poem, published in 1842 and drafted as early as 1833, was rather penned in the age of *ascent* of the British Empire, depicting a restlessness in the heroic spirit during imperial flourishing.

Three paradoxical versions of one mythos here reverberate: M's recital proposes that an imperial project is in a state of decline, but that some of the spirit of adventure, fight and resilience nevertheless remains. Tennyson's poem is about an imperial adventurer who, while having returned safely home and is growing old, sets out for yet a new venture, because it is in his nature to seek out vitality (the first lines read: "I cannot rest from travel: I will drink / Life to the lees") even at the cost of death ("my purpose holds / To sail beyond the sunset, and the baths / Of all the western stars, until I die") (Tennyson 1842). In contrast, *Skyfall*'s plot is about an aging agent who, like Odysseus, having visited Hades (M: "Where the hell have you been?—Bond: Enjoying death"; Mendes 2012, 00:25:40–00:25:43), returns home to the place of his childhood, only to destroy it in a blaze of loathing ("I always hated this place"; Mendes 2012, 02:03:46). In this respect, *Skyfall*'s implicit message is that national/imperial nostalgia is false: M misreads Tennyson about venturing out, and Bond returns home only to wreck it. *Skyfall* is an anti-nostos, and doubly so. However, it sets up the establishment for Bond's future as the agent that we already knew from the time before Craig: what he returns to is not his biographical past (Bond's family home; Bond as Fleming, the Scot) but rather his own mythological past as an agent of Her Majesty, with a male M, with a desk job Moneypenny, and so on. Everything old is new again: ultimately, the usual hierarchies are reestablished. Decryption here only serves renewed encryption of power.

The beginning of *No Time to Die*, refracted through *SPECTRE*, is therefore the rectifying mirror image of *Skyfall*. At this point, everything that was established has been relinquished. For the first time since the first film, *Dr. No*, James Bond is back in Jamaica, however this time not on a mission for empire to a latter-day colony, but in retreat from the specter of neoimperialism. *No Time to Die* is the true return, just as *Skyfall* was the false one—Jamaica, not Empire; an island, not the highlands; the archipelago, not hierarchy. The Bondian Odysseus has returned home by pushing to extremes his westward adventure: he has left service under British sovereignty to live freely on his Caribbean island, hidden away from the world, Calypso style.

If Jamaica (or the Caribbean) is Bond's home, then the Bond movies trace the story of his nostos, comparable to the *Odyssey*: a warrior venturing out into the world to fight for some sort of imperial ambition, only to long to return home but being fatefully frustrated in succeeding. The cinematic Bond appears as a modern-day Odysseus, tossed from land to land and island to island, "lost at sea, adrift," as he says in *Tomorrow Never Dies* (Spottiswoode 1997, 00:35:26)—and as we often find him at the end credits, from *Dr. No* and on, while the credits assure us that "James Bond will return." The insistence that Bond will return is however never really a return home, only the repeated promise of a new adventure, once again thrown into the world. *No Time to Die* is the first time that he actually returns to his point of origin, to a Fleming-like lifestyle by a Jamaican bay much like where he was first conceived.

Two things follow, though. One is that *a new return of another 007* is staged on the very island of Jamaica, in the guise of a black woman who has inherited the number—a

British agent posing as a Jamaican, played by an actress of Jamaican descent, and playing at a future of the character beyond the biography of James Bond himself. This points to the extreme of Bond's creolization: his future might be as a black Jamaican woman. Much of the movie consists in resisting this extremity: to get back to being the 007 that he once was, while not fully surrendering to the sovereignty that held him at service, supplanting it for the bonds of family. The ultimate tragedy of Bond is that his Odyssean epos, both as return to his home island and to his family, is proved to be an ephemeral fantasy. This is the second thing that follows: the *complete reversal of the Odyssean myth*. Bond sacrifices himself for the family he will never really have, as he faces the full might of the collected contenders for world domination (the equivalent of the suitors). In one more case of fatal irony, it is the missiles of the supposed home country that ultimately kill him: the last act of the ghostly vestige of the British Empire is to direct its weapons at some contested, liminally situated island in the Russo-Japanese archipelago, where Bond finally accepts his fate. In the end, Bond simply finds himself in the wrong archipelago, on the enemy's deadly Poison Island, not a paradisiacal isle of life. Not all archipelagos are the same; some are awash with vital force, while some just give way to the hadal chasm.

Conclusion

Trying to work out thought's relation to the Earth, to territorialities and landscapes, in ways that do not frame them as domains of power, we have moved from the dialectics of geopolitics to the tidalectics and hadalectics of geopoetics. As regards Bond, dialectics could be seen as the logical form of a stereotypical narrative conflict between East and West, in that Britain retains its power, in nostalgia of its imperial status, by sublating the opposition of the capitalist and communist empires (the United States vs. the USSR). Bond encrypts resistance to dominion within a discourse of power. Or, keeping the Caribbean in view, we might instead imagine a different kind of dialectics between opposite values, which pertains to the differences in territorial coloniality: an opposition of the idea of empire as essentially continental and the idea of the archipelago as resisting the principle of imperialism, the sublation of which would be the notion of Great Britain as an archipelagic empire par excellence (a singular case of solving the conflict between land and sea, in the conceptions of both Deleuze and Glissant).

The tidalectic movements of history would then be the processes of returning to the Caribbean to reinforce or renegotiate a sort of social contract of the British archipelagism: what is this strange hybridity of an "island empire," the romance of a world of islands as a "bond of empire"? The many returns of Bond to the Caribbean paint the palimpsest portrait of a figure that never quite moves on, but rather shores up the past until it can be washed away. The Bond series as a whole seems to fit this tidalectics. But with Daniel Craig, the tides turn back and wash away like never before; starting out again, once more as if never before, he is the one to also come to an end. With Craig, Bond not only finally returns to affirm his true origin in Jamaica, but also faces the abyss by foreign isles. From the Bond saga in general, it is therefore possible to map out a logical unfolding of different ways of thinking territoriality and spatiality in relation to power.

One would be the geopolitics of Bond, representing a dialectics of powers. Essentially, the geopolitical aspect conceives space as domains of power in opposition, the object of which we could say is "world domination." This is continental thinking in terms of masses of space at a surface level, guided by principles of expansion and continuity (Glissant's two imperial movements); and this is where we find the matter of the tectonic plates, symbolizing power blocks in balance or shifting dominance, as if there were hidden forces determining the state of affairs.

Another would be the geopoetics of Bond, of which we may discern two types. First, the Bond saga in general demonstrates a tidalectics of forces, a dynamic play of elemental forces that gives a sense of vitality to the world. This is archipelagic thinking of fractal space at the surface, of fragments and dispersals in place of expanse and continuity, like islands scattered precariously across the sea and held together only by the winds and waves that sweep along their path. Instead of shifting balances of centrifugal and centripetal motions of intent, this is the movement of repetition and returns, of coming-and-going, of trying again and anew. Here we could say that we are "island hopping."

The second geopoetical type would then be the hadalectics of fate. There is always the risk, both in venturing out and in returning, to be swallowed up by the earth. This is abyssal thinking, in terms of fractures of space in the deep, namely the cracks and hollows in what continental thinking assumes to be solid mainland—chasms that open up between the tectonic plates. This is a thinking of the pelagic depths in their most uncompromising obscurity, as a dominion of death (hence a double fatality); it is a poetics of sinking and rising, of demise and resurgence, of unearthly resurrections, perhaps.

The general geophilosophy of Bond, if we integrate both geopolitical and geopolitical perspectives, is then the following.

Continental thinking is the idea governing the Cold War impasse—the dialectical logic of opposition implies an affirmation of negation (world as conflict) and the assumption of synthesis in sublation (the goal of winning). This is the case both regarding the narrative conflict between East and West, or North and South, and the logical conflict between the (very real) fantasy of imperialism/coloniality and the (surreal) imaginary of Caribbean anti-imperial creolization.

Archipelagic thinking is dramatized in the Caribbean adventure and incessant attempts to return; the tidalectic logic of repetition functions as a negation of opposition (the world as peace), in search of a place to be realized but which seems impossible to reach or return to (the nostos/nomadism of utopia).

Abyssal thinking is the idea of the catastrophe, the sense of a risk of in fact not "returning" (thus a negation of repetition); in this we see the hadalectic logic of what we might call "subtraction" (the antithesis of sublation: loss/death), the fatality of withdrawing from the world in face of the impossibility of nostos.

These three perspectives resemble the Odyssean themes of adventure (the romance of imperialism, the glory of conquest), return (the ideal of *nostos* as the quest for a life worth living), and ruse (*mêtis*, the adaptability to fate and the tricks trying to cheat death). They are all in some way part of the Bondian palimpsest: when we see Bond, there is an Odysseus behind him, just as when we see the Caribbean, there is a reflection of the Aegean archipelago. (The palimpsest thus shows a multilayered mixing of images, a sort of spatial *métissage* of what appears, rather than dimensions of depth for what is concealed.) But the epic or mythic association has some complexity. The Odyssean connection between the Mediterranean (Homer), the Caribbean (Walcott), and the British (Tennyson) is the overarching problematic of the Bond mythos: the question of an archipelagic power and its refusal, a tidalectic logic of its history and possible repeatability, and a hadalectic logic of its origin and demise. James Bond doesn't really have the power to dominate, but rather to live and let die—and not least to return, even from death.

The question is, however, what it will mean to return under present political conditions. From the perspective of American hegemony, between *SPECTRE* and *No Time to Die*, Bond managed to skip over the Trumpian chasm, from the administration of Obama to that of Biden. One might say that in the EON canon, he made time to die at the right moment, before Trump's second coming. If he is resurrected once again, it seems fated that 007 will return as an agent of Jeff Bezos, incorporated into the prime of Amazon mass entertainment and the bulimic, unabashed American neoimperialism of Trump 2.0. What rough beast now slouches toward Bethlehem? The final, most fatal irony of James Bond is perhaps that the legacy of the character's Caribbean dreaming will manifest in the nightmare guise of a Zombie Bond in servitude to the plutocrats of Eldollarado.

References

Antonioli, Manola. 2003. *Géophilosophie de Deleuze et Guattari*. Paris: L'Harmattan.

Apted, Michael, dir. 1999. *The World Is Not Enough*. 20th Century Fox Home Entertainment, 2 h 8 min. Blu-ray, 1080p, 2012.

Aurélia, Dominique, Alexandre Leupin, and Jean-Pierre Sainton, eds. 2020. *Édouard Glissant, l'éclat et l'obscur*. Pointe-à-Pitre: Presses universitaires des Antilles.

Barker, Ernest. 1944. *The Ideas and Ideals of the British Empire*. Cambridge: Cambridge University Press.

Bennett, Tony, and Woollacott, Jane. 1987. *Bond and Beyond: The Political Career of a Popular Hero*. New York: Macmillan.

Black, Jeremy. 2005. *The Politics of James Bond*. Lincoln: University of Nebraska Press.

Bogetoft Mogensen, Ann-Sophie. 2023. *Tidalectic Poetics*. PhD diss., Roskilde University.

Bonta, Mark, and John Protevi. 2004. *Deleuze and Geophilosophy: A Guide and Glossary*. Edinburgh: Edinburgh University Press.

Brathwaite, Kamau. 1994a. *Barabajan Poems*. New York: Savacou North.

Brathwaite, Kamau. 1994b. "Newstead to Neustadt." *World Literature Today* 68(4): 653–60.

Britton, Celia M. 1999. *Edouard Glissant and Postcolonial Theory: Strategies of Language and Resistance*. Charlottesville: University Press of Virginia.

Carbone, Mauro, Parde Broggi, and Laura Turarbek, eds. 2012. *La géophilosophie de Gilles Deleuze: entre esthétiques et politiques*. Sesto San Giovanni: Mimesis.

Comentale, Edward P., Stephen Watt, and Skip Willman, eds. 2005. *Ian Fleming and James Bond: The Cultural Politics of 007*. Bloomington: Indiana University Press.
Compton, Wayde. 2001. *Bluesprint: Black British Columbian Literature and Culture*. Vancouver: Arsenal Pulp Press.
Coombes, Sam. 2018. *Édouard Glissant: A Poetics of Resistance*. London: Bloomsbury Academic.
Crane, Ralph, and Lisa Fletcher. 2017. *Island Genres, Genre Islands: Conceptualisation and Representation in Popular Fiction*. New York: Rowman and Littlefield.
Dash, J. Michael. 1995. *Edouard Glissant*. Cambridge: Cambridge University Press.
Deleuze, Gilles. 1968. *Différence et répétition*. Paris: PUF.
Deleuze, Gilles. 1986. *Foucault*. Paris: Minuit.
Deleuze, Gilles. 1990. *Pourparlers*. Paris: Minuit.
Deleuze, Gilles. 2002. *L'île déserte et autres textes: textes et entretiens 1953–1974*. Paris: Minuit.
Deleuze, Gilles, and Guattari, Félix. 1975. *Kafka—pour une littérature mineure*. Paris: Minuit.
Deleuze, Gilles, and Guattari, Félix. 1980. *Mille plateaux: capitalisme et schizophrénie, 2*. Paris: Minuit.
Deleuze, Gilles, and Guattari, Félix. 1991. *Qu'est-ce que la philosophie?* Paris: Minuit.
DeLoughrey, Elizabeth. 1998. "Tidalectics: Charting the Space/Time of Caribbean Waters." *SPAN: Journal of the South Pacific Association* 47: 18–38. www.academia.edu/760559/Tidalectics_Charting_the_Space_Time_of_Caribbean_Waters_SPAN_1998.
DeLoughrey, Elizabeth. 2009. *Routes and Roots: Navigating Caribbean and Pacific Island Literatures*. Honolulu: University of Hawaii Press.
Drabinski, John E. 2019. *Glissant and the Middle Passage: Philosophy, Beginning, Abyss*. Minneapolis: University of Minnesota Press.
Fleming, Ian. 2012. *Casino Royale*. New York: Vintage.
Fleming, Ian. 2019. *Live and Let Die*. New York: Vintage.
Funnell, Lisa, ed. 2015. *For His Eyes Only: The Women of James Bond*. New York: Columbia University Press.
Funnell, Lisa, and Klaus Dodds. 2017. *Geographies, Genders and Geopolitics of James Bond*. London: Palgrave Macmillan.
Gilbert, Lewis, dir. 1977. *The Spy Who Loved Me*. 20th Century Fox Home Entertainment, 2 h 5 min. Blu-ray, 1080p, 2012.
Glissant, Édouard. 1990. *Poétique de la Relation: Poétique III*. Paris: Gallimard.
Glissant, Édouard. 2005. *La cohée du Lamentin: Poétique V*. Paris: Gallimard.
Glissant, Édouard. 2009. *Philosophie de la Relation: poésie en étendue*. Paris: Gallimard.
Glissant, Édouard, and Patrick Chamoiseau. 2022. *Manifestos*. Translated by Betsy Wing and Matt Reeck. London: Goldsmiths Press.
Goldberg, Jeffrey. 2025. "The Trump Administration Accidentally Texted Me Its War Plans." *The Atlantic*, March 24. www.theatlantic.com/politics/archive/2025/03/trump-administration-accidentally-texted-me-its-war-plans/682151/
Hoa, Jen Hui Bon. 2012. "'That Which We Are, We Are': Hong Kong and Postcolonial Identity in *Skyfall*." *Situations: Cultural Studies in the East Asian Context* 6: 1–11. http://situations.yonsei.ac.kr/product/data/item/1535538575/detail/e0581787bf.pdf
Homer. 2007. *The Odyssey of Homer*. Translated by Richmond Lattimore. New York: Harper Perennial.

Khalfa, Jean. 2023. *Poetics of the Antilles: Poetry, History and Philosophy in the Writings of Perse, Césaire, Fanon and Glissant*. Lausanne: Peter Lang.
Kinane, Ian. 2022. *Ian Fleming and the Politics of Ambivalence*. London: Bloomsbury Academic.
Leupin, Alexandre. 2016. *Édouard Glissant, philosophe: Héraclite et Hegel dans le Tout-Monde*. Paris: Hermann.
Lovatt-Smith, Lisa, and Novia McDonald-Whyte. 2023. *Jamaica Vibes*. New York: Assouline.
Martel, James. 2019. "An Anarchist Power Amidst Pessimism." *The Comparatist* 43: 125–46. www.jstor.org/stable/10.2307/26824951.
Martel, James. 2020. "The One Who Made the Lock Also Made the Key: Thomas Hobbes on Encryption and Decryption in the Face of Sovereign Power and Authority." *Revista da Faculdade Mineira de Direito* 23(45): 34–48. https://doi.org/10.5752/P.2318-7999.2020v23n45p34-48
Maximin, Daniel. 2006. *Les fruits du cyclone: une géopoétique de la Caraïbe*. Paris: Seuil.
McCreesh, Shawn. 2025. "'This Is Going to Be Great Television': Trump Sums Up His Zelensky Showdown." *New York Times*, February 28. www.nytimes.com/2025/02/28/us/politics/television-trump-zelensky-ukraine.html.
McDonald, Angus. 2020. "Crypt, Mausoleum, Cenotaph; Sepulchre: Metaphors of Encryption." *Revista da Faculdade Mineira de Direito* 23(45): 49–59. https://doi.org/10.5752/P.2318-7999.2020v23n45p49-60.
Mendes, Sam, dir. 2012. *Skyfall*. Metro-Goldwyn-Mayer, 2 h 23 min. Blu-ray, 1080p, 2013.
Mitchell, Peter. 2021. *Imperial Nostalgia: How the British Conquered Themselves*. Manchester: Manchester University Press.
Musiol, Hanna. 2018. "Metaphors of Decryption: Designs, Poetics, Collaborations." In *Decrypting Power*, edited by Ricardo Sanín-Restrepo. London: Rowman and Littlefield, 157–78.
Nesbitt, Nick. 2013. *Caribbean Critique: Antillean Critical Theory from Toussaint to Glissant*. Liverpool: Liverpool University Press.
Parker, Matthew. 2015. *Goldeneye: Where Bond Was Born: Ian Fleming's Jamaica*. London: Windmill Books.
Pugh, Jonathan, and David Chandler. 2023. *The World as Abyss: The Caribbean and Critical Thought in the Anthropocene*. London: University of Westminster Press.
Putin, Vladimir. 2022. "Vladimir Putin Meets with Members of the Valdai Discussion Club. Transcript of the Plenary Session of the 19th Annual Meeting." https://valdaiclub.com/events/posts/articles/vladimir-putin-meets-with-members-of-the-valdai-club/
Riley, Charlotte Lydia. 2023. *Imperial Island: A History of Empire in Modern Britain*. New York: Vintage.
Rosello, Mireille. 1992. *Littérature et identité créole aux Antilles*. Paris: Karthala.
Sanín-Restrepo, Ricardo. 2016. *Decolonizing Democracy: Power in a Solid State*. London: Rowman and Littlefield.
Sanín-Restrepo, Ricardo, ed. 2018. *Decrypting Power*. London: Rowman and Littlefield.
Sanín-Restrepo, Ricardo. 2021. *Being and Contingency: Decrypting Heidegger's Terminology*. London: Rowman and Littlefield.
Sanín-Restrepo, Ricardo, and Marinella Machado-Araujo. 2020. "The Theory of Encryption of Power: Itinerary of an Idea." *Revista da Faculdade Mineira de Direito* 23(45): 18–33. https://doi.org/10.5752/P.2318-7999.2020v23n45p18-33.
Shakespeare, Nicholas. 2023. *Ian Fleming: The Complete Man*. London: Harvill Secker.

Spottiswoode, Roger, dir. 1997. *Tomorrow Never Dies*. 20th Century Fox Home Entertainment, 1 h 59 min. Blu-ray, 1080p, 2012.
Stokes, Robert. 1930. *New Imperial Ideals: A Plea for the Association of the Dominions in the Government of the Dependent Empire*. London: John Murray.
Tennyson, Alfred. 1842. *The Early Poems of Alfred Lord Tennyson*. www.gutenberg.org/cache/epub/8601/pg8601-images.html.
Tertrais, Bruno. 2023. *La guerre des mondes: le retour de la géopolitique et le choc des empires*. Paris: L'Observatoire.
Trump, Donald J. 2025. "Presidential Action: Restoring Names that Honor American Greatness." www.whitehouse.gov/presidential-actions/2025/01/restoring-names-that-honor-american-greatness/.
Walcott, Derek. 1990. *Omeros*. New York: Farrar, Strauss and Giroux.
Walcott, Derek. 1993. *The Odyssey: A Play*. New York: Farrar, Strauss and Giroux.
Walcott, Derek. 1998. *What the Twilight Says: Essays*. New York: Farrar, Strauss and Giroux.
Wald Lasowski, Aliocha. 2015. *Édouard Glissant, penseur des archipels*. New York: Pocket.
Wald Lasowski, Aliocha. 2020. *Les cinq secrets de James Bond*. Paris: Max Milo.
White, Adam. 2025. "Amazon Has Taken Control of Bond—and May Have Just Killed Him." *The Independent*, February 21. www.independent.co.uk/arts-entertainment/films/features/james-bond-amazon-future-b2702254.html.
White, Kenneth. 1987. *L'esprit Nomade*. Paris: Grasset.
White, Kenneth. 2007. *Dialogue avec Deleuze: politique, philosophie, géopoétique*. Torino: Isolato.
White, Kenneth. 2018a. *L'archipel du songe: voyage transcendental parmi les petites îles de l'Atlantique tropical*. Translated by Marie-Claude White. Marseille: Le mot et le reste.
White, Kenneth. 2018b. *Le plateau de l'albatros: introduction à la géopoétique*. Marseille: Le mot et le reste.
Wiedorn, Michael. 2018. *Think Like an Archipelago: Paradox in the Work of Édouard Glissant*. New York: SUNY Press.
Wilson, Kathleen. 2002. *The Island Race: Englishness, Empire and Gender in the Eighteenth Century*. Oxfordshire: Routledge.

8

Decrypting the Mexican *Enforced Disappearance Apparatus* in the *Soft Dictatorship*

María Bacilio

This chapter presents a short genealogy that decrypts the transformation of enforced disappearance in Mexico from the second half of the twentieth century to the twenty-first century. The genealogy makes evident that enforced disappearance has to be understood as a *power apparatus*, that is an *archic* network in terms of command and knowledge that is exercised over populations to cope with any given crisis (political, economic, etc.). A new concept, the *enforced disappearance apparatus*, is presented as a result of what Michel Foucault calls a historical a priori (discourse, time, and space). Time is situated within the period known as the *soft dictatorship*. This temporal framework, that articulates "democracy" and dictatorship, is decisive for understanding the emergence, consolidation, and transformation of the *enforced disappearance apparatus* up to the present day. The *soft dictatorship* also constitutes a central element in this research because it operates as the foundational logic of the legal-political topology in Mexico. As such, it has shaped in different manners the space, the subject's experience (the disappeared and his/her family), and it has given place to micro-sovereignties.

The chapter is divided into seven parts. "*The Arcana Imperii* of Mexico" presents how Mexico saw the emergence, just after the Mexican Revolution, of what is known as *soft dictatorship*, contrary to Latin American dictatorships. This means an encrypted regime that combines democratic and authoritarian elements in such a way that dictatorship becomes imperceptible. Here the first generation of victims of the *enforced disappearance apparatus* is presented. It is also argued that the national and neoliberal project cannot be separated from drug trafficking. "The *Enforced Disappearance Apparatus*" presents the need to talk of enforced disappearance as a *power apparatus*. "Origin of the Term 'Dictablanda'" discusses the origin of the word "dictablanda" (*soft dictatorship*) in the Mexican context and how this paradoxical term conjugates encryption and archism. "Time or *Dictablanda*" argues that the *soft dictatorship* is key in understanding the emergence and consolidation of the *apparatus*. The notion that space is affected by the zone of indistinction of the *soft dictatorship* is presented in "The Space or Threshold of Indistinction." The question of the disappeared as bare life is presented in "Subject or Bare Life." Finally, "*Enforced Disappearance Apparatus* as Sequestration" presents the changes experienced by the *apparatus* in the new millennium and the need to understand it under the logic of what Michel Foucault calls sequestration.

The *Arcana Imperii* of Mexico

In 2000, Mexico had the possibility of becoming a real democracy after having the same party in power for seventy-one years. This party, which continues to exist, is the Institutional Revolutionary Party (PRI, according to its Spanish acronym), which was created in 1929 after the end of the Mexican Revolution. Despite the long ruling of this party and the systematic use of repression against social movements (such as the peasant and urban guerillas, the student movements, Indigenous movements, labor movements, etc.), this period is not fully recognized as a dictatorship, as was the case in Central or South America. This side of the American continent experienced particularly harsh military dictatorships, mostly in the second half of the twentieth century. One of the most striking results of these dictatorships was the disappearance of thousands of guerilla fighters and activists, which meant that enforced disappearance was one of the privileged ways in which the State would silence and repress its opponents. The PRI was no stranger to enforced disappearance; it began using this method at least from the 1950s against peasant and guerilla movements such as the *Jaramillista* movement led by Rubén Jaramillo (McCormick 2016, 156–7) in the State of Morelos; the National Revolutionary Civic Association led by Genaro Vázquez and the Party of the Poor led by Lucio Cabañas, both located in the State of Guerrero. In the 1960s, the PRI used it against student movements and urban guerillas such as the September 23rd Communist League.

The similarities and differences between military dictatorships and the PRI was what led Peruvian writer Mario Vargas Llosa to propose that Mexico was experiencing during that time the perfect dictatorship or *soft dictatorship* (*dictablanda* in Spanish), namely, a regime that combines democratic and authoritarian elements in such a way that dictatorship hides in plain sight. Following this idea, we could affirm that during that time, Mexico found itself in a zone of indistinction, between nomos and anomie. The fact of being in such a zone prevented the PRI, at least for a while, from being internationally recognized as part of the same constellation of authoritarian Latin American regimes, which would systematically use enforced disappearance to shut the opposition down.

We can give five reasons for understanding how the PRI managed to present itself as a democratic party. First, during the seventy-one years in power it did not prevent elections, yet the members of the party would always finish by having the most important positions, like the presidency. Second, between the 1960s and the 1980s the Mexican government welcomed thousands of exiles fleeing Latin American dictatorships, showing itself to be a country that was against authoritarianism and a defender of human rights. Among these exiles was Rigoberta Menchú, an Indigenous Guatemalan activist and winner of the Nobel Peace Prize in 1992. Her activism included the denunciation of enforced disappearance carried out during Guatemala's Civil War (1960–96). Third, in 1975, Mexico hosted the first World Conference on Women during the presidency of Luis Echeverría. He served from 1970 to 1976 and was responsible for implementing the systematic disappearance of guerrilla fighters. In his opening speech, Echeverría stated that "the improvement of the 'status of women' could only be achieved through the establishment of a new world economic order that would be fairer to the countries of the 'Third World'" (Valey 2022, 133). His speech was praised by nonaligned countries. This too gave the appearance of a benign and tolerant government. Fourth, while a number of persecuted Central and South American intellectuals and activists went into exile in European countries, thus drawing international attention to the atrocities committed under dictatorships, there was no comparable diaspora in the case of Mexico during that time. Finally, the number of people who disappeared under those dictatorships was significantly higher than in Mexico. In Argentina, it is estimated that 30,000 people suffered this terrible fate, while in Guatemala the number of missing people during the Civil War reached 45,000.

Since paramilitary drug-trafficking groups have taken over enforced disappearance, Mexico has far exceeded the number of missing people in comparison to some Central and South American countries. In 2025, it is estimated that more than a 100,000 people are missing, which is a crisis. The use of enforced disappearance as a counter-insurgency practice during the second half of the twentieth century has therefore been more deeply studied as a way of historicizing it. It has also led scholars to ask about the changes Mexico has experienced at the hands of what is commonly now known as "criminal groups" or, more recently, "terrorist groups," namely drug traffickers. For example, some scholars consider that a necropolitical approach helps to explain the way in which missing people have been found: cut into pieces in mass graves or in abandoned structures (such as houses or wells).

There are still important questions that have not yet been asked among scholars. The first question is: how is it possible that with the arrival of democracy, enforced disappearance stopped being used in such a systematic way in some Latin American countries that experienced military dictatorships, whereas in Mexico not only have such practices remained with the arrival of the democratic transition (which took place in 2000), but in fact became even more deadly? The second question is: is it appropriate to talk of enforced disappearance as a mere "technique of domination" or as a "terror technique" used by the State and drug-trafficking groups to repress, punish, threaten or terrorize the population, or should it be looked upon as a *power apparatus*[1]?

The latter question reflects what Foucault calls a historical a priori (of discourse, time, and space). Reading enforced disappearance as a *power apparatus* allows us to stress the differences between enforced disappearance in Mexico during the second half of the twentieth century and the new form that it took at the beginning of the twenty-first century. In addition, this concept helps to show how such practices have affected the life of the population in this country and how these missing people have become, following Giorgio Agamben, bare life (2016, 25).

The third and last question we will pose concerns sovereignty and domination. If enforced disappearance is a *power apparatus*, then the members of drug-trafficking groups and anyone who uses it to eliminate or to keep someone in the zone of indistinction (either dead or alive), should not just be seen as a criminal, but rather as a kind of sovereign. This is to say that an approach to power based on the social contract (Hobbes–Locke–Rousseau) should be partially abandoned in order to show how power can only exist thanks to *micropowers* (the police, the family, lovers, drug-trafficking groups, paramilitary, etc.), which can decide on the life or death of anyone. This decision is what offers such *micropowers* the ability to act as a sovereign.

Before answering the first question we have to historically locate the Mexican drug traffickers who, despite gaining more visibility mainly because of Operation Condor (1977–88), constituted themselves and became a paramilitary and economic power at the same time as the PRI. When this party took power in the 1920s, it wanted to gradually turn Mexico into a modern and eventually neoliberal nation. Such an ambition, which became more evident during the Cold War, is one of the reasons why the guerrilla movements arose in the first place.

The drug traffickers, who were mainly peasants coming from the northwest State of Sinaloa (home of the most important drug bosses like the "Chapo" Guzmán), took power during those same years. During the twenties, the Mexican government, following a series of international meetings, adopted a more repressive stance concerning drug consumption, aligning themselves with the widespread global condemnation of drugs. In the 1930s, the first campaigns to destroy plants like marijuana and poppy took place. These sources of drugs, according to the Mexican discourse, could provoke "racial degenerations" (Astorga 2016, 34). The increasingly latent prohibition in Mexico, the lucrative business on drug sales, as well as the return of soldiers who had fought in the two world wars (who used drugs to endure the harsh conditions they experienced), allowed drug trafficking to consolidate as an extremely profitable business.

We must also consider the alliances that were forged between the PRI and drug traffickers. As Mexican sociologist Luis Astorga reminds us, we cannot separate the consolidation of the PRI from drug trafficking, since their own members (politicians, military, policemen, and even ambassadors) protected and helped drug-trafficking groups. Furthermore and vice versa, the drug-trafficking groups or, as Astorga calls them "mafioso paramilitary groups," enriched and protected members of the government. This is why for Astorga, these groups did not gradually become a "parallel power," as some political scientists or analysts claim, but were in fact the basis of power itself or, at the very least, they constituted a form of power that could not have existed without the aid of State institutions and actors. Likewise, it is not appropriate to view these groups as "corrupt barbaric hordes" (Astorga 2016, 199) that allegedly tainted otherwise pristine institutions, for corruption and violence were already present long before, from the very moment Mexico consolidated itself as a modern and neoliberal nation.

Rather than designating drug-trafficking groups as the primary culprits of Mexico's woes, it is necessary to analyze their existence and history in an interdependent and simultaneous manner with that of the State or, more precisely, with the *soft dictatorship* and the global capitalist economy. It is this dangerous entanglement that helps explain the failure of the various "Operations" to eliminate drug trafficking. Indeed, each time the Mexican government had to offer someone up to the United States, it merely handed over the most easily replaceable figures rather than those occupying strategic positions, as doing so would have meant sacrificing the government itself: "From north to south, from one border to the other, from the beginning to the end of the century and into the new millennium, spanning from governors to the presidential family, what has remained constant is the exposure of the relationship between political power, police power, or both, and drug trafficking" (Astorga 2016, 228–9).

In saying this, we can already see why members of mafioso paramilitary groups should not be understood as mere criminals, but rather as micropowers or, better, as micro-sovereignties and why Mexico's Constitution as a nation cannot be understood without an understanding of the alliance between at least two forms of what Foucault calls illegalisms. The first form is the PRI, which thanks to the *soft dictatorship* stayed in power for seventy-one years and, the second form, are the mafioso paramilitary groups. Further developing enforced disappearance as a *power apparatus* will let us show why the legal-political structure of the *soft dictatorship* is an encryption of power and, hence, the *arcana imperii* (the secret of power). That explains why it has not been possible to rid Mexico of enforced disappearances.

The *Enforced Disappearance Apparatus*

In his text *What Is an Apparatus?* Agamben sets out to define what Foucault meant by the term *apparatus*. The French philosopher first used this concept in a vague manner in his 1977 seminar *Society Must Be Defended*, in his 1978 seminar *Security, Territory, Population*, and more systematically in the first volume of *The History of Sexuality*, published in 1976. Here, all of his efforts are devoted to understanding sexuality as a *power apparatus*. Yet, according to Agamben, despite his frequent use of the term, he never really defined it.[2] What the Italian philosopher then does is to frame and specify this concept.

The first thing that Agamben says is that he finds in this concept a possible form of the universal in Foucault's work, or at least, a term that functions as if it were a universal. The philosopher is obviously aware of Foucault's distance from phenomenology, such as that of Husserl, whom he reproaches, among other things, for his universalist intentions, his quest for the teleology of a unified reason and a transcendental subject (or the unity of the subject). Foucault, in order to counter phenomenology and following Nietzsche, proposes a new method that he first calls archaeology and later genealogy.[3] This method enabled him to diagnose the present and the everyday, as well as to situate each problematic in a contingent context.

Another reason why Foucault turns down anything resembling a universal is his rejection of any general use of categories such as State, sovereignty, law or power. By the latter, Foucault does not mean a set of institutions, structures or a *puissance* with which some would be enabled to subject a population. This means that the philosopher does not analyze the State or the law as the only sources of sovereignty from which derivative and descending forms of power are produced. Thus, following

Philipe Chevalier's suggestion, rather than answering the question "what is power" or "the substance of power" or "the essence of power." Foucault asks, "how does [power] happen?" (2011, 25). This empirical way of questioning power frees the historical and even political field of any substance or essence, because it puts an end to the idea that there is a single form of rationality with unequivocal ends instituted by a single group. On the contrary, those in charge of administering and exercising power would be multiple and sometimes unsuspected figures, such as: the military, the paramilitary, the doctors, the intelligence service, the police, the neighbors, the entrepreneurs, among others. Now, even if Foucault excludes a single form of power from which derived forms of power would arise, this does not mean that he completely denies the existence of a general form of power. In order to give consistency to local power strategies or micropowers, the latter must nevertheless create regularities that enable them to reproduce themselves in different forms. The State and the law would thus be the result or terminal forms of a series of micropowers:

> By power, I do not mean "Power," as the set of institutions and *apparatuses* that guarantee the subjection of citizens in a given state … The analysis, in terms of power, must not postulate, as initial data, the sovereignty of the State, the form of the law or the global unity of a domination; rather, these are only the terminal forms. (Foucault 1976, 121)

"Terminal form" should not be understood as a "total form," for then we would once again be falling back on the form of the universal from which the philosopher detaches himself, or at least tries to detach himself. For instance, Mexico as the terminal form of the nation State can only be understood as such thanks to the different micropowers that emerged at the same time. We mentioned above how the mafioso paramilitary groups contributed to the consolidation of the PRI and vice versa. The PRI should not, however, be understood as a "total form" because Mexico as a nation State continues to experience changes concerning the exercise of power and sovereignty, mostly after the 2000s when the rule of the PRI came to an end.

Despite Foucault's distancing from the various forms of the universal, Agamben nonetheless sees in the *apparatus* a general term that would occupy the place of what the French philosopher critically calls universals (2006, 27). However, according to Agamben, the term "universal" should not be understood as a generality resulting from abstraction, as this would once again lead us into the phenomenological trap. What we need to understand instead is a network that brings together a series of elements in a moment of crisis.

The crisis to which Agamben refers concerns, in a Foucauldian or archaeological-biopolitical sense, the way in which practices of power are led to update themselves in response to new social, political, economic, and health emergencies. The *apparatus* in this sense is what brings together the *micro*- and *macropowers* (the State, the law, etc.), as well as what produces several scissions within the subject itself, giving rise to the process of subjectivation. By this the French philosopher means that the subject is shaped by various discourses and practices, which causes the subject to: (1) separate him/herself from the nontruth of him/herself, (2) to be seized by the *apparatus* that leads him/her to produce a new subjectivity or truth of him/herself, (3) to produce a subject capable of freely assuming his/her new subjectivity and (4) to keep experiencing the same operation of separation and assumption in different moments of his/her life. It is at this point that the *apparatus* is able to respond to a crisis (such as population deviances, guerrilla movements or a high demand on drugs), but it is also here that it becomes at the same time a mechanism of government as well as a mechanism of the production of subjects (Agamben 2016, 32).

A crisis is thus controlled or neutralized by the network that can be traced between a set of practices, multiple forms of knowledge, and institutions. It is the setting in motion of this network that ensures the infinite production of subjectivities, behaviors, discourses, and gestures. It is clear, then, why Foucault rejects the possibility of a transcendental subject. If the subject results from the place he or she occupies in an *apparatus*, the subject cannot simply precede it, or get rid of the *apparatus* altogether. This does not mean, however, that the subject cannot resist it and set in motion a counter-conduct or a form of self-invention. The nonidealistic sense that Foucault gives to his historical a priori allows us to follow the idea that everything that appears in language, space, and time will eventually produce a network of power knowledge (an *apparatus*) that will be exercised over populations to cope with any given crisis.

The crisis of the PRI after the Mexican Revolution consisted of consolidating a modern nation and a liberal project. This was not easily achieved because of the presence of social groups (peasants, workers, Indigenous people, middle class, etc.) who could not be easily integrated into the modern nation project and capitalist interests. The State also had to deal with the rise of *counter-conducts* such as those of trade unionists, guerrilla fighters, feminists, student movements, queer movements, countercultures, among others. The birth of these *counter-conducts* ended up becoming another source of the crisis that had to be fought, first and foremost, by a nominalist project that consisted in creating a whole series of discourses.

Discourse or language is what first gives power the possibility of deciding on the fate of objects and subjects, this is why one of the first counter-insurgency acts of the Mexican government was to produce an enemy by calling "terrorist" or "bandit" everyone who took part in either insurrection or protest. Criminalization of such behavior is then what led the PRI to systematize an illegal and violent action (enforced disappearance) executed by *micropowers* and *macropowers* as a response. But if these two forms of power ended up finding the ideal framework of communication, coordination, and action, it was thanks to a particular encrypted form of temporality and legality, which was put in place as a backdrop to the *apparatus*, namely, the state of exception. In Mexico, the state of exception takes the form of *soft dictatorship*.

What is particular about the period of exception that occurred during the seventy-one years the PRI remained in power is that thanks to the zone of indistinction created by a paradoxical dictatorial democracy, the government did not have the need to openly declare a state of exception before implementing the *enforced disappearance apparatus* (as was the case of openly dictatorial regimes). The state of exception was implicitly present in the moment the *soft dictatorship* became the ground of existence of Mexico as a modern nation. The state of exception was imperceptible and, hence, encrypted. It "secured the smooth installation of a perfect predatory system, and it guaranteed the destruction of democracy in its name" (Sanín-Restrepo 2018, XVII). One of the most striking results of this encrypted exceptionality was the consolidation and perpetuation, until the next century, of the *enforced disappearance apparatus*.

Now, we will show how the indistinction of the *soft dictatorship* shaped the time and space of the first network of power of the *enforced disappearance apparatus* and what kind of subjectivity it produced. We will also sketch out how the exceptionality produced by the *soft dictatorship* determined the second moment of existence of the *enforced disappearance apparatus*, which appeared in 2000 and which is mainly, but not only, implemented by mafioso paramilitary groups. This will explain why, unlike in Central and South America, this *apparatus* did not cease at the end of the hybrid regime of the PRI, but instead was only strengthened.

Origin of the Term "Dictablanda"

In 1990 in Mexico City, Octavio Paz invited a number of intellectuals to take part in a television program broadcasted by *Televisa* (a hegemonic telecommunications company renowned for its historical support and collusion with the PRI and the right wing), to discuss the "experience of freedom." Among the guests were right-wing historian Enrique Krauze, Mario Vargas Llosa (before becoming Nobel literature laureate), and non-Latin American intellectuals such as Adam Michnik and Bronislaw Geremek. The aim of the program was to discuss the various dictatorships experienced in Latin America and Europe. Tensions quickly flared when Vargas Llosa objected to Paz's exclusion of Mexico from the dictatorial tradition. The Peruvian writer with great lucidity in his political analysis (although we do not normally agree with him), offered some explanations as to why Mexico constituted a special case of dictatorship or, to be more precise, what made this country the "perfect dictatorship." The secret formula of this disguised dictatorship, which he believed is not to be found in communism, the Soviet Union or even in Fidel Castro's regime, consists of a series of hybrid and paradoxical strategies. In this case, it is not a single man who imposes himself on an entire country, but rather a party. The party leaves enough room for criticism as long as it serves to reinforce the idea that it is seeking to guarantee democracy. However, when criticism challenges its hold on power, it eliminates the source of such criticism at all costs (Vargas Llosa 2010).

Vargas Llosa argued that the party used left-wing rhetoric (positioning itself as an heir to the revolution), to justify its right to power and its supposed openness. Such rhetoric was created and transmitted by intellectuals "subtly" co-opted by the PRI, through official functions or appointments (Paz himself held several diplomatic posts under the regime). Finally, Vargas Llosa also said that the party was incapable of bringing about social justice.

After unrolling this list of arguments, Vargas Llosa ended by saying "this dictatorship is a dictatorship … to the extent that all Latin American dictatorships have tried to create something similar to the PRI … The dictatorship in Mexico has had *the same consequences* as those of other Latin American dictatorships" (Vargas Llosa 2010). Before Krauze, who was moderating the debate, gave the floor to Paz, he clarified, "thank you for your valiant intervention on dictatorship or rather on *soft dictatorship*?," "*Soft dictatorship*!" responded Vargas Llosa. Paz replied to the Peruvian writer saying that in Mexico it is a fact that we had not experienced a military dictatorship, but rather the hegemonic domination of a party.

The Mexican intellectual's response only confirmed what Vargas Llosa had criticized him for: this authoritarian regime, by creating a gray zone, succeeded in misleading (or manipulating and encrypting) public opinion. Paz thus appeared to be a victim of the zone of indistinction, this assuming that his answer had not been biased by his own diplomatic commitments to the PRI, nor by the cultural control exercised by the party, nor by the fact that it was a televised program that could expose him to public scrutiny. Admittedly, after the Mexican Revolution there was no military coup or dictatorship in the style of Porfirio Díaz (a military dictator who remained in power for thirty-four years and whose regime gave rise to an uprising: the Mexican Revolution). Yet, after the Mexican Revolution and with the consolidation of the PRI, the presidency was in fact occupied solely by the military until the arrival of Miguel Alemán, who governed from 1946 to 1952. However, despite the arrival of a civilian in power and the omnipresent encrypted rhetoric and propaganda of demilitarization, the reality, as proposed by historian Thomas Rath, is that this was merely a camouflage (2014, 90). Not only did the military wield power openly and tacitly throughout the existence of this hybrid form of dictatorship, but worse still, it created a reticular power by supporting armed *groupuscules* that operated as *micropowers* during the PRI's regime.

What Vargas Llosa has brought to light are all the invisible forms established during the *soft dictatorship*, those which gave this regime a power envied by more open or fully fledged dictatorships. On September 2, 1983, General Augusto Pinochet declared in a speech: "We have never been a dictatorship, we are a *soft dictatorship*, but if necessary, we will have to shake hands, because first we have to save the country, and then we will look back" (Pinochet 2017).

The *soft dictatorship* is, in our view, an extremely consequential term for the philosophical analysis we are developing in terms of encryption and archism. Firstly, because the word itself in its semantic construction plays with hardness and flexibility. *Dictablanda*, in Spanish can be contrasted to hardness (*Dicta~~dura~~*), something that is permanent, that anchors, that defines, that dominates, that takes root, and so on. As Paul Gillingham and Benjamin T. Smith remind us, the seventy-one years of the *soft dictatorship* (1929–2000) were only surpassed by the Liberian Truth Party (1878–1980), the Mongolian People's Revolutionary Party (1921–96), and the Communist Party of the Soviet Union (1917–89) in terms of longevity (2014, 1).

The term *Dictablanda* also refers to softness (*blanda*), something that is flexible, penetrable, mutable, amorphous, plastic, and so on. Following Vargas Llosa's historical approach to the term, the adjective soft allows us to include a singular form of democracy and all the different forms of military *groupuscules*. It also allows us to include the same proven effects of more rigid dictatorial regimes. The Peruvian writer mentions the inability to bring about social justice, but another effect, this time of the hard side of the term (*dicta*), was the origin, consolidation, and perpetuation until the next century of enforced disappearance. However, unlike the dictatorships in Central and South America, whose regimes had a clearly defined beginning and end as well as a cessation in the systematic use of enforced disappearance (at least systematically in some regions), Mexico remains far from witnessing the end of this *apparatus*. Indeed, the most dramatic consequence of the *soft dictatorship* is that the rise of the modern and liberal nation took place at the same time as the rise of the *enforced disappearance apparatus*. This could be interpreted as a cursed sign: Mexico is a nation that cannot be understood without this *apparatus*. This intrinsic link could thus partly explain why enforced disappearance has been exacerbated in this country and has penetrated the most unsuspected corners of Mexican society, such as the household.

Time or *Dictablanda*

The tactical power that the term *soft dictatorship* offered the PRI (and hence our analysis), leads us to consider its reign as the time of the historical a priori of the *enforced disappearance apparatus*. This is a time that continues until today but with new forms of sovereignty. The *soft dictatorship* is thus the preliminary condition that will define all the paradoxical phenomena that remain to be defined: space and subject. But to understand all the consequences of such a paradoxical meaning, its relationship to the state of exception has to be shown. The PRI or *soft dictatorship* was created as an exceptional and transitional solution after the armed period of the revolution (which could be seen as the rise of a permanent state of emergency). But under this party's authoritarianism, the only thing that happened was that the exception became the rule. In other words, the *soft dictatorship* was presented as a figure of necessity (Agamben 2016, 199) or as a transitional phase after armed confrontations.

The aim of the PRI was to establish a constitutional or democratic order. But such an order was not quite established, because in reality, what was put in place was an illegal measure that managed to become legal and constitutional, given that "democratic" elections were held despite the permanence of a single party. It is precisely because of this, that the analysis becomes more complicated, as it is no longer a question of identifying and analyzing well-defined constitutional and temporal structures, but rather an extra-legal structure whose effectiveness is indebted to legal fictions that have made it possible to conceal its nebulous nature. Not surprisingly, as we saw, Latin American dictators (like General Augusto Pinochet) envied such an *arcana imperii*.

Following Giorgio Agamben's analysis of the state of exception in *Homo Sacer*, it seems to us that his insights shed relevant light on that hybrid or nebulous period constituted by the *soft dictatorship*. What Agamben does is precisely to show the point of intersection between the "traditional" legal-institutional model (as political techniques) and the biopolitical model of power (as technologies of the self). The point of intersection that the Italian philosopher proposes starts from the observation that it is not possible to separate these two models of power, given that what is the original core of sovereign power consists precisely in the involvement of natural life (or *bare life*) in the political sphere. Agamben considers that what characterizes modern politics is not the simple fact that natural life has become an object to be managed or administered, but rather that the state of exception as a juridico-political space, where *bare life* is both excluded and included, has become the rule. The zone of indistinction and the double bind produced by the way *bare life* is affected by the state of exception are thus, for the Italian philosopher, the hidden foundation on which the entire political system rests. This is the zone that makes communication between political and technologies of the self possible and what gives rise to the "new biopolitical body of humanity" (Agamben 2016, 17) (bare life or *homo sacer*).

The state of exception is thus a topological structure that appears, at least in the beginning, at the heart of or underlying the legal-political duality. This means that, although Agamben first studies the dialectical form of the legal-political duality, later in *Homo Sacer* he introduces new dualities as well (*zoē–bios*, state of nature–law, violence–justice, constitutive violence–constituent violence, nature–culture, etc.). In the midst of these dialectical couples, the only constant is the state of exception. The hyphen that unites these pairs could even be seen as a visible sign of such exceptionality, given that it is exactly in the threshold created between these two sides, in this "empty" space, that Agamben situates the new biopolitical body (bare life).

The questions that have to be asked then are: (1) who decides to set up this threshold of indistinction between anomie and nomos? (2) Why is it precisely the absence-presence of a legal-political order that makes certain political regimes, such as the *soft dictatorship*, extremely effective? And (3) What does this threshold produce in terms of time, space, and subject?

With regard to the first question, it is necessary to distance ourselves from Foucault's treatment of the question of sovereignty, since for Agamben it is precisely the sovereign who legally decides on the exception. This capacity still grants him a central place in the exercise of power, a centrality that, as we have seen, Foucault no longer reproduces in his analysis. Thereby, for the Italian philosopher it is the sovereign who, when suspending the law, not only establishes the state of exception, but also finds himself defined by this exception, a situation that creates within the very figure of the sovereign an oxymoron *of* ecstasy-belonging (Agamben 2016, 205) that, paradoxically, situates him in the same space as bare life (in the zone of indistinction occupied by the hyphen). In other words, when the sovereign legally decides to suspend the law, he or she seems to be outside the law. However, being "outside" does not mean no longer having any relationship with the law. Indeed, the sovereign must maintain a certain relationship with the law if he or she is to deactivate it. Thus, the sovereign's relationship with the law becomes paradoxical, given that the only link the sovereign maintains with the law is the one by which he is excluded from it (Agamben 2016, 53). Sovereignty must therefore not be conceptualized as something entirely above and beyond the legal order. On the contrary, it must be understood as something that is included in it, in the paradoxical sense of an inclusive exclusion.

This *ecstasy-belonging* is also experienced by the law itself. Agamben's use of the syntagma "force-of-law" shows that this technical term, which originated in Roman and medieval law but acquired its modern meaning during the French Revolution, designates what occurs at the moment when the state of exception is declared. According to the logic of this syntagma, what happens with the exception is, on the one hand, that the law is in force, but does not apply (has no force) and, on the other hand, those acts that did not have the force of law acquire it. This presence-absence of law is what leads Agamben to write this syntagma in the following way: “force-of-~~law,~~” to indicate that in order to apply a norm, its application must be suspended. Yet, despite the suspension and withdrawal of the law, it remains operating at the very moment when illegal decisions are being made about life. In this case, the law appears as something that exists only as a result of anomie. This anomie is what gives the law its strength and legitimacy. This is why one of the characteristics of law is that it can remain inert in the face of anomie. The state of exception is therefore the prerequisite for understanding the relationship between the living and the law.

Concerning the second question, the effectiveness of the legal-political order of the *soft dictatorship*, the latter can be considered a state of exception that succeeded in establishing itself over time without the need for legal modifications or explicit declarations for seventy-one years. If the PRI achieved such permanence, it is because it put in place an encrypted structure, or “death machine” (Agamben 2016, 251), which operated throughout the authoritarian period. The distinctive feature of this structure is that its archetypal legal-political logic is sacrificial, despite the democratic fiction it has put in place. This means that the “force-of-~~law~~” of the *soft dictatorship* lies not so much in the anomie (or exception) concealed behind the law, but on the contrary in an exception placed openly before the law, erected as a rule. Whereas democracy was merely a fictional façade, enabling dictatorship to maintain and mask its anomie.

The *soft dictatorship* is thus a legal-political order that makes intelligible the national and democratic lie on which Mexico was built. The lie consists in having Mexicans believe that the nation could be built without sacrifice, namely without violence. This is how the effects of the zone of indistinction created by this hybrid and encrypted structure manifested themselves and continue to manifest today. The *enforced disappearance apparatus*, although not the only *apparatus* to have come into being during these years in Mexico, is undoubtedly one of the most dangerous.

To sum up, we could say that the soft dictatorship can be defined

> as the establishment, by means of a state of exception, of a legal civil war, which enables the physical elimination not only of political opponents, but of entire categories of citizens who, for one reason or another, appear to be unable to integrate into the political system. Consequently, the voluntary creation of a permanent state of emergency (even if not declared in the technical sense) has become one of the essential practices of contemporary states, including so-called democratic one. (Agamben 2016, 178)

It is striking to note that by modifying a few words of Agamben’s quotation, which refers to the Third Reich in his text, we find a definition of what the *soft dictatorship* really was. Let’s now look at how it affected the space of the *enforced disappearance apparatus*, as well as the subject within that space.

The Space or Threshold of Indistinction

The space in the logic of sovereignty is the materialization of the *soft dictatorship*, which will make visible the legal-political structure proper to the *enforced disappearance apparatus*. One of the most obvious effects of the *soft dictatorship*, as a temporality, was the persistence of the party, but the series of events that took place within these seventy-one years, such as the creation of the *enforced disappearance apparatus*, completely overturned the conception of time and space. Time and space exploded. This means that the historical a priori of this *apparatus*, as well as its effects on subjectivity, are so multiple that they implode any linear conception of time and any Euclidean form of space.

Before Foucault came up with his analysis of biopolitics, in the 1970s, he devoted his work to anatomo-politics or to a "physics of power" (Revel 2010, 196), which means disciplining individual subjects through strategies and practices that shaped their bodies and perceptions. As the term anatomo-politics implies, the aim was to focus on direct effects on the body and mind of individuals, such as punishment. The prison, the school, the workshop, the factory, the army or the hospital are just some of the spaces that embodied such individual orthopedics (individual physical constraints). But these spaces could not have appeared without the support of a series of discourses and knowledges that provided the enunciable material through which the space could materialize. For example, Gilles Deleuze reminds us that for the criminal to exist it was first necessary to insert the criminal matter into the law (the offender, offenses, punishments, etc.), so that it could then be inscribed into stone (e.g., build a prison).

If the architectural structure of the prison, particularly the well-known panopticon, became important, it is because of what it allows us to see. Not only does it make crime and criminals visible, but it also ensures that inmates feel observed (Deleuze 2004, 39). A social effect and an individual effect are therefore the consequences of both discourses and milieus. It should be added, however, that the discipline not only makes itself visible through spaces, but also through objects. In *The Will to Know*, Foucault mentions the effects on children of simply putting or not putting up curtains in residence halls (1976, 39).

Later, but still in the 1970s, the French thinker turned his attention to the control of entire populations or "social orthopedics" (Revel 2010, 200–1). In this moment, he proposed the biopolitical turn. But the transition from punitive societies to biopolitics should not be understood as a moment in Foucault's analytics of power that leaves anatomo-politics behind. Rather, what happened was that the latter has been incorporated into new configurations of power. In some cases, this has meant softening and rendering less visible the techniques needed to "fit life and its mechanisms into explicit calculations" (Foucault 1976, 188). As an example, we have the grid of time, space, and movement of individuals. This grid, which acquired its shape in confined spaces, was later applied, with the development of the modern metropolis, to all cities and even to the countryside (which had long been excluded from logics of power similar to those of urban spaces).

The transition from a logic of individual orthopedics to a logic of social orthopedics has enabled a plurality of *apparatus* to be put in place. As a result, unsuspected spaces acquired new meanings thanks to the different interpretations that have been made by thinkers who are heir to biopolitics. We have thus moved from disciplinary spaces, such as schools, to biopolitical spaces, such as homes; and from spaces between biopolitics and thanatopolitics, such as concentration camps, to necropolitical spaces, such as, according to Achille Mbembe, plantations or the occupation of the West Bank. The question with regard to the *enforced disappearance apparatus*, that was put in place during the *soft dictatorship*, would be how to correctly situate the spaces that were used to neutralize guerrilla movements and any protest movement in the "bio-history" (Foucault 1976, 187). The space of the *enforced disappearance apparatus* of the second half of the twentieth century was the result of a chain of forms of biopolitics (bio-, thanato-, and necropolitical) whose combination has turned enforced disappearance into such an effective *apparatus*. Thus, it is possible to identify disciplinary, biopolitical, and thanatopolitical logics in the same space, for example a guerrilla fighter in a torture chamber.

In *The Camp as Nomos of Modernity*, Agamben proposes that the structure of concentration camps makes it impossible to decide between fact and law, exception and rule, because every event (however banal) that occurs in this space enacts the decision on *bare life* (2016, 153). According to Agamben, the structure of the camps appeared in moments of explicit exceptionality such as in the Second World War or during ethnic cleansing, where the camps manifested their hidden topological logic. Open exceptionality, however, is no longer necessary for this logic to appear. There are camps everywhere whenever a decision on life becomes devoid of any legal-political protection. This is irrespective of the nature of the crimes committed in the camps. The Italian philosopher means that it does not matter how someone's life is taken or denigrated, as long as it is always virtually feasible to create spaces where absolutely everything becomes possible.

The threshold of indistinction created by spaces who follow the biopolitical logic of camps, can be useful for thinking about the implosion of time and space concerning enforced disappearance. The particularity of this *apparatus* lies precisely in the active and continuous production of the threshold of indistinction. It is this threshold that creates doubt as to the fate of the missing person: is he or she alive, dead or a "living-dead?" (Mbembe 2006, 59). The missing person, however, is not the only one affected by this threshold; space and time also embody this indistinction, which is why virtually anything can happen within the historical a priori.

The topological structure of the camp, as a threshold of indistinction, can also make possible that the most unlikely spaces accommodate a hybridization between law and fact and thus become spaces of exception. For example, during the Argentine dictatorship, the Orletti mechanical workshop functioned as a clandestine detention, torture, and extermination center, where some 300 people were abducted and tortured, many of whom are still missing. The *threshold of indistinction* of these spaces also affects the experience and perception of the missing person within the *apparatus*. This is why sociologist Pamela Colombo proposes that spaces where disappearance that occurred during the Argentine dictatorship should be analyzed as spaces still under construction, despite the end of the *enforced disappearance apparatus* in that country, because in the moment victims or collateral victims remember and talk about their experience, the spaces continue to change (2017, 134).

Time is not spared from this opening up of meaning. Military time during the dictatorships of Latin America and the seventy-one years of *soft dictatorship* affected the temporality of the missing people, as well as that of their loved ones. In clandestine detention centers, Kirsten Mahlke argues, that the military could inflict torture simply by manipulating biological, physiological, and customary rhythms. Detainees who disappeared, for example, could not tell whether it was day or night during interrogation, they were also exposed to the interruption of sleep and meals. Space-time distortion was even part of CIA military manuals, as evidenced by the "Alice in Wonderland" section of one of the manuals (Mahlke 2014, 111). Those who survived being disappeared during the counter-insurgency period in Latin America, known as "ex-detainees-disappeared" (Gatti 2022, 150), also imagined their temporality during their detention enabling them to resist torture.

The fragmentation of space and time can also be materialized in objects. Let's not forget the importance of certain police and military cars in the operational implementation of enforced disappearances. In 2014, the kidnapping and disappearance of the forty-three Ayotzinapa students in the Mexican State of Guerrero could not have taken place without specific transport such as Ford Ranger pick-up trucks (Univision Noticias 2016). Colombo reminds us how in Argentina the Ford Falcon became the symbol of transportation for the disappeared, as it was considered a powerful, fast, and above all spacious car with great storage capacity (it had a large trunk). The Ford Falcon was the car of choice for the repressive *apparatus* (Colombo 2017, 112). Inside these cars, drivers alternated speeds and took winding roads to disorient detainees, enabling the police to create new spaces and temporalities.

The structure of the concentration camp is of interest to Giorgio Agamben because it enables a spatial paradigm. When thinking of the way in which the *enforced disappearance apparatus* came into being during the *soft dictatorship*, one inevitably sees that the spaces and the times were created by a proliferation of zones where the most unimaginable violence could occur with impunity. The subtle and encrypted way in which the biopolitical and legal-political form of the *soft dictatorship* took root in Mexico meant that even after the fall of the PRI, it continued to exist. The exception thus became the rule. It should come as no surprise, then, that the *enforced disappearance apparatus* is the nomos of the political space in which this country still finds itself. The question now is to grasp what the historical a priori of this *apparatus* has produced in terms of the subject.

Subject or Bare Life

The threshold that is initially created between legality and illegality, as well as between the legal and the political, creates a dangerous ambivalence for all those who have the misfortune to be captured in such a zone of indistinction. This danger lies in the intimate relationship that their lives, now considered bare life or *homo sacer*, come to have with sovereignty. For Agamben, following the meaning of an archaic Roman figure that he tracked back in the article "Sacer Mons" of grammarian Pompeius Festus, what is key concerning *homo sacer* is that his or her life is not executed or sacrificed. Life is not executed because the murder of bare life is not considered a crime, and life is not sacrificed because his or her sacrifice is not considered as such: "the specificity of *homo sacer*: impunity for those who kill him, and the prohibition on sacrificing him" (Agamben 2016, 70–1). This double condition places *homo sacer* or bare life in an ambivalent legal-political structure, close to the sovereign exception, as he or she is the victim of a double exclusion: bare life is excluded from human law (*ius humanun*), as well as from divine law (*ius divinum*). Yet despite this double exclusion, he or she is nevertheless doubly captured, a state of being that places *homo sacer* in the same topological logic akin to that which the sovereign and the force-of-~~law~~ occupy in the state of exception.

Such an inclusion-exclusion allows the Italian philosopher to situate this figure at the threshold of indistinction upon which the sovereign himself rests. This reveals not only their intrinsic relationship, but also the violence to which bare life is exposed. What is more, it is precisely because of the shared topology of the sovereign and bare life, within the threshold of indistinction, that it is possible for any individual to become both potentially sovereign (or, better, *micro-sovereign*) and potentially *homo sacer*. The first violence experienced by bare life is precisely the sovereign ban of the political body: "The sacred character of life that today one seeks to affirm as a fundamental human right against sovereign power expresses, on the contrary, at its origin, the subjection of life to a power of death, its irremediable exposure within the relation of abandonment" (Agamben 2016, 79). This is why the founding act of the city lies in the erasure of juridico-political boundaries, as this erasure gives place to indistinction and, therefore, carte blanche for cruelty.

The disappeared embodies perhaps more accurately than any other figure of the *homo sacer* the zone of indistinction, due to the position between life and death of the missing person. One consequence of such a location is the impossibility of knowing whether the person is dead or alive. Added to this is the fact that anyone may act as sovereign in relation to them. The disappeared is thus a paradoxical being: if the person cannot be found, they cannot belong to the realm of the living; and without a corpse, the person cannot be admitted into the realm of the dead. Neither the profane world nor the sacred world is inhabited by the missing person. Hence the *disappeared* is subject to a double exclusion-inclusion. Yet, the main question that appears is how to justify such a topology not only theoretically but also genealogically. The researcher finds herself in the delicate position of attempting to identify historical limits that may serve as examples of the *homo sacer* in the Mexican context. The *soft dictatorship* is for this research a strategic historical limit of the production of bare life in Mexico, given that it was during that period that the *enforced disappearance apparatus* appeared and strengthened. Thus, through time the *soft dictatorship* gave place to a structure that welcomed legality and illegality, inclusion and exclusion.

By way of conclusion and to summarize what has been outlined so far, this analysis has focused on biopolitical and juridico-political practices that became paradigmatic in Mexico and that strengthened through the production of a particular subject: bare life, which manifests in the figure of the disappeared. When the *enforced disappearance apparatus* first appeared in Mexico, the ones who experienced it were the opponents to the regime, such as the guerrilla fighters. Their disappearance was first enacted through discourse: "he/she is a criminal" or "he/she is a guerrilla member." The discourse condemns the "bandit" to become a half human, half animal figure whose life can be condemned, sacrificed or disappeared with impunity. This logic of power shows that to justify itself, sovereignty must, first, give a face to bare life in order to banish it from the political body (thus from the city). This confirms, following Agamben, that what politicizes human life is its abandonment to the unconditional power of death:

> The semantic ambiguity, already noted, whereby *abandonment* means both "at the mercy of" and "freely," finally becomes intelligible. The *ban* is, strictly speaking, the force—both attractive and repulsive—that binds together the two poles of sovereign exception: *bare life* and power, *homo sacer* and the sovereign. It is for this reason alone that it can signify both the emblem of sovereignty and expulsion from the community. (2016, 101)

The fact that death or enforced disappearance is the condition through which life becomes politicized allows us to insist, once again, that discourses directed against the guerrilla fighters or activists were neither innocuous nor merely symbolic. This is why a president such as Luis Echeverría did not hesitate to publicly condemn these people to death,[4] almost as if the triumph of the modern Mexican nation should be measured in terms of bare life. This was confirmed shortly after the beginning of Echeverría's presidency, through the emergence of what is now known as the crisis of the disappeared. It is now time to speak about this crisis and to show who is the sovereign and who the *homo sacer* in the second moment of existence of the *enforced disappearance apparatus*. This second moment concerns those who have been disappeared mostly by mafioso paramilitary groups.

The *Enforced Disappearance Apparatus* as Sequestration

The dawn of the new millennium was marked by a series of significant events. In Mexico, the long-awaited political shift took finally place with the electoral victory in 2000 of a different political party. The second wave of globalization gained momentum and the global war against terrorism took root following the 9/11 attacks. As the Mexican journalist and writer Sergio González Rodríguez reminds us, this event was a decisive factor in the escalation of violence in Mexico, given that the United States intensified its covert interventionist policies. This not only led to the infiltration of US military and paramilitary forces in Mexican territory, but also facilitated the influx of advanced weaponry and cutting-edge technologies. Such interference not only exacerbated levels of violence and corruption, but also shaped the very strategy of warfare adopted to combat mafioso paramilitary groups. According to González Rodríguez, 9/11 served as a pretext in 2002 for the United States to derecognize the principle of absolute State sovereignty. The erosion of State sovereignty on a global scale, however, had already been underway well before 2002; "Operation Condor" in Mexico is an example.

All populations suffer during the war on terror. González Rodríguez argues that the "New World Order" declared by George H. W. Bush entailed a push to homogenize the world and maintain control over regions, particularly those considered potentially dangerous, and/or rich in strategic natural resources. The "New World Order" also required the implementation of a model of population control and surveillance, made possible through panoptic technological networks. This surveillance effectively introduced civil war into households, because under a terrorist threat anyone can potentially become an enemy. The economy, unsurprisingly, did not emerge unscathed from these new global configurations. At the beginning of the century, a certain distance between the State and the oligarchs still appeared to be maintained or, at least, the oligarch's influence was more subtly concealed. However, this boundary has gradually eroded because of the increased concentration of wealth in the hands of a minority, the deregulation of certain markets, the reduction of some public services in favor of the private sector, the rise of individualism and consumerism fueled by social media, and the advent of anarcho-capitalism (Malabou 2022, 16). Malabou states that this shift brought about the rise of political figures, like Argentine president Javier Milei, who embody a hybrid combination of violence and a belief in a form of governmentality entirely disconnected from institutions and founded instead on pure transaction (2022, 53).

The mafioso paramilitary groups aligned themselves to the transformations brought about by the new millennium. In the 2000s, the alliances forged between these groups and the PRI shifted and their ability to maintain power even after the party's defeat revealed that the State's monopoly on sovereignty is a myth. This signaled that the systematic reduction of anyone to *bare life* was becoming a far more tangible reality. Indeed, from the start of the new millennium to the present day, more than 100,000 people have been reported missing across Mexican territory. Several things changed during this period: the relationship of the drug-trafficking groups to new technologies like espionage systems and the use of advanced weaponry, for example, drone-based bombings of civilian populations as occurred in 2024 in the Chiapas highlands. There was also the rise of electronic currencies, the demand of synthetic drugs such as fentanyl, widespread poverty, and mass migration to the United States.

Even though the power of the mafioso paramilitary groups was initially consolidated through illicit goods and activities (human trafficking, organ trade, oil theft, natural resource exploitation, and the imposition of "taxes") this does not mean that they failed to find pathways into the legal economy, such as real estate or agricultural exports like avocados. The weakening of the political party that birthed and protected the mafioso paramilitary groups allowed these groups to continue to exert pressure on the State, to the point of subjugating it. Hence, drug-trafficking groups represent now the "hard" side of the *soft dictatorship* that continues to be the legal-political logic of power even during the arrival of a real democracy, which currently embodies the "soft" side of the *soft dictatorship*. The hard or dictatorial side of this new version of the *soft dictatorship*, *soft dictatorship* version *2.0*, manifests itself in the numerous assassinations of political candidates and journalists, the collusion of the military and police forces with drug traffickers, and so on. The other thing that also changed was the network of power of the *enforced disappearance apparatus*. Instead of being merely used to protect a national and neoliberal project, it is currently used to nourish and maintain what we call a*narcho*-capitalism.[5] This is why we see in this new *apparatus* a logic of what Foucault called sequestration.

In his course at the Collège de France titled "On Punitive Society," Foucault made a distinction between the spaces of confinement in the eighteenth century and those in the nineteenth century. In the former, the goal was to marginalize individuals or to isolate those who were already marginalized, such as the poor, and fix them in a particular location. In the nineteenth century, confinement was no longer limited to isolating individuals, but also to integrating them into a productive system, in other words, to "sequestrate" them. Foucault mentions, for example, children sent to agricultural colonies or young female workers placed in factory convents. Another difference between these two forms of confinement is that while the first was about State control mechanisms, the second was mainly the result of private initiatives. These private initiatives, however, were not entirely separated from the State because they still relied on its institutions to exist. The philosopher discusses how, for example, a workshop could not function if the police or the military were not nearby.

The importance of spaces of sequestration is that they allow full control over an individual's time and force. Here, life is entirely consecrated to the time of production, which is exactly what happens today inside the *enforced disappearance apparatus*. Currently the reasons for making someone disappear are multiple (crimes of passion, neighborhood conflicts, corruption, feminicides, extortion, political repression, human trafficking, migrant smuggling, among others.) and disappearance has become a banal everyday crime; indeed, anyone can act as a *micro-sovereign* (a jealous or possessive man, a neighbor, the police, the army, drug traffickers, entrepreneurs, government officials, etc.). Still, many of the reasons for disappearing someone have to do with keeping an illegal economy alive, therefore part of the people who disappear are put inside spaces of sequestration. This means that the teleocracy of this second moment of the *enforced disappearance apparatus* is no longer the same as it was when guerrillas and activists were reduced to their bare life. During the counter-insurgency period, what happened inside the *apparatus* was more about setting someone in a space (in the manner of the eighteenth century). The idea was mostly about excluding "criminals" to places of confinement (clandestine prisons, buildings, etc.) and prioritizing their execution. With the arrival of the new millennium and the empowerment of a*narcho*-capitalists, however, the historical a priori adopted forced labor. Understanding spaces of sequestration seems key to uncovering the new logic of sovereignty and archism in this country.

In 2019, the existence of forced labor camps was spoken about by an escapee from one of these sequestration places located in a mountain in the State of Jalisco (Guillén and Petersen 2019). He gave his testimony under the pseudonym of "Luis." His testimony states the way in which mafioso paramilitary groups kidnap young men through fake job offers and force them to work for them after a series of cruel "training exercises." For example, burning bodies of other kidnapped people. These men are kidnapped and disappeared with the intention of: making them work in drug labs, cultivating and guarding poppy fields, become drug dealers and hitmen, construction workers, and so on. The "training" these men had to endure borders madness and horror. The words, actions, and spaces of the drug-trafficking groups make evident their *a*narcho*capitalistic* procedures. The logic behind the camp and sequestration spaces is to satisfy the needs of production in a country that provides one of the most profitable goods of our time: illegal drugs. What takes place in the camp therefore obeys an organization based on a perfectly rational legal-political structure that makes the captives both bare life and micro-sovereign once they are introduced into the *apparatus*. Despite Luis's explicit warning about what was going on in the camp, the State did nothing. In 2025, a ranch located also in the State of Jalisco was discovered, which contained fragments of burned bones, as well as 400 pairs of shoes, 400 clothes, suitcases, and abandoned IDs. The discovery was made by a group of people known as *buscadoras* (searchers), whose struggle consists of looking for missing people in Mexico. The discovery of this ranch sparked national outrage and the *buscadoras* named this space as an extermination camp. The pain of the families with missing members intensified in the face of the State's cruelty, inaction, collusion, and injustice. According to the topology provided by the *soft dictatorship* everything seems to indicate that action, truth, and justice might never come from the State, as it itself is trapped in the zone of indistinction of the *enforced disappearance apparatus*. The *buscadoras*' struggle will be crucially remembered in Mexico's history, because they are fighting against an *arcana imperii* that began earlier than the twenty-first century.

Notes

1 The notion of enforced disappearance as an *apparatus* was first introduced by the Argentine political scientist Pilar Calveiro in her book *Poder y desaparición: los campos de concentración en Argentina* (1998). The author, however, never explicitly elaborates on what she means by "*apparatus*," at times even using the term "technique" in its place. Our contribution to the analysis of enforced disappearance as a *power apparatus* lies in situating it within the framework of bio-history and Mexican history. We have also sought to give this *apparatus* a kind of embodiment through the concept of the historical a priori (discourse, time, and space), as developed by Michel Foucault in *The Archaeology of Knowledge*. Giorgio Agamben, for his part, in his essay "What Is an Apparatus?," does not integrate the historical a priori into his analysis.

2 In an interview given in 1977 he mentions that he tried to define the term.

3 Phenomenologists such as Nathalie Depraz point out that, in fact, Husserlian phenomenology and Foucauldian archaeology still share a certain continuity and

several points of proximity. Depraz highlights, first, Husserl's interest in history, albeit belatedly, in *Krisis*; second, the critical distance both the French and German philosophers adopt in order to analyze historical content, termed archaeology in Foucault and *epoché* in Husserl; and finally, their use of the notion of historical a priori and of a descriptive diagnosis to trace the transformations of subjective rationality (2013, 335).

4 See entries 36–56 of the published statement delivered by former president Luis Echeverría in 1974. In these entries, he mentioned, among other things, how these terrorists (urban and rural guerrilla groups) undermined the national project and how he would be ready to repress them with the full force of the law. See also Luis Echeverría, "4to Informe de gobierno de Luis Echeverría de 1974," public statement, April 2021, www.youtube.com/watch?v=A1S3dlCqcD4.

5 Following the economic logic of anarcho-capitalism, it seems to us that the drug traffickers, particularly with the arrival of the new millennium and with the end of the PRI, rather than just being considered as mafioso-paramilitary groups should now be understood as a*narcho*-capitalists (*narcho* in italics). This neologism serves to highlight the transformations drug trafficking and drug traffickers (as oligarchs) have undergone with the advent of the new expression of capitalism. Whereas they once depended on a government structure (the PRI) that required them to spare part of society from violence, they are now unchecked by any State institution: violence is exercised mercilessly in the name of economy.

References

Agamben, Giorgio. 2006. "Théorie des dispositifs." *Po&sie* 115(1): 25–33. https://doi.org/10.3917/poesi.115.0025.

Agamben, Giorgio. 2016. *Homo Sacer. L'intégrale 1997–2015*. Paris: Seuil.

Astorga, Luis. 2016. *El siglo de las drogas. Del Porfiriato al nuevo milenio*. México: Debolsillo.

Chevalier, Philippe. 2011. *Michel Foucault et le christianisme*. Paris: ENS Éditions.

Colombo, Pamela. 2017. *Espacios de desaparición: Vivir e imaginar los lugares de la violencia estatal (Tucumán, 1975–1983)*. Buenos Aires: Miño y Dávila.

Colombo, Pamela, and Estela Schindel, eds. 2014. *Space and the Memories of Violence*. New York: Palgrave Macmillan.

Deleuze, Gilles. 2004. *Foucault*. Paris: Les éditions de minuit.

Depraz, Natalie. 2013. "De Husserl à Foucault: la restitution pratique de la phénoménologie." *Les Études philosophiques* 106(3): 333–44. https://doi.org/10.3917/leph.133.0333.

Foucault, Michel. 1976. *Histoire de la sexualité I. La volonté de savoir*. Paris: Gallimard.

Foucault, Michel. 1997. *Il faut défendre la société*. Paris: EHESS/Gallimard/Seuil.

Foucault, Michel. 2004. *Sécurité, territoire, population. Cours au Collège de France (1977–1978)*. Paris: Gallimard/Seuil.

Foucault, Michel. 2013. *La société punitive*. Paris: Gallimard/Seuil.

Gatti, Gabriel. 2022. *Desaparecidos: cartografías del abandono*. Madrid: Turner.

Gillingham, Paul, and Benjamin T. Smith, eds. 2014. *Dictablanda: Politics, Work, and Culture in Mexico, 1938–1968*. Durham, NC: Duke University Press.

González Rodríguez, Sergio. 2014. *Campo de Guerra*. Barcelona: Anagrama.
Guillén, Alejandra, and Petersen Diego. 2019. "El regreso del infierno: los desaparecidos que están vivos." ¿A dónde van los desaparecidos? https://adondevanlosdesaparecidos.org/2019/02/04/los-desaparecidos-que-estan-vivos. Accessed January 5, 2025.
Malabou, Catherine. 2022. *Au voleur! Anarchisme et philosophie*. Paris: Puf.
Mahlke, Kirsten. 2014. " 'All Limits Were Exceeded over There': The Chronotope of Terror in Modern Warfare and Testimony." In Space and the Memories of Violence, edited by Pamela Colombo and Estela Schindel. New York: Palgrave Macmillan, 105–18.
Mbembe, Achille. 2006. "Nécropolitique." *Raisons politiques* 21(1): 29–60. https://doi.org/10.3917/rai.021.0029.
McCormick, Gladys I. 2016. *The Logic of Compromise in Mexico: How the Countryside Was Key to the Emergence of Authoritarianism*. Chapel Hill: University of North Carolina Press.
Pinochet, Augusto. 2017. "Esto no es una dictadura señores esto es dictablanda." Declaration. www.youtube.com/watch?v=4aKP4s8LcNQ.
Rath, Thomas. 2014. "Camouflaging the State: The Army and the Limits of Hegemony in PRIísta Mexico, 1940–1960." In *Dictablanda. Politics, Work, and Culture in Mexico, 1938–1968*, edited by Paul Gillingham and Benjamin Smith. Durham, NC: Duke University Press, 89–107.
Revel, Judith. 2010. *Foucault, une pensée du discontinu*. Paris: Mille et une nuits/Fayard.
Sanín-Restrepo, Ricardo, ed. 2018. *Decrypting Power*. New York: Rowman & Littlefield.
Univision Noticias. 2016. "Reveladoras imágenes sobre los 43 desaparecidos." www.youtube.com/watch?v=NxGPsF9q0JU.
Valey, Marion. 2022. "La conférence onusienne pour l' 'Année internationale de la femme,' Mexico, 1975. Un éveil international aux droits des femmes?" *Histoire, Europe et relations internationales* 2(2): 133–6. https://doi.org/10.3917/heri.002.0133.
Vargas Llosa, Mario. 2010. "Vargas Llosa y la dictadura perfecta." Debate. www.youtube.com/watch?v=kPsVVWg-E38&t=463s.

Notes on Contributors

María Bacilio (Mexico) is a philosopher and writer. She holds a PhD in philosophy from École Normale Supérieure de Paris (ENS) and an MA in Contemporary Philosophy from the same institution. In 2025–6 she will be a postdoctoral fellow in Princeton University at their Program in Latin American Studies. Her work focuses on violence, biopolitics, power, civil war, ontological anarchy, insurrection, justice, and memory with a special focus on Mexico and the Democratic Republic of the Congo. She has worked as a temporary lecturer in the Philosophy Department at the ENS and at the Cycle Pluridisciplinaire d'Études Supérieures de Paris. In 2017, she was awarded the Gustavo Baz Prada Medal from the Universidad Nacional Autónoma de México after her internship in a women's psychiatric prison in Mexico City.

Jonnie Eriksson (Sweden) is Senior Lecturer in the History of Ideas and Science, and director for a programme in cultural studies at Halmstad University, Sweden. His research chiefly concerns utopianism, vitalism, athleticism, biopolitics, geophilosophy, and their intersections, especially with regard to bodily and spatial conditions for thought and action.

Anthony Faramelli (UK) is a psychosocial researcher and group practitioner whose research is grounded in issues of coloniality and the theories and practices of institutional psychotherapy. Anthony is Lecturer in visual cultures at Goldsmiths, University of London, where he teaches in the Centre for Research Architecture and across the visual cultures programmes. He is a member of the executive committee of the Association for Psychosocial Studies, the advisory board for the Centre for Migrant Futures, and a founding member of the Transversal Institutional Analysis Network. In addition to multiple articles on digital cultures and the theories and practices of institutional psychotherapy, Anthony is the author of *Resistance, Revolution and Fascism: Zapatismo and Assemblage Politics* (2018) and an editor of *Spaces of Crisis and Critique: Heterotopias beyond Foucault* (2018). His current research projects examine digital cultures of the Alt-Right, psychotherapy's aesthetics practices, and the resistant networks formed by Latin American diasporic communities.

Kalle Jonasson (Sweden) is Associate Professor of Education Sciences and heads the Department of Education at Halmstad University, Sweden. He specializes in the philosophy of movement, particularly concerning how movement connects to knowledge and images.

Marinella Machado-Araujo (Brazil) holds a PhD in administrative law from UFMG-Brazil. She is a professor of graduate and postgraduation programs of the Pontifical Catholic University of Minas Gerais (PUC Minas), Brazil, where she teaches general theory of public law, administrative law, and urban and environmental law. She coordinates the Legal Nucleus of Public Policies (NUJUP) at the Faculdade Mineira de Direito, PUC Minas. She has been a visiting researcher at Università de Firenze, Florence; Max-Planck Institute, Heidelberg; and a visiting professor at the University of Bologna.

James R. Martel (USA) teaches political theory in the Department of Political Science at San Francisco State University. He is the author, most recently, of *Anarchist Prophets: Disappointing Vision and the Power of Collective Sight* (2022). He is currently working on a new book called *Continuous Assembly: The Power and Promise of Non Archism*. He is also a political activist and a labor organizer.

Andityas Soares de Moura Costa Matos (Brazil) is a full professor of philosophy of law at the Federal University of Minas Gerais (UFMG), Brazil. He holds a law degree, as well as a master's and PhD in philosophy of law from UFMG, and a PhD in philosophy from the University of Coimbra, Portugal. He completed postdoctoral studies in philosophy of law at the University of Barcelona, Spain, and in philosophy at the University of Campinas, Brazil. He has held visiting professorships at the University of Barcelona and the University of Córdoba, Spain. He is a productivity fellow with the National Council for Scientific and Technological Development (CNPq), Brazil, and currently coordinates the research group "The State of Exception in Contemporary Brazil." His main areas of interest include philosophy of law, political theology, civil disobedience, state of exception, radical democracy, anarchism, post-foundational contemporary philosophy, alchemy, and philosophy of image. His latest books are *Political Representation against Radical Democracy: An (A)theological Archaeology of Separated Power* (2020), *The Coming An-archy: Fragments for a Dictionary of Radical Politics* (2023), and *Counterpolitics of Alchemy* (2024).

Vincent Pisters Møystad (Norway) is a lecturer in the Department of Media, Communications, and Cultural Studies at Goldsmiths, University of London. He is a researcher and educator in the Sound System Outernational network and the Open Book Project and an active trade unionist. His research interests include popular sonic culture, labor organization, working-class practices of self-education, and histories of Black liberation movements.

Simón Royo-Hernández (Spain) is a philosopher and writer with a PhD. A secondary school teacher and lecturer and tutor at the Universidad Nacional de Educación a Distancia, he currently works at the Ministry for Inclusion, a task he combines with his philosophical work. He was one of the finalists for the 2007 Pensar a Contracorriente Award (Havana, Cuba), Fourth Edition, with his essay "Construir un arte y repensar el comunismo: una ética de las verdades." He has written several philosophical articles, including "Nietzsche and Unamuno: The Meaning of the Earth," *New Nietzsche Studies* 5 (1/2): 42–56 (2002). The books that he authored include *Pasajes al posthumanismo: historia y escritura* (2012), *El sujeto anárquico. Reiner Schürmann y Michel Foucault*

(2019), and *Anarkia/anarcolepsis* (2024). He currently collaborates with the *Redes Libertarias* magazine.

Ricardo Sanín-Restrepo (Colombia) is the author of *Decolonizing Democracy: Power in a Solid State* (2016), *Being and Contingency: Decrypting Heidegger's Terminology* (2021), and the editor of *Decrypting Power* (2018). He has also authored *Ser y Contingencia* (2023) and *Teoría Crítica Constitucional* (2014).

Zackary Taktuk Smith (USA) is a graduate student in the Indigenous Studies program at University of Alaska, Fairbanks. He has recently been appointed as an Assistant Professor in Iñupiaq Studies at Iḷisaġvik College. Taktuk's area of study focuses on Indigenous critical theory, Indigenous sovereignty, cosmology, and the political imaginary from an Iñupiaq perspective. Being Iñupiaq himself but raised outside of his cultural heritage, Smith's studies have been a vehicle toward reconnecting family, culture, language, land, and place. His research and contributions come from a place of intergenerational healing and an unwavering passion and love for his community.

Index

www.ingramcontent.com/pod-product-compliance
Ingram Content Group UK Ltd.
Pitfield, Milton Keynes, MK11 3LW, UK
UKHW020212290926
15470UKWH00001B/138

9 781666 978711